BRIDGES
TO
HUMANITY

BRIDGES TO HUMANITY

NARRATIVES ON ANTHROPOLOGY AND FRIENDSHIP

BRUCE GRINDAL
FRANK SALAMONE

WAVELAND
PRESS, INC.

Prospect Heights, Illinois

For information about this book, write or call:

Waveland Press, Inc.
P.O. Box 400
Prospect Heights, Illinois 60070
(708) 634-0081

CONTENTS

PREFACE

This story begins more than thirty years ago, when Joe Casagrande edited a book about friendships in the field. That book, *In the Company of Man* (1960), depicted fieldwork situations. Joe, however, was quite aware that the field of anthropology, as well as the anthropologist's field, was changing. His awareness of these changes was clearly apparent to any who spent more than a few moments in serious conversation with him.

The story continues with Frank Salamone, who spoke at length with Joe about those changes during the course of his 1976 NEH postdoctoral work. He had arrived at Joe's seminar on the history and theory of anthropology a bit later than the other participants because he had been in Nigeria conducting some research. He duly reported to Joe's office in international studies and found that Joe's sleepy eyes belied an active interest and attention to people.

Soon Casagrande had drawn him out, and Frank rambled on enthusiastically about a man named Matthew whom he had met in Nigeria a few years before in 1970. Matthew had emerged from the bush, spoke good English, and became a Catholic catechist, one of his many jobs in the years that came after 1970. In early summer 1976, Matthew had taken Salamone with him on his catechitical trips. Furthermore, he had conducted some studies for him and in many other ways had made his trip successful.

When Salamone finally paused for air, Casagrande asked him why he didn't update *In the Company of Man*. He replied honestly that he did not know whether he could find a theoretical peg on which to hang his story of Matthew. In common with many in his anthropological generation, Salamone felt that anthropology was no longer interested in works that were "merely descriptive." He regretted that fact—but there it was. Joe, who had seen many anthropological trends come and go, smiled his peaceful smile and repeated his advice. If the story was good, he ventured, it would be read.

vii

Over the years, Salamone has often reflected on that advice. As the idea percolated, the field of anthropology was transforming itself into shapes that would be more amenable to Salamone's and Casagrande's persistent adherence to the belief in the holistic nature of anthropology based on fieldwork.

At the 1974 meetings of the American Anthropological Association in Mexico City, two symposia were held on topics broadly related to something that is now called humanistic anthropology. The two chairs of these symposia, Bruce Grindal and Toni Flores, sat down afterward and discussed what they had done. Both of them agreed that they were onto something, and in that year the Society for Humanistic Anthropology was formed. In 1976, the journal of the society, the *Anthropology and Humanism Quarterly*, was founded, and in 1980 the society was officially recognized as part of the American Anthropological Association.

What was that something that Grindal and Flores were onto? It was the idea that humanistic anthropology must take as its premise the basic humanity of all people and condition of people as cultural creatures. We as anthropologists have a particular vantage point as multienculturated intelligentsia; we are capable of both perceiving a world culture in the process of creation and helping to fashion its shape and direction. Humanistic anthropology, moreover, attempts to capture the "felt life" of human experience through narrative and poetically written materials that capture those whose lives we have entered and about whom we have chosen to write. We must be primarily concerned with human life and experience and continue to affect a voice that allows us to communicate those experiences that, although born of specific cultural circumstances, nonetheless transcend culture and thereby enhance our sensibility and awareness of the human condition. We have to study human beings, and we must study what concerns them most intimately—that is, the hold that life has on them. We must affect a voice that renders the human story both compelling and true.

For Grindal, humanistic anthropology has been and continues to be an intensely personal endeavor in which inquiry is intimately related to the conduct of life. The acquisition of knowledge, meaning, and truth is intimately tied to the interpersonal relationships formed in the field.

The opportunity for Grindal and Salamone to meet presented itself in 1991. Salamone placed a notice in the *Anthropology Newsletter* soliciting contributions to a proposed volume on fieldwork that would build on Casagrande's work and place it in the context of modern developments in fieldwork. Grindal, upon reading Salamone's notice, became excited by the possibility of collaboration and proposed to

Salamone that they test the waters through organizing a panel for the 1992 American Anthropological Association meeting in San Francisco. Each of the papers at that session emphasized, through narratives about the field experience, how anthropological or ethnographic fieldwork has changed in the last thirty years, particularly since the publication of Casagrande's *In the Company of Man*. The response to these papers, moreover, was so positive that the editors continued the project with the encouragement of Tom Curtin of Waveland Press. The results of that work are here in this volume.

In closing we wish to give special thanks to Patricia Dietrich for her editorial assistance and to Robin Rhodes whose "fresh eyes" aided us in the formulation of the book.

Bruce T. Grindal
Frank A. Salamone

INTRODUCTION

Very few occasions in life can duplicate the solitude of an anthropologist's early days "in the field." In those days the anthropologist feels like both an outsider and a child. There may be language barriers. There will certainly be social barriers restricting and channeling interactions. Bearing down heavily on the anthropologist will be the knowledge that some tangible result should ensue from the expedition.

Repeatedly, in these early days, some person has entered the anthropologist's life to assume the position of teacher and friend. Francis Bacon notes, in a passage that speaks somewhat directly to the anthropological experience, that friendship "maketh daylight in the understanding, out of darkness and confusion of thoughts" (1992:159). Without being aware of the fact, anthropologists often parallel Bacon's sentiments when discussing their field experiences.

Throughout a good part of its history, however, anthropological writings, with some notable exceptions, were written as if the anthropologist were merely a recording instrument and, as befits a machine, incapable of friendship. As is appropriate to such a measuring device, the anthropologists seemed to have no feelings. Nothing, it seemed, could move the anthropologist to tears or laughter. Such displays were unseemly, and when indulged, often appeared in fictionalized writings under pseudonyms, such as Laura Bohannan's *Return to Laughter* (Bowen 1964).

1

It wasn't that anthropologists were unfeeling machines. Rather, the profession and the entire social science enterprise aspired to attain scientific status through emulating the supposed detached behavior of physical scientists. Most physical scientists were not dealing with living people, however, and the anthropologist was. The ethnographer, consequently, assumed a pose that pretended the fieldworker was an objective observer able to record with the utmost precision all aspects of a society's sociocultural life.

The ethnographer, moreover, made the assumption that all members of a society were interchangeable parts, each fully socialized and enculturated into a monolithic culture. Thus, students read about "the Nuer," or "the Arapesh." Individuals tended to disappear into the mass, with some exceptions. Important statuses, such as "the Leopard Skin Chief" or "the shaman," were written about. Again, however, the impression was given that all people who occupied these cultural positions were more or less interchangeable. Little, if any, room was left in the typical ethnographies for individual variation or style.

Students would have been forgiven if they had also concluded that anthropologists, as well, were more or less interchangeable. Rarely did students discover how ethnographers ate, slept, loved, or felt about their research and the people among whom they conducted it. Anecdotal tales that spiced up classroom discussions provided some idea of what life was really like in the field. These, however, were rarely published, lest the admission of human feelings disqualify one as an anthropologist.

In recent decades, however, the tide has turned. Personal narrative has assumed a rightful place in anthropology as ethnographers have become increasingly aware that their own personal backgrounds affect their studies and presentation of their research. That research, moreover, is presented in a shrinking world in which our friends and collaborators can and do read our products. Moreover, in our modern time the native is not so distant as once was the norm. He or she can, and often does, reenter our lives on our front porch. This appears especially true in the situations Ruth Behar, Patricia Beaver, Robin Ridington, and Jeanne Simonelli discuss.

And yet—can the anthropologist truly continue the friendships begun in the field when the native enters her or his world? The question requires further thought and investigation and raises serious questions regarding the anthropological enterprise. Can even the best-intentioned anthropologists bridge the gap between humanistic science and true friendship? Can the native truly enter the anthropologist's world, and, more importantly, will the anthropologist accept the native as an equal on the anthropologist's turf? We hope the answer is yes but, as some of the papers in this volume suggest, at least a portion of some field friendships is based on mutual, even if unacknowledged, gain; and once that gain is no longer present, the friendship no longer has active value.

Furthermore, other realities have prompted passionate probing of the fieldwork enterprise, including friendships. Of great importance to this reflective mood is recognition of the fact that the political realities in which fieldwork takes place have changed. Decolonization and feminism have worked to make anthropologists more aware of and sensitive to the wider implications of their writings. Appropriately, anthropologists who identify themselves as humanists have been in the forefront of the movement to explore and present the human dimension of fieldwork. Only through an understanding of that dimension, in fact, can the significance of anthropological work for the understanding of the human condition be appreciated. For these anthropologists, the goal of anthropology, which is to understand meaning and value, is central. More specifically, their stories are attempts to elucidate the meaning and value of friendships.

The contributions to this volume span a wide geographic area. Three are from Mexico. Alan Sandstrom, working in northern Veracruz, recounts his struggle to establish friendships through the barriers of miscommunication and misinterpretation. Gregory Reck's ethnographic stay, in the eastern Sierra mountains of Mexico, results in a transformation of his person, enabled by his informant, who dramatically becomes his friend. And Ruth Behar's ethnographic experience moves with her from Mexico to North America with her friend who relocates nearby in Detroit.

Four narratives focus upon Native Americans. Edith Turner, in her study of healing among the Alaska Inuit, encounters in the person of Claire, a teacher who opens her mind to alternative explanations of reality. Simonelli's narrative ascends from the geography of Canyon de Chelly in Navajo country and chronicles the friendship and spiritual journey's of two women. Claire Farrer's long-term relationship with Bernard Second, a Mescalero Apache "singer" in northern New Mexico, is an account of psychic intimacy and mutual knowingness. And Ridington's collaboration with the Omaha people of the northern Plains is an example of how modern narrative includes the informant as co-author.

Other ethnographic contexts are located in India, China, Portugal, Trinidad, and the United States. Kirin Narayan narrates her discovery of the affection that emerges from the telling of and listening to stories, both traditional and personal, while doing fieldwork in India. Beaver observes in China that friendship emerges from simple, sincere, and strategic reciprocities. Robert Roy Reed's touching portrayal of his field experience in Portugal draws the reader into a deeply emotional aspect of fieldwork. John Stewart's emphasis on ethnography as self-discovery is embedded in his engrossing portrait of Trinidad's carnival and the revelations of remembered friendships. And Michael Angrosino provides insights into American culture through his investigation of Eutaw Jack and his particular view of society, demonstrating how much the "mentally disturbed" can teach about "normal" society.

Finally, the book transports the reader to Africa. Bruce Grindal, in his fieldwork in west Africa, recognizes the pain of friendship and the powerlessness to prevent tragedy. Frank Salamone "takes you there," to northern Nigeria where a common interest in music creates the magic of a budding friendship. Both reflect on the manner in which field experiences can be therapeutic in aiding fieldworkers who must deal with some of their own deepest feelings.

The book has also sought a balance between male and female anthropologists, as well as in "years of service." The editors were surprised at the relative uniformity of vision among the contributors: neither age nor gender provided any significant difference in the relationships addressed here. Such might not have been the case twenty-five years before anthropologists became more self-reflective about our enterprise. It is interesting to note that common themes override differences of gender and age.

A central theme is an inherent ambiguity underlying the anthropologist's position in the field. The anthropologist is a scholar, but also, and primarily, a human being. Beaver, Reed, Salamone, Sandstrom, and Reck confront the issue directly. Reck's phrase, "a closeness in the shadow of separate paths," captures the poignancy of the phenomenological experience of field friendships, which are often situation specific and haunt the anthropologist's memory after a return to normal routine. As Beaver and Narayan reveal, the purpose and agendas of anthropologist and native often differ. Beaver, for example, found her Chinese colleagues shaping her research in ways that would advance their own interests. Narayan, in turn, found her collaborators directing the course of her fieldwork. The fact that her field site was also the home of her American mother further complicated her position.

And yet—do our collaborators really take us where we do not wish to go? The bittersweet nature of our friendships may be, after all, what we seek. Reck's quotation from Stanley Diamond (1970) certainly suggests a kind of psychological determinism. If "anthropology is the study of men [and women] in crises by men [and women] in crises," then it seems that a certain self-selection is operating. The miscommunication and mistrust that Stewart, Sandstrom, Grindal, and Reck note—as well as Reed's and Behar's recognition of the bittersweet nature of field friendships—seem inherent in the nature of the field context.

The authors further demonstrate another fact about the anthropological enterprise; namely, there is always some element of autobiography contained within ethnography. It may, it is true, be disguised or even repressed ethnography. It may take years before the field experience is seen as self-revealing, as in the examples of Reck and Grindal, or almost instantaneous, as in the portrayals of Narayan and Salamone. In any event, the theme of self-discovery is a key to most of the articles and demonstrates the idea of the field experience as rite of passage.

In most of the pieces, the anthropologist discovers some personal truth about his or her friend that is also a self-truth. In the pieces by Turner, Farrer, Beaver, and Grindal something is perceived out there, another truth, that defies the rules and methods of our scientific culture but can be known through personal experience and interaction with people who "know" in different ways. Stylistically, most of the pieces conclude with a denouement in which the plot of the narrative reaches a climax in which the anthropologist achieves that truth. The portrayal of anthropology as a quest for meaning indeed appears to dominate these vignettes.

Finally, while a majority of the works are straightforward narratives, each has been somewhat influenced by the trends in anthropological writing. There is a great deal more of the native speaking in his or her own voice in these chapters. Stewart, Farrer, Ridington, and Simonelli, however, present the boldest departures from more traditional anthropological presentation with the use of the poetic voice and the inclusion of the informant as a second major voice.

In sum, this book has brought together some of the best writers in anthropology today to communicate their personal encounters in the field, about the mutual and often painful exchange of personhood and value that informs the reader not only about people living in other cultures but also who *we* are: the ethnographer, the observer, the reader. Each author has written about friendship in the field with the firm belief that without friends we anthropologists could not do anthropology. We are, alas, not all-seeing measuring machines. In contrast to the classical portraits of our anthropological ancestors, we are subjective beings, deeply moved by events that occur in the field. We cry at tragedy and rejoice at good tidings. We are painfully aware of our shortcomings and the limitations of our backgrounds. In spite of that awareness, however, we are also cautiously optimistic about our ability to arrive at some understanding of another culture, especially with a little help from our friends.

MICHAEL V. ANGROSINO

EUTAW JACK

THE MAN BORN BLIND

Anthropologists working in the United States must deal with a society with many different faces and voices, despite its overall familiarity. They must confront the challenge of being strangers in need of friends to guide them through the maze of assumptions that shape life just around the corner.

Angrosino's story concerns his attempts to enter into the world of deinstitutionalized mentally retarded adults through autobiographical narratives. Eutaw Jack is a man who has lived in that world for most of his life although he is not, in the technical sense, mentally retarded. Through their sharing of a common passion for understanding the lives behind the inarticulate public facade of mental retardation, Angrosino and Eutaw Jack come to a place at which they can reach out to each other at a time of emotional crisis.

My project has grown over the years to deemphasize the manifest content of the narratives and to focus instead on what those narratives reveal about the storytelling capacities of people with supposedly limited cognitive and communicative skills. In effect, I've come to look on the old and honored anthropological technique of the life history as a way of understanding the strategy of storytelling as a means to bridge barriers to communication. (See, e.g., Angrosino 1992b, 1994.) I am not convinced that people with mental disabilities form a separate culture, but I am sure that they process their experiences of the world in ways different from those of the mainstream. (See, e.g., Angrosino 1992a.) If we truly wish to serve such clients, we must know not merely whether they think this or that service is good or bad; we must learn how to experience the world as they do, so that we can make better sense of their evaluations. That shift in emphasis was due in no small measure to Eutaw Jack.

Eutaw Jack

Would it be too preciously post-modern to say that he entered my life as a text? No matter: that's the truth of it. It happened like this.

Back in 1984, a friend told me about someone he'd met through his church's social service group. As a child, this man had been diagnosed as mentally retarded, and he spent most of his life in hospitals or other forms of custodial care. After many years, a sympathetic psychologist discovered that he had been incorrectly tested. He was reclassified and released, sent into the world as an adult with absolutely no knowledge of that world. He quickly "took the wrong path," became an alcohol-abusing street person, and then found salvation with Alcoholics Anonymous. This remarkable man called himself Eutaw Jack after the small Florida town where he was born, and he was then about forty years old. He had, moreover, written his autobiography, which he had given my friend, asking him to use his university connections to "do something with it." My friend in turn, knowing my then-newfound interest in the life stories of the deinstitutionalized (as well as an earlier research interest in AA) wanted me to read the autobiography and perhaps even help get it published.

I was eager to help, as my project was off to a slow start. It was proving difficult to convince caregivers that their mentally impaired clients had anything worth recording; a number of them worried that I would simply upset the delicate balance of their clients' fragile lives. From the few interviews I had managed to carry out up to that point, I had come to realize that the process would be slow and painful and very different from working in the life history genre with the articulate and forthcoming West Indians among whom I had conducted earlier fieldwork. So I jumped at the chance to deal with a life story that had already been rendered in finished form, the product of someone who clearly understood the importance of research like mine.

I was, however, disabused of my fantasy of pain-free research the minute I unwrapped the package. I found 948 sheets of onionskin paper, covered front and back with single-spaced typescript. It had been produced on an old manual typewriter whose ribbon had long since been drained of its vital juices. Worse, the entire tome was constructed in a single sentence with neither section breaks nor paragraphs. Eutaw Jack might well have been the next James Joyce or William Faulkner, but I knew at a glance that I'd never have the time, the patience, or the editorial talent to do anything with his manuscript. I toyed with the idea of shipping it off to Norman Mailer or Truman Capote, who had done so well by other real-life down-and-outers with literary aspirations, but I just gave it back to my friend, saying I couldn't help. (I guess I also meant it couldn't help me, either.)

A few days later I got a phone call—a furious voice demanding, without preamble or introduction, who the fuck I thought I was, some fancypants college boy without the fucking guts to come to terms with real life, and how would I like my ugly face made even uglier. It could only have been—and it was—Eutaw Jack.

I didn't dare hang up, although I made a mental note to ask my friend why in hell he had given my name and phone number to a maniac. So I listened to the oral version of the torrent of words I had seen on the typescript. He finally paused for breath, and I weakly said, "Look, I'm sorry—I didn't mean your story wasn't good. It's just that I didn't have the time . . ."

Much to my surprise, his tone changed immediately and he said cheerily, "Oh, I know you're busy. I just needed a few pointers, is all."

"Pointers?" I quavered.

"Yeah," he replied, sounding almost jaunty. "Meet me Saturday at noon at the Wendy's over by the Stadium. I just need you for a few minutes, just to get clear on a few things."

As it happened, the Wendy's in question had begun a program to give adults with mental retardation supervised job training, so at the very least I could take the opportunity to say hello to one or two of my life history collaborators away from the agency setting. But even so, I felt compelled to meet Eutaw Jack.

From the heft and boom of his voice, I expected Eutaw Jack to be a huge bruiser, and I thought I'd see him enthroned at a table behind a mountain of fries, terrorizing the girls at the salad bar. As I pulled into the parking lot, a wizened man with a small, sad face was taking out the trash. He waved at me feebly and said, in a tired and forlorn whisper, "You must be Mike. Otis [one of the clients with whom

I'd begun to work] told me you had a piece of crap car." He glanced mournfully at my ancient, nobly scarred Volvo.

"You're not Eutaw Jack, are you?"

"That's me," he said in a fading-fast voice. "I'll meet you inside."

Otis Blevins was on duty. He had recently graduated to sandwich-wrapper and was beaming behind the counter. "You'll like Eutaw Jack," he shouted. "He's the best guy ever. He taught me everything I know."

Lew Rainey, the manager who had taken an interest in the training program, leaned over and said, "He's right. Eutaw Jack's something else. I don't know how I'd run the program without him." Still puzzling over the several versions of Eutaw Jack I'd already encountered, I ordered lunch and sat down to wait for him to finish his duties and take a break.

After a while he appeared under a fresh head of steam, his voice once again transformed. This time it could have been that of a brisk, no-nonsense executive, not harsh but certainly not friendly.

"So, it was too long?" he snapped.

"Well, yes, it was long, but . . ."

"Too much detail?"

"Yes, definitely too much detail. And . . ." I groped for a diplomatic way to raise the matter of his grammar and style.

"Bad English?"

"Well, maybe not bad when you're talking to someone in person, but in writing . . ."

"OK," he said drily. "That's all I needed to know." His tone sounded as if the interview were at an end, but he made no move to go. He continued, in fact, to look me straight in the eye. After what felt to me like an uncomfortably long pause, I reverted to my experience as a life/oral history interviewer:

"If you only had one thing about yourself that you'd like people years form now to remember about you, what would it be?" I expected that he would pick out a specific incident from his autobiography or perhaps talk in a more general way about how he had turned his life around after a hard youth. His gaze did not shift, but after a while he broke into the merriest of grins, and said, "Why—I'm the 'Man Born Blind' come to real life!"

This statement—both its unexpected content and the firmness with which it was uttered—took me aback. I hadn't heard that he had experienced a physical challenge in addition to his mental and emotional ones. He grasped immediately that I was lost.

"The Man Born Blind. John 9."

"You mean, in the Bible?"

He sighed. "Yes, the Bible, college boy."

I was to become very familiar with John 9 as a result of Eutaw Jack's comments. It is indeed a fascinating story, the miracle tale told with the greatest circumstantial detail in all the Gospels. In it, Jesus and his disciples are discussing a certain blind beggar. They ask if his own sins or the sins of his parents had caused his misfortune. Jesus denies the connection between sin and the man's physical problem and proceeds to cure his blindness "so that the works of God might be made visible through him." The beggar is soon accosted by a group of Pharisees who demand to know what happened. The beggar tells them that Jesus cured him by smearing clay on his eyes. They are aghast: the cure took place on the Sabbath, and some of them fume that Jesus cannot be a man of God because he violated the Sabbath prohibition against work. The Man Born Blind sticks to his guns: "He is a prophet," he declares. The Pharisees summon the parents of the beggar, who affirm that their son was truly born blind. Fearful of the authorities (and probably peeved at having lost a source of income), they disavow any knowledge of how their son's sight was restored, and they abandon him to his fate. The Man Born Blind is summoned back by the Pharisees, who repeat their accusation that Jesus is a Sabbath-breaking sinner and insist that the beggar tell the story of his cure one more time; they imply that he is one of Jesus' disciples and party to some sort of scam. The Man Born Blind stands his ground, saying that no sinner could have effected such a miracle. The Pharisees are furious at this lowly character giving them lectures, and they fling him out of the temple. Jesus reappears, and the Man Born Blind affirms his faith that Jesus is the "Son of Man," the messiah. Jesus says that his plan is to bring sight to the blind. The Pharisees, who do not understand that Jesus is speaking allegorically, assert that since they are not blind, they have no need of his healing. Jesus leaves them, saying sadly, "If you were blind, you would have no sin; but now you are saying, 'We see,' so your sin remains."

I came to understand that Eutaw Jack saw himself as having been born in "darkness"—abandoned by indifferent parents and unfeeling medical and educational authorities and then at last liberated. But like the beggar in the first flush of his healing, he didn't know what to make of his new condition. The beggar had his physical sight restored and then in the bargain had been given a profound glimpse into the divine plan of salvation. Eutaw Jack had wanted only to get out of the awful state hospital; he had, in addition, been told that he was never retarded at all. He hadn't minded the label so much, only the condition to which it had consigned him—much as the beggar, in his naiveté, probably had no grander plans for his sight than to stop being a beggar. Both were unprepared for the existential shock; in Eutaw Jack's case, not only did he get out of the hospital, but he was certified as not retarded after all. The beggar at least had Jesus close at hand for guidance. Eutaw Jack, who needed several years of hard knocks before coming to terms with Jesus, understood that liberation was no picnic in the park—it would demand sacrifices of its own, much as the Man Born Blind was flung out of the temple and branded a cohort of a notorious sinner.

What was startling to me as I pondered Eutaw Jack's response was that he had consciously used what I assumed to be a sophisticated rhetorical device, an extended metaphor based on a very specific and complex literary allusion, to cut through the narrative jumble of his life story. I took it for granted that formal autobiographers did so, and I could imagine life/oral history informants of normal intelligence doing so as well. But although Eutaw Jack was not retarded, he had lived until adulthood being treated as if he were; the residual effects of those early decades of intellectual deprivation had left him with many of the surface traits of one with mental disabilities. That he could still— confidently and without prompting—shift from the innumerable concrete details of his life to the overarching abstraction of a metaphor that encapsulated his life was surprising. "Retarded" people are supposedly deficient in abstract thinking.

More surprising still was the fact that the metaphor was not a simple, homespun attempt (such as, "My life is a toilet," which is what one of my other informants later told me), but one that tapped into a key passage, chewed over by philosophers and theologians for two millennia, that gets at the heart of the Christian ethic of redemption through absolute faith in the saving power of Jesus.

Eutaw Jack, however, denied that he had done something remarkable. Later in our conversation, he pointed out that "every retard I know" could do the same. They wouldn't all pick the Bible, of course, and most of them wouldn't think of an explicitly literary analogue to their condition. But almost all of them, he asserted, would be able to answer the direct question I had put to him. He had spent almost his whole life learning how such people behave, he said, and after we had gotten to know each other better, he liked to joke that he had deliberately checked himself into the hospital at a young age so that he could do "participant observation." The reason that retarded people "out in the world" metaphorize their experience, he explained, is because they have a hard time dealing with ambiguity; they do better with simple, repetitive tasks in controlled situations. They like to eat the same foods, wear the same clothes, stick to the same time schedules, deal with the same people. The world, of course, rarely accommodates them, and so they are bombarded with an apparent chaos of events and motivations. They seek the security of consistency within themselves. "It's who they think they are—that's what they hang on to, no matter what other shit is flying around them. You people do the same thing, don't you—only it ain't so vital, and you can play around with it. People like us, we gotta stick to one idea that holds us together."

Eutaw Jack and I talked for the rest of the afternoon, and we met regularly thereafter. He seemed to lose a direct interest in writing his own life story as he took on a powerful interest in helping me work on the stories of others. His comments that first day were, indeed, the catalyst that allowed me to reformulate my research and break out of the tangle of (often factually erroneous) specifics to reach the safe place of the consistent metaphor of identity.[1] I could not, I found, ask others the same direct question that had prompted Eutaw Jack's response; despite what he thought, he really was unique in my circle of mentally disabled collaborators in his ability to understand the question and provide a coherent answer. Nevertheless, over the course of the next several years, with much trial and error, it has become possible for me to construct interviews that tap into the metaphorical "rearrangement of self" (Hankiss 1981) that guides the self-identification process of retarded, as well as "normal" autobiographers. (See, e.g., Norton 1989.)

Throughout the process, Eutaw Jack was my reality check. I was cautious at first in accepting his view of my informants; his own experiences, after all, had not been common ones, and although he was insightful, he did tend to view the world through the lens of his own life. Even so, he gave me excellent, if occasionally unorthodox advice. For example, one potential interview subject was a man so shy and tentative in his manner that he could only giggle and blush when spoken to. I was about to write him off as someone I could work with, but Eutaw Jack said, "Ask him to sing for you." In a what-the-hell mood, I did so the next time I saw him, and he immediately burst into an off-key, but confidently full-throated rendition of a sobby country song about a truck driver.

"So what?" I asked Eutaw Jack later on.

"Keep doing it. See what happens."

So every time I saw Charlie Hastings I asked him to sing, and immediately his goofiness vanished and he took center stage. He had a surprisingly large repertoire, although I noticed that *all* his material concerned truck drivers, their cheatin' wives back home, their encounters with honky-tonk angels, their sense of aloneness on the road.

"So what?" I said again to Eutaw Jack.

"I don't know, exactly," he admitted. "But it must mean *something*. Don't you college boys think *everything* must mean *something*?"

"Do you think Charlie thinks of himself as a truck driver—like you think of yourself as the Man Born Blind?"

"Could be. I just knew he liked to sing, except no normal person ever asks him to. I thought it'd make him feel more kindly to you. But damn—wouldn't it be a pisser if that's what he's doing?!''

Charlie, as it turned out, did see himself as a loner, playing by his own rules, just like the truck drivers of legend. He did not have the wherewithal to take off in his own rig and have the sad and colorful romantic adventures he sang about, but he never felt he was really ''where I really am'' when he had to stay put. Talking about his sense of himself and about his aspirations gave Charlie a whole new way of relating to himself—and of relating that self to others—that was far more meaningful and rewarding than my initial invitation to tell me about the things that had happened to him, a boring and depressing chore in his mind. No one was more pleased than Eutaw Jack for having made this fortuitous discovery.

The breakthroughs weren't always happy ones, however. I was, for example, particularly interested in working with one man who had graduated from his training program but who seemed to prefer to live on the streets. Robert Elgin was articulate—almost glib. He had a sly, streetwise charm, and he always seemed glad to talk to me. I could never get him to say much about himself, but it was shockingly easy for him to get me to reveal things about myself—like where I lived and how much money I earned. Eutaw Jack repeatedly said, ''I just don't trust him—don't know why, just don't.'' He apparently did some sleuthing on his own and subsequently told me that Robert had a perfectly nice garage apartment in a house his sister owned; he didn't live on the streets at all. I refused to believe it, but after several months of my giving Robert ''a little bit to get me by'' (and getting nowhere near to learning anything about him), I ruefully admitted that Eutaw Jack was probably right. ''He's a user, is all. Even a retard can be smart enough to use somebody else. Especially a do-gooder college boy.''

All the while, Eutaw Jack worked at Wendy's, doing a variety of menial jobs. He never wanted to do any one thing on a steady basis, and he had a major panic attack that kept him huddled in his bedroom for several days when Lew suggested that he apply for management training. ''I just want to help out,'' he told me. ''I'm not cut out for big responsibilities.'' I pointed out that a lot of people already depended on him—Lew certainly did, and the various clients who went through the program all looked to him for advice and support. He'd make a very good manager, I told him. ''No,'' he said in a way that left no possible room for argument.

He spent his time at church, at AA meetings (he belonged to a group composed mainly of street people), and at work—with spare time given to consulting with me and serving as a liaison between me and potential interview participants. His church activities were primarily concerned with the social service service committee, in which capacity he dealt mainly with homeless mentally ill people. Therefore, almost everyone in his social network was "deviant," or "dysfunctional," or a "marginal" person. He explained this situation with another reference to the Man Born Blind. "Do you ever hear about him later on—like, was he one of the big-time apostles? No, you do not. I mean, even after that big introduction, he kinda disappears. But you know what? I bet he didn't disappear at all—I bet he did all his apostling with other nobodies like him and that's why you never hear about him. He *knew* people like him could only be reached by people like him." This attitude also explained why he invariably referred to himself— and asked others to refer to him—as Eutaw Jack, even though he had been taken away from his home town as a young child, had never been back, and no longer had even remote family connections there. "Everybody's gotta be from some place. You never really are anything but what you were. The Man Born Blind didn't stay blind, but that's how he was born, and that's how we still talk about him all these years later."

Eutaw Jack had a very clear notion of what he could do, and he didn't aim to tempt fate by stepping out of those bounds. He believed that his goal should be depth rather than breadth. In his "blindness" he had tried to "play the bigshot" and do everything. Now he just wanted to "bloom where I'm planted." And he was planted squarely in the world of those who, in the eyes of the mainstream, were on a par with the blind beggar—tainted nobodies who had value in the eyes of the Lord, if not of anyone else.

Although Eutaw Jack seemed at first to be a volatile character, he turned out to be one of the most controlled people I've ever known. Even his jarring mood swings were, I came to understand, part of the plan. He had a repertoire of voices and attitudes that he put on and took off as the occasion seemed to demand. He worked very hard not to give in to spontaneous emotional reactions. "That's what retards do," he told me on more than one occasion: "Real people [as he and so many of my retarded informants called the nonretarded people they dealt with in their daily lives] always know what they're doing." It did not occur to him that the arbitrary switching among moods and tones would strike "real people" as far more disordered than the simple giving way to honest emotion; he had great difficulty looking at himself and seeing the impression he might make on someone else in a specific social situation—surprising in one who had taken such pains to write a complete autobiography and who had such striking insight into his own overarching identity. Most of the "real people" in his life, like Lew and the church members, were so used to him that they didn't pay attention to his play-acting, although they were amused when a newcomer was caught off guard, as I had been by his first telephone outburst. I sometimes had to stifle an urge to tell someone he was yelling at, "But he's not really like that, you know!" knowing that

Eutaw Jack would have been genuinely angry had I presumed to "explain" him to others. He wanted very much to be the sole mediator between himself and the world.[2]

Eutaw Jack had come to believe that his own tortuous path to independent maturity had been marked most clearly by the development of his sexuality,[3] and it was he who urged me to explore this dimension of the question of deinstitutionalization. He had had casual and forgettable encounters with other residents (of both sexes) at the hospital, but after his release he went "hog wild." He convinced himself that in order to live up to his "free man" status, he'd have to do what all "real men" did, which he interpreted as "tomcattin' around." He did not hide his previous homosexual encounters but felt that they were simply matters of expediency, not of real preference. Given his odd behavior, he was not very successful in wooing "real women," and so he made do with prostitutes, often spending all his money on a quickie with a lady of the evening. He liked the prostitutes—they were nonjudgmental and seemed to empathize with others who were looked down on by mainstream people. But it hurt his pride to have to "pay for what a real man ought to have by right." After his "salvation," he swore off prostitutes—not out of moral fervor, but because he thought of such traffic as a symbol of his failure to be a "real man." He preferred to "do without" rather than have to pay for a woman's company. "It makes you even stronger," he averred, "when you do without because it's a stand for a principle."

I asked him about a year ago if this decision ever made him feel lonely. "No," he said decisively. "I have Jesus. And all my friends." We were at a back table at Wendy's at the time, and he suddenly stood up. I thought for a minute that he was going to poll the room and tally up his friends, but he immediately sat down. "Listen," he whispered. "I've got something to tell you." His eyes searched mine for several long minutes, and I knew he wasn't acting out a friends-tell-each-other-secrets minidrama. I knew enough about him by then not to prompt; he would say what he had to say in his own good time. He dropped his eyes, dabbled a straw in his Coke, and then swung his chair around to look out the window.

I waited.

At length, he turned to face me again and said, very softly, "I've got it."

"What?" I asked, thinking he had come up with the solution to one of my research problems. (Ever the self-absorbed researcher, I was hoping he had an opinion as to whether a certain informant, who had turned hostile, was abusing alcohol again, and, if so, what he thought I ought to do about it.)

"I mean, I've got *it*." He pronounced the word with peculiar vehemence and stopped, as if waiting for me to acknowledge that I knew what "it" meant, so that he wouldn't have to say the dread thing—whatever it was—out loud. I was, however, stumped, and stared back with what I hoped was a friendly, encouraging smile.

"You know . . ."

I waited.

"I'm . . . positive."

"Positive about what?"

He shook his head and laughed, heartily but mirthlessly, and snorted, "You really are one dumb fuck of a college boy!"

The light bulb finally clicked on and I gasped, "You're HIV-positive?"

He nodded and shrugged his shoulders, saying nothing. I reached out to take his hand, but he pulled back. "You'll catch it!" he hissed. "I don't think so," I said, withdrawing nonetheless. I told myself that I did so to spare him embarrassment—it wasn't the time to give him a lecture on AIDS hygiene. But I wasn't as sure about my motives as I seemed to be. I knew other people who were HIV-positive, but Eutaw Jack was different. There was almost certainly a part of me that felt that he was less a friend to be accepted uncritically than someone I had used for my own academic purposes; actually taking his hand might have meant a commitment to him beyond our anthropological dealings, a commitment I was grateful enough to be allowed to avoid.

"When did you find out?" I asked after a while.

"Just yesterday. I already told the pastor, and he said not to worry about any of the expenses and all—the church people will take care of me." He, of course, had no insurance of his own.

"What made you get tested? Did you think something might have happened . . . ?"

"A lot of things happened. I never put two and two together, you know. But Doc Grace—he takes care of all the guys at OH ["Opportunity House," my pseudonym for the agency for deinstitutionalized mentally retarded adults from which I had drawn most of my informants]—knew about some of what I done, and he said maybe I oughta. Guess it's better to know than not to, even though I ain't doing none of that shit no more."

"Well, you know that you may not start feeling sick for a long, long time, especially if you do what the doctor says."

"I know. But it don't matter. I'm ready."

How could anyone ever be "ready"? I thought as I stared at him. He was as serene as I'd ever seen him, but I was too confused to tell whether he truly was calm or simply playing a don't-show-emotion game. He may have guessed my thoughts, because he said, "You know, it's that damn ole Man Born Blind again. I can't get away from him!"

"How do you figure?"

"Well, it's like Jesus said about him. It wasn't his sins or nobody else's that made him the way he was—it wasn't nobody's fault, but it was a way to show that God heals us all in the end, if only we got faith."

"Do you really have that kind of faith?"

"I gotta believe I do, else I'm sunk."

Another silence descended as I tried to sort out my feelings and gauge Eutaw Jack's reactions. After a while I asked him, "Do you think now you'd like to get back to your own life story? You must have spent so much time on it before." Leave it to a professor to assume that the completion of an academic project would help someone face eternity with a clear conscience.

"Thanks, but no. I already wrote all that stuff down. It didn't take but a couple of days anyhow. I did it for me, I guess. I don't care if nobody else never reads it. Well, maybe at first it mattered, but no more. Maybe what I'm called to do is to help you help them other guys who don't know how to talk as good as me tell their stories. I gotta think that's what the Man Born Blind must've done: he didn't puff himself up and parade himself around like he done something great. He *knew* he didn't do nothing. But I bet—I truly bet—he went around to other guys like him and helped them understand that they could see too, if only they knew that Jesus was with them. He brought 'em to Jesus, don't you know."

"You're not saying I'm Jesus, are you?" I laughed nervously.

"Hell no!" he guffawed.

"So if you're the Man Born Blind and the guys who tell me their stories are like other blind beggars, but I'm not Jesus, then who am *I*?"

"Well, college boy, you figure it out—who else is there in the story?"

Afterword

Eutaw Jack remains asymptomatic as of this writing, and his life has not changed substantially. My project has come to an academically satisfying close, but taking to heart his metaphorical categorization of my role, I no longer assume that I "see" just because I can make a plausible theoretical analysis of a body of narrative data. I learned from him that people with mental disabilities are not defined and stereotyped by their condition—they are people first, with a range of moods and motivations and very definite ways of thinking of themselves. It is only we who assume that their condition is all-important, who typically interact with them as if they were walking embodiments of a diagnostic category. Eutaw Jack showed me that they were members of our own culture, using elements of that culture (like storytelling) to help them cope with an environment, just as we all do; mental disability is simply one factor in this coping repertoire—a powerful one to be sure, but not its sole defining character.

Eutaw Jack and I still meet for lunch at Wendy's, and I shake his hand gratefully whenever we get together.

Notes

[1] My analytic approach has been based on the rhetorical use of the formal properties of the autobiographical narrative, a genre of life history study that has been characterized by Peacock and Holland (1993:371) as "story-focused," as opposed to "life-focused," analysis.

[2] Eutaw Jack signed a release statement permitting me to contribute this essay to the published collection. In it, he acknowledged that he had read the essay and believed it to be accurate. I was uneasy at first, in light of this assessment of his self-awareness. But as he signed the form, he smiled and said, "You really got me dead to rights!" I suspect that circumstances in his own life at the time he read the essay (to be discussed below) explain his mellow reaction to something that earlier would probably have made him very angry.

[3] Sexuality is one of the key areas in the search for identity among adults with mental retardation. Vulgar stereotypes feature either the sweet, innocent, asexual retarded person or the amoral, insatiable sexual monster. In truth, retarded people exhibit the same range of sexual appetites and tastes as "real people," although they have an even more difficult time sorting out the nuances of "relationship behavior." (See, e.g., Angrosino and Zagnoli 1992.)

PATRICIA D. BEAVER

THE CHINESE CONSTRUCTION OF AN AMERICAN ANTHROPOLOGIST

Beaver's work explores the relationships that develop in China when the anthropologist is an American wife and mother, a Chinese colleague, and an American researcher of Chinese culture. Traveling to China in the aftermath of the Democracy Movement and the Tiananmen Square massacre of June 4, 1989, Beaver found a climate of repression that accentuated the gap between the freedom of movement and life choices available to American and Chinese scholars. A university teacher in China, Beaver was greeted with enthusiasm by her Chinese colleagues, who shaped the direction and content of her research. She entered the field to learn more about Chinese culture and found herself defined by her colleagues in ways that would serve their ends as well as her own. Rather than subjects of her research, her colleagues became active collaborators and friends in enduring relationships that continued after the fieldwork period had ended.

Reciprocity *(guanxi)* is a central fact of all Chinese (and all human) relationships, and a principle that Beaver more fully understood when confronted — after she returned home — with obligations to reciprocate the multiple acts of kindness that made her fieldwork successful. She entered into the study of *qigong*, a form of traditional Chinese spirituality, as a retreat from the daily demands of work and family. Yet her understanding of both qigong and guanxi were informed by her childhood experiences with Christianity and her Chinese friendships.

September 4, 1990

"Lao Bai?" I hesitantly whispered to the old night watchman. His sleep now disturbed, he muttered groggy morning greetings. Then gathering himself from the couch, he padded across the floor of the dimly lighted hotel lobby and rattled the cumbersome keys to open the padlocked front doors. Thanking him profusely, I stepped into the stillness before dawn, startling in contrast to the brash daytime noise of trucks and car horns. The unusual quiet alerted all my senses to the shadows of the night; yet the sounds of crickets soothed my padded footfalls. I hurried along the road between silent gray buildings, stark in their quietude, to the nearby park. Winding my way through the well-worn paths between scrubby bushes and scattered pines, I sighted the familiar trees, and then the liquid motion of the human forms in the movements of *qigong.* I silently assumed a place nearby in front of a tree that would become my familiar focus of these morning rituals of renewal. Beginning the journey through the five balance movements these new friends had taught me two days before, I tried to remember to breathe, to move, to count the twenty-four repetitions of each movement, while focusing on the movement of *qi,* of spirit, breath, life force, from the tree and into my outstretched hands, through my body and into the earth.

May 4, 1992

Today I received a letter from a Chinese friend, written in
green ink, which she explains is the color of love. She reminds
me of the good times we had together in China, that she
dreams of seeing us soon, and that we are her best friends.
She closes her long, newsy, yet thoughtful letter with a
request to come to my university and study with me—to be
my Ph.D. student. Yet my university has no Ph.D. programs,
nor do we offer a graduate degree in anthropology. I am at a
loss as to the proper response.

This paper reflects upon dynamics in the practice of ethnographic field research, particularly the entanglements of fieldwork,
what Clifford Geertz calls the "anthropological irony" of relationships
that are simultaneously sincere and "bordering on deceit" (Geertz
1968: 155). While in China, I unwittingly participated in a complex
system of reciprocity, called *guanxi*, receiving cultural knowledge and
friendship in exchange for the fulfillment of unspecified requests. In
marked contrast to the polarities formed through my scholarship, I
simultaneously studied *qigong* with people in whom I found comfort
and peace, in part from the balanced quality of our relationships.
Qigong, like its more familiar cousin *tai chi*, is derived from Taoism.
It involves the practice of specific exercises and movements to achieve
health and well-being. While novices focus on morning exercise
routines, skilled masters reputedly can heal illness and injury, and
traditional Chinese hospitals frequently offer qigong as a treatment
option.

I began field research in China in the fall of 1990 with great
uncertainty, not knowing if any research agenda would be tenable. In
the wake of repressions following the 1989 Democracy Movement and
rumors of repression of faculty and students at the university where
I worked in China, I had no feeling for the climate that might exist for
social science research. However, within the first two weeks of arriving
in China, I was approached, indeed embraced, by the social science
department. Social sciences in China suffered repression during the
Cultural Revolution (1966–76) and were only rehabilitated in the
mid-1980s. The existence of the three-year-old department at the
Chinese engineering university was a happy surprise to me. Within
a month of my arrival in China, the two department heads had helped
me outline a research program on the impact of the decade of economic
reform policies on Chinese women and the urban family, had assigned
me two research assistants, and had proposed the creation of a
cooperative center between their university and mine. As the months
wore on, our research proceeded, with frequent communication and
meetings, as I sought to work carefully with my Chinese colleagues

and to fulfill my own research objectives for qualitative and interview data.

Previous research experience in China during the 1983–84 academic year had shown me the difficulty of gaining access to Chinese communities. Foreign experts are routinely housed in foreign guest areas and restricted in their access to local residential areas. Official channels, littered with bureaucratic obstacles, are necessary for approval of research agendas. My earlier experience, and those of others working in the northeast, had proven that the best research plans were often allowed implementation only in the last two months of a year-long stay in China, and many colleagues have left China angry and frustrated with the bureaucratic morass. While I had inquired about alternative housing, I knew that my family would be required to live in foreign guest quarters, removed from the Chinese communities we sought to know.

My study of qigong was part of a fascination with Chinese spirituality, healing, and curing not directly related to my scholarship. My Southern Baptist upbringing and anthropological training have bequeathed to me a respect for other forms of spirituality, coupled with a generous dose of skepticism. I participated in an exercise program with a spiritual core to understand this belief system, and to get some regular exercise. The group of three allowed me into their midst and shared with me their knowledge. I came to the group through my long-term friendship with one of the participants, a woman I have known since 1983. As friends, we enjoyed each other's company. Unlike the social world that began after dawn, this group asked nothing of me, and of them, I asked only to be tolerated. They chose to share knowledge, to include me in workshops, to lead me into further steps in qigong, because they were inspired by an understanding that once one becomes a master of qigong by opening the flow of *qi* into one's own being, then one can see the illness, the imbalance in someone else's heart. One must help others interpret the experiences that may occur along the way of practicing qigong.

September 2, 1990

> In the first light of dawn, my friend led me to a wooded area of the park. There I saw a man and woman conversing as they moved their arms in graceful arcs; then pausing, they would continue to converse as if discussing some point of interpretation. My friend introduced me to the man as a qigong master and to the woman as one whose qigong movements were particularly praiseworthy. As I stood awkwardly in their midst, they talked among themselves in barely audible tones before addressing me directly. Then my friend patiently explained that I should not learn carelessly or

incorrectly, lest my qi (energy/life force) be misdirected into the wrong part of my body. The master then turned with his palms toward me and stood quietly, eyes closed in meditation. I too stood still, in my uncertainly attempting to maintain a semblance of calm. After a few long moments, he began to speak to me of my health. He said that I had three problems of concern, which he labeled female problems, fatigue, and a heart condition that sometimes makes my heart beat rapidly. I listened in stunned amazement, feeling somehow exposed, as a complete stranger in an alien land had seen beneath my skin. Yet aware of possible nonspecific "female problems," the restless night before spent fighting periods of wakefulness in anticipation of this encounter, and a long diagnosed history of paroxysmal atrial tachycardia (PAT), a heart condition manifest in sudden periods of rapid heart beats, I discarded my misgivings, abandoning myself to trust in these strangers. Following their instructions in the first five balance movements, we began these graceful exercises, completing the session with a quiet cooling-down period, in which the qi is allowed to dissipate from every pore of one's body into the earth beneath one's feet, the air, and the sky. Then, as the sun rose full in the morning sky, we parted, and I reflected upon this new experience. We must be open to those exquisite moments of clarity, of understanding, or of beauty that may occur on the morning path worn smooth by countless numbers of feet in search of awareness and well-being. In becoming consumed by the demands of the days, we can overlook these gentle paths to knowledge.

The political climate in 1990 was indeed confusing. Radical economic changes resulting from the roughly ten years of new economic reform policies were in evidence at every turn. New markets, vast arrays of consumer goods, and a variety of clothing fashions were dazzling to the eye accustomed to the more conservative style of the early 1980s. Bold and aggressive ventures in international business were likewise evident to us, particularly situated as we were in the hub of the international community on campus. Daily encounters with Russian, Korean, Japanese, Hong Kong, and American business and technical experts enlivened our residence in the hotel.

Yet a quiet undercurrent of repression likewise was in evidence. Social science department faculty and students had been in the forefront of massive demonstrations as part of the 1989 Democracy Movement. Across China, reprisals against intellectuals had sent young teachers into factories for a year's reeducation and had caused the virtual blacklisting of graduating students seeking jobs. In addition, new government regulations required that college graduates must work for five years before being permitted to travel out of China for higher education. Thus, despite a comparatively relaxed political environment on the surface, there was an undercurrent of suspicion, repression, and fear. Indeed, as the year wore on, this undercurrent became more evident. Despite the freedom I exercised in my Chinese classroom, a Chinese colleague was criticized for having had me lecture on Western philosophical ideas and feminism to his social science class. Similarly, an invited lecture I prepared on the Western family for a social science class was abruptly canceled on the day it was scheduled, and the six seminars I had been asked to present for the social science faculty never materialized.

With the uncertain political climate in mind, I had agreed to teach English and was quite satisfied with the assignment of a class of graduate students preparing for the English examination (TOEFL) necessary for admission to graduate programs abroad. I met with this class of 22- to 40-year-old teachers and graduate students ten hours a week for the fall semester. Politically dissident opinions were not uncommon in class discussion, although I neither encouraged nor discouraged such expression. I conducted multiple interviews with several of the students for whom I became a confidante for the articulation of politically unacceptable ideas. Needless to say, we became intensely involved with each other. For example, Mr. Jing, as the class monitor, was responsible for assisting me and keeping track of the other students. Though extremely cautious politically, he often chatted with me, and I interviewed him. He also translated some materials for my husband, and our friendship developed. My family was invited to attend his sumptuous wedding, including being carried to the festivities in a taxi. We brought a small pair of cloisonné vases as a wedding gift, a generous but not immodest gift. I had intended my gift to be a thank-you for his attentiveness to my needs in class and, I guess, to settle my social debt. However, the evening before we left China, Mr. Jing and his new wife came to call, bearing a complete set of eight tricolor Tang dynasty reproduction porcelain horses, each approximately nine inches high. I thus left China in his debt.

The concept of guanxi is central to all social relationships in China. "Literally, *guanxi* means 'relationship,' but in the context of the gift economy it has the sense of social connections, connections which must be carefully initiated, preserved and renewed through the giving and receiving of gifts, favors, and dinners or banquets." It involves social capital built upon "pre-existing relationships of classmates, people from the same native-place, relatives, superior and subordinate in the same workplace" (Yang 1988:411). I have been aware of the importance of guanxi, a commonplace term in everyday life, as long as I have worked in China. However, I had viewed guanxi relationships as internal to the everyday workings of *that* society; I did not perceive myself as significantly connected into this system because of the relatively shallow depth of my associations, my inability to maintain reciprocal relationships on the basis of one-year stays seven years apart, and the fact that I am not Chinese. For many Westerners, be they teachers, researchers, or business and industry representatives, guanxi is an impediment, an annoyance, an obstacle to the smooth operation of a sometimes dysfunctional social and economic order. While scholars of China recognize the importance of guanxi relationships in all Chinese social interactions, guanxi is commonly described as internal to the Chinese social order, grounded in Chinese kinship or in school- or work-based friendships of long duration. Thus, outsiders are implicitly part of the guanxi system only insofar as they must be taught the proper gift to give for certain favors.

We were constantly bombarded with the term guanxi—in my formal research and that of my historian husband, in my private interviews with students and colleagues, in the day-to-day relationships of dealing with my children's schools, the marketplaces, or buying train tickets. The Foreign Affairs office was unable to purchase train tickets for us after the new train station opened because they had no guanxi with the new station's employees. My husband was given explicit instructions on the proper gift to give each official whom he wished to interview or request permission to access specific historical documents. In March of 1991, as we prepared to ship most of our belongings back to the United States, we were annoyed by the fact that we had to purchase cartons of Marlboro cigarettes as guanxi for the customs officials in order to expedite inspection of our personal belongings.

Despite the initial and continuing uncertainties, obstacles, and misunderstandings, the 1990–91 academic year proved to be a fruitful research year. Doors were opened to me that had been barred in 1983, homes were open to my family as we dined on the simpler family fare in small, crowded apartments that we were rarely allowed to glimpse before. Relationships established in those earlier years were rekindled, and new friendships formed. We were included in department celebrations and festivities and the round of parties celebrating changing seasons.

Well into the fall of 1990, I received a quiet request from a Chinese colleague to sponsor her so that she could join her husband in the United States. I began preparations, and soon the news that I was preparing to sponsor *someone* spread through the Foreign Affairs and Social Science departments, contributing to a climate of suspicion and intrigue. Before long, another colleague inquired about the possibility of admission to a graduate program at my institution. Again, I began to make inquiries on her behalf; yet our separate discussions were conducted in a climate of secrecy. As the year wore on, various students began to inquire about how to get into American graduate schools. I carefully explained the absolute requirements of successful completion of GREs and TOEFL and submission of completed application materials. However, I learned of the difficulty of gaining permission to even take the GREs and TOEFL, which frequently requires guanxi relations as a way around the long wait on a long list that may take years for one's name to reach the top. I was often confronted with requests for me to assist this son, this daughter-in-law, in gaining admission to this, or that, or any engineering or computer science Ph.D. program.

My research and family needs kept me from responding to the professional needs of many who inquired. My husband and I had research agendas in China, but we had a life in China as well; we were raising children, whose well-being and adjustment was of the utmost importance. I was teaching and supervising two of my American students who had come to China as well. As in the United States, and unlike my first fieldwork in rural Appalachia, my life was compartmentalized, or so I thought at the time. *This* relates to research; *this* is my personal life. My Chinese students' accounts of trying to get out of China through the back door were professional concerns, related to the Chinese bureaucracy; my youngest daughter's severe bronchitis and our dealings with the Chinese medical care system was a family crisis relating to my role as a parent; our necessary guanxi gifts to unknown bureaucrats and officials were annoyances, just another hassle and hazard of working in China.

October 14, 1990

I like being here in China. Life has a graceful, dare I say gentle, feel, but perhaps that's the influence of qigong. Qigong is the perfect belief system; it makes one's body feel wonderful, since the focus is on well-being, both spiritual and physical, with its origins in Taoism. I'm enjoying the community with my qigong companions, although primarily in silence. For the past few days, my friend has been teaching me new movements and a new cosmology. One steps along the sides and corners of an invisible square, whose center is divided into *yin* and *yang*, and whose sides and corners represent the four elements, the cardinal directions, and the organs of the body.

It is still remarkable to go out early in the morning to meet friends with whom I barely communicate and have them allow me into their belief system, their community, with so little communication necessary. Today my friend was not there, but the other woman led me through the new movements, and I am grateful, for they are indeed complex. Yet following her exquisite movements made the complicated process seem easy. She also taught me another set of movements, building on the previous diagrammatic representation, but including an overarching symbolism of the sun (I think).

To move my hands and arms in this way is graceful and relaxed, yet full of power. It makes me see my hands, and like my hands. I try to remember revelations of early dawn to record, but they slip away as quickly as I step back into my other life.

May 1992, Boone, North Carolina

Reaching for my office mail, I see that another letter has arrived from China. While I don't immediately recognize the surname, the address is all too familiar, and I open the thick letter with a sinking feeling. It is another poignant request from a Chinese colleague for sponsorship to my university, a request that I cannot fulfill.

Returning to the United States, I am blessed with a wealth of research materials, including a completed economic survey of 400 households, a number of interviews with unique constituencies, and materials that I acquired through my own relationships. I also have facilitated directly or indirectly the foreign study abroad for several Chinese faculty. Yet this is not enough.

I enter my freshman anthropology class and lecture my students—about the obligations we have to those we study, the embeddedness of culture, about reflexivity in field research—and feel very stupid.

My ultimate research strategy and research accomplishments were shaped by my Chinese colleagues, by the guanxi, the social capital established between myself, my husband, and individual scholars, by the guanxi built up in my university's ongoing relationship with the Chinese university. Only in coming home from China did I begin to understand my own embeddedness in the guanxi system and my obligations to reciprocate the negotiated social contracts. Guanxi relationships are part of my social capital whether or not I like it, and whether or not I return to China.

July 1992

Today, I received a letter from Mr. Jing, my TOEFL class monitor, who writes that he and his wife miss us after our year's absence. His letter closes with an eager request for my help in facilitating his graduate study in the United States. While in China, I had provided materials on various graduate engineering programs, encouragement of his pursuit of the TOEFL and GRE exams, advice on getting strong and specific references. There is really nothing more that I can do for this promising young engineer.

Simple reciprocity I learned from Marcel Mauss as a beginning student of anthropology and have taught to beginning students of anthropology for nineteen years. Yet how I am so easily manipulated by it, with the evocation of intense emotional response. Joseph Casagrande wrote, "One or a few individuals . . . may become [the anthropologist's] particular mentors and close associates" (1960:xi). My friend writes, "I dream of seeing you soon. You are my best friends in life."

Sometimes I never want to go back to China or have to deal with, much less think about, these entanglements. Sometimes I hate to receive letters from China, as each one comes with a request I cannot or sometimes do not want to fulfill. Casagrande wrote that "one's capacity for imaginatively entering into the life of another people becomes a primary qualification for the enthographer" (1960:xii). Yet I want to alienate myself from the entanglements with these people so that I can write the book that I have carefully researched about them and their lives. My friend writes, "an idea is bursting into my mind that whether you can accept me as a cooperator to study what you are working for one year." Yet I love China, I love the way it smells, feels, tastes, I love the smokey air that makes my eyes water on a cold morning, the calls of vendors selling tofu, that, remarkably, remind me of the vegetable woman who sold her wares on my grandmother's street in Macon, Georgia, when I was a child (My children find the imagery hilarious: "Miz Rankin, want to buy some to . . . fu?") I love the way women hold each other's hands in friendship and comfort. I love the liquid movements of human forms in the stillness of early dawn.

Yet the question lurking within every personal relationship with a Chinese friend remains: what will they ask of me; when and how can I accommodate it?

Nothing has prepared me for the personal impact of the current political climate in China or the social inequality existing between the Chinese and American intellectual communities—the United States the First World, China the Third. My American students and colleagues and I come and go, into and out of China, travel to Tibet or the Mongolian grasslands with impunity; my students may return to college, take a job for a while and drop out for a year, marry whomever they choose, transfer to another institution with a more appropriate curriculum. Jing, Han, Li, Wang, and all of the other intellectuals with whom I worked do not have such luxuries of indecision, of casual relationships, particularly since the Democracy Movement and the repression of intellectuals following the Tiananmen massacre of June 4, 1989. Yet Chinese intellectuals emerge from one of the world's oldest and most sophisticated scholarly traditions. Western imperialism has aggravated China's instability, contributing to the rise of the current regime. Like all Western scholars, I represent the imperialist forces. Like all Westerners, I also am a means of escape from political and economic repression within the current system. Many Westerners do sponsor Chinese friends or their children and permanently alter their lives. Prerequisite to sponsorship is a solid relationship of trust, a relationship of friendship. Friendship with a Westerner is an avenue out of China, into a romanticized existence from which few choose to return. Not many friendships turn into sponsorships, but for Chinese, it's worth a try; friendship is a profitable investment. By these definitions, I have many Chinese friends. Within a repressive situation limiting our separate quests, I have benefited from the multiple forms of research assistance and from the gestures of friendship clearly offered. I hope that my friends and colleagues have benefited equally from their relationship with me and my family, but I cannot offer all that they want or need.

What was my motivation for conducting research in China? To satisfy my intellectual hunger, to know China better so that I could teach my American students more effectively, to conduct research so that I could publish scholarly articles and gain prestige within the American academy.

What was my colleagues' motivation for working with me? Their collaboration was intended to facilitate my research. It was, above all, to cultivate me as a Sinologist, who could then facilitate their participation in the intellectual world outside China. It was to facilitate their departure from China. Their investment of social capital in me was a way of achieving greater options for their professional lives, and I was an instrument whereby they might gain passage out of China.

In 1960, eleven years after the Chinese Revolution, when few Americans were allowed into the People's Republic of China, Joseph Casagrande wrote that "Field work by its very nature is at heart a collaborative enterprise" (1960:x). He also noted that the anthropologist "needs the active cooperation of the people if he is to succeed in his work. That such cooperation is so often freely given is eloquent testimony to the universal good will of men. Let it be admitted, too, that the successful outcome of field research depends not only on the anthropologist's own skills, but also on the capabilities and interest of those who teach him their ways" (Casagrande 1960:x). My Chinese collaborators not only taught me their ways but became collaborators in an active sense, shaping not only my understanding but the very research design, all the while entrusting their futures in the hope of my goodwill.

October 10, 1990

My friend and I rode our bicycles across town amid the evening's traffic congestion to attend a qigong seminar. Her excitement that this famous master was in town was matched by my own excitement that she had invited me to come with her. We found our places among about 300 other participants gathered in a large gymnasium as the master began to lecture. He talked of opening one's inner vision through the *xue mu tian*, *xue* being the midpoint of one's forehead; *mu* the midpoint inside one's head between the temples; and *tian*, further inside one's head directly below the *bai hui*, or midpoint on the top of one's skull. The qi should travel into one's being along the path formed by these three points.

Following the lecture, we assumed cross-legged positions of meditation on the cushions brought for that purpose. One of the master's students and several local assistants moved through the silent throng as the master's voice directed the qigong exercises. My friend interpreted in hushed tones many of the movements, as we focused on bringing the qi (or light) from far away closer in, finally into the xue, the mu, and ultimately the tian. At one point I was aware that someone was working with me—I felt a tingle in my hair (at the bai hui) and the lightest hint of a touch on my back, then heard the voice of the master right behind me. Next we focused on moving the qi down through the spine, then through internal organs in a certain pattern. We repeated each of these and other movements, resting after each release of energy. The last fifteen minutes or so were a puzzle, as I could no longer understand the master's quiet Chinese and my friend became silent. No longer able to follow the process, I became conscious of my body, particularly my legs, which began to scream with pain after the hour and a half of immobility. The master and his assistants had bamboo sticks that they swung through the air to spread the master's powerful healing qi around to benefit everyone. The sounds of the bamboo poles slicing the air was like birds whistling to each other. At one point during my restless agony I felt the end of the bamboo lightly touch my knee, a reminder to be still.

As we pedaled through the smokey darkness on the way home, my friend and I discussed the events of the evening. I had been amazed to sit among so many people who were so quiet and still for so long. In fact, I had been agonizing over the pain in my legs, determined not to move and be outdone, when I heard the barely audible sound of a woman's quiet sobbing. I was thrilled that someone had achieved the opening of the inner eye, the master's goal for the evening's workshop. As we pedaled home, I remarked to my friend about this, and she looked at me in dumbfounded surprise. She patiently explained that the woman was crying because her legs hurt. I

had interpreted her weeping in the Southern Baptist way,
assuming that an emotional outburst was a sign of revelation.
Of course, Chinese don't experience enlightenment in qigong
in the Southern Baptist tradition of ecstasy.

Along with the weight of sin, evil, and ecstatic religious
expression, the other legacy of my Southern Baptist upbringing is
intense guilt over unfulfilled obligations. Unable to respond to my friend
and colleague in green ink, unable to take her on as a student to study
with me, I have let our correspondence wane. In the sinless, guilt-free
balance of qigong I found escape from the demands of reality in the
social world. Yet to be studying the relations in which one is embedded,
like fulfilling one's obligations on more familiar home territory, is
stressful and challenging and absolutely necessary.

RUTH BEHAR

MY MEXICAN FRIEND MARTA
WHO LIVES ACROSS
THE BORDER FROM ME
IN DETROIT

In this ethnographic story, Behar plumbs the cultural, psychologic, social, and medical factors leading to her Mexican friend Marta's decision to have a hysterectomy at the age of twenty-six. Behar analyzes Marta's life story as well as their own relationship, exploring the racial, class, and national differences between them that create borders that need to be crossed sensitively, and sometimes painfully, for friendship to flourish. By investigating the relationship between Marta's life in Detroit and the author's life in Ann Arbor, this story explores the predicaments of maintaining the fiction of ethnographic research between two women living as "neighbors" in an unequal society.

Marta and I live a half-hour away from each other, but there is a gaping-wide border between the corner house she and her family are borrowing from her brother-in-law in Detroit and my two-story Victorian house in a quiet tree-lined neighborhood of Ann Arbor. Neither of us ever pretends that this border is inconsequential. Yet the circumstances of our lives have brought us at once so close and so far, and within that space we've managed to build a friendship.

It is June of 1993, and I am preparing for a return visit to Marta's hometown in Mexico, where my husband and I have lived, off and on, for ten years. She herself can't go back, because her husband Saúl has just lost his job and their economic situation is shaky. So this year I will be the one to hug her parents and sisters, and to spend afternoons chatting in the patio with her *abuelitos*.

Marta arrives with her husband Saúl to drop off a Sears catalogue for me to take to her family. And she brings their video camera to shoot some footage of my house. For Marta my house is a museum. She goes around talking into the camera as she points out highlights in our living room and dining room. "We come to this house a lot. Our friends like to invite us over," she says, chuckling.

An earlier version of this essay, titled "My Mexican Friend Marta Who Lost Her Womb on This Side of the Border," appeared in *Journal of Women's Health*, vol. 2, no. 1 (1993): 85–89.

My house is filled with books, embroidered cloths, and antique furniture; and there are clay pots, enameled trays, and bark paintings brought from Mexico. It is a house of many rooms, wood-paneled windows, and a garden. I sometimes can't believe it is my house, bought with my own money. As a Cuban immigrant kid, I grew up in a series of cramped apartments in New York, so when Marta tells me she loves to come to my house, that it is her dream house, I understand, but feel odd that the things I have acquired are inspiring wanting and longing in someone else. She takes notice of anything new—a wicker chair, a used piano, a Turkish beaded good luck charm, new tiles in the bathroom with whimsical nopal cactuses, also brought with us from Mexico.

Marta focuses her camera on all of my Mexican wares. "Look at all the beautiful things from Mexico," she says into the camera. She seems to be displaying for her family back in Mexico all the Mexican things the anthropologist has in her house, which the Mexican herself, namely Marta, doesn't want to have. Marta, for whom Mexico is her grandparents, her seven siblings, and her mother and father, who were always working not to become poor, desires none of these things; she dreams of packages filled with pretty white linens, edged in lace, that you order from catalogues, and she wants elegant, gold-trimmed porcelain dishes, the kind you can sometimes find on sale for fifteen dollars, service for four, at K-Mart.

I am always the one who phones Marta. When Marta decided to marry Saúl and come live with him in the United States, I made a promise to her parents and grandparents in Mexico that I would always look out for her on this side of the border. I haven't been able to explain to her family that another border separates us here.

"Marta, how are you?" I ask in Spanish, addressing her in the informal *tú*. We have spoken our native Spanish to each other since we met ten years ago in Mexico. We may both speak English to our sons, but our friendship is lived in Spanish.

"I'm fine. And you?" Marta always addresses me in the formal you, as *usted*. She won't let me forget that I am ten years her senior; that when we met in Mexico she was a young girl finishing high school, and I was already a married woman embarking on a career as a writer. Even after seven years in the United States, and my continual requests that she address me as *tú*, Marta insists on maintaining certain formalities that acknowledge the age, cultural, educational, and class differences between us.

"And how is Saúl?"

"He's okay. He got that job teaching high school Spanish. Says he's going to earn almost as much as he used to at his old job. Says he's looking forward to the long summer vacations. We're just waiting for them to call about his physical exam."

I have known Saúl for about as many years as I have known Marta. Born in the United States of Mexican parents, Saúl grew up in Michigan, working summers with his four brothers and their parents in the cherry, apple, and cucumber harvests. When I met Saúl, he was searching for his roots in the same Mexican town in which my husband and I were searching for a topic to study. He'd usually visit around Christmas, hosting lively *posadas* at the house of his mother's cousin, where the *tamales* were plentiful and a big *piñata* bulging with sweets was never lacking. On one of his first visits, when I met him, he came with a girlfriend, a *gringa* with long curly blond hair; and years before, he had come with a different girlfriend, also a *gringa*.

But during the Christmas season in 1983, he came alone. Marta, who had won a scholarship to attend a state boarding school, was home on a vacation from her job teaching in a rural school. Her hair was permed, she wore a pink knit blouse and fitted pants, and she danced an entire night with Saúl at a fifteenth-birthday party, the *quinceañera*, of a cousin. Soon after, when he returned to the States, they wrote letters to each other every day. Two years later, they decided to get married, against the objections of Marta's father. He described Saúl, thirteen years older than Marta, as a *gallo*, an old rooster, who wanted the hand of a *pollito*, a little chick.

Marta and Saúl were married in a big church wedding in Mexico in December of 1985 and moved to East Lansing, where Saúl worked in the personnel department of Michigan State University. In the university setting, Marta met other women from Latin America and studied English. Saúl, who realized he'd taken Marta away from her job, hoped she'd prepare to become a teacher of bilingual education. But Marta soon decided she wanted to have a child and, without letting Saúl know, she let him get her pregnant. What she hadn't expected was that it would happen so quickly.

Their son, Eduardo, was born in 1988, when Marta was twenty-three, and in 1989 they moved to the Detroit area, where Saúl found a better-paying job in a state government office. For the next three years they lived in a garden apartment in Romulus, under the flight paths of the Detroit Metro airport, where few families with children lived. Marta felt unsafe and stayed indoors all the time, shut within the four walls of their apartment, with her baby and the television as her only companions. Marta says she learned English watching soap operas. Later they moved to another apartment in Westland, where there were more families with children, and the stores were within walking distance. It was not yet Marta's dream house, but at least she felt less isolated.

Then Saúl lost his job. To save money he and Marta gave up their garden apartment and moved into his brother's house. It was a difficult moment, especially because they had taken on the added responsibility of caring for Marta's brother and sister, who had come from Mexico with all their papers in order thanks to Saúl's efforts. Polo and Lisandra planned to complete their last year of high school in the United States and then study in a community college. The two of them had learned English quickly and progressed rapidly in their schoolwork. Saúl was proud of them and hoped their presence would cheer up Marta, who had grown depressed and moody in her new surroundings.

"Guess what?" Marta suddenly announces. "I've signed up for a course. Saúl says it would be good for me. It's a course about relationships, about letting go of the anger you've been carrying around since you were a child. Do you know I still have dreams in which I get angry because my mother isn't home to take care of me?"

Women think back through their mothers, and, indeed, Marta wants to become a different kind of mother than her mother. Marta tells me that her adult self comprehends that her mother had to work hard, first as a peddler and then as a schoolteacher, to care for her eight children; but even so, she says with anguish, she can't forget how as a child she felt neglected and wished she could be wrapped inside her mother's arms, those arms which were always busy working. In the United States, Marta imagined she could become the mother she didn't have, the mother who would plan her pregnancy and be exclusively devoted to her child. And so she chose to have one child, Eduardo, for whom she has cared singlehandedly during the early years of his childhood. And she has chosen, too, to make it impossible to ever have another child.

It is October of 1992, five months after Marta's hysterectomy. With some hesitation I have asked Marta if I can write about her operation for a conference on women's health. I fear that treating her as an anthropological subject will hurt our friendship, but Marta immediately agrees to let me write about her. She considers it an honor, she says, that I am interested.

We sit on her bed with the white lace coverlet. A mirror is behind Marta, and I try not to look at my own face as I look at her. Little Eddy is in the living room playing with my husband, David, who has accompanied me on this trip because I don't like to drive to Detroit alone. The tape recorder is on the bed, and I hold up the microphone toward Marta. We don't know that the tape recorder is not recording anything; only later, when I get home, will I learn that David forgot to put the batteries in the microphone.

On three sheets of lined looseleaf paper, Marta has begun to write her life story in a few broad strokes. I read her handwritten words and notice how careful she has been to leave out anything painful; but her sense of solitude is profound and it surfaces, unwittingly, several times in her brief text, which ends in midsentence, with the words, "I have tried not to be an abnegated wife, but a . . ." She has held within herself all the pain of social and cultural displacement, all the tension of her rite of passage from virgin to wife, and all the anxieties of losing her womb so soon after becoming a mother.

Knowing that she planned to have only one, or maybe two, children of her own, Marta tells me she tried to enjoy every moment of her pregnancy. It was a special time that she remembers with joy. But giving birth was a nightmare for her. At the hospital, when she became fully dilated, the doctors told her that the baby's head was too big and that they needed to perform a C-section. They had given her a spinal block for pain relief, and later they put her under total anaesthesia to perform the C-section. Saúl was not allowed to be present at the birth, and the staff delayed bringing the baby to her. Apparently the anesthesiologist was sloppy, because after giving birth Marta suffered from terrible spinal headaches and body pains for four months. She cries, remembering how she could barely take care of Eddy at first. For Marta, having a C-section, especially one that was botched and alienating, made her feel that her womb wasn't worth much. She told me that the doctor who took out her uterus cut along the dotted line of her C-section scar.

Marta found the doctor who performed her hysterectomy, a board-certified obstetrician, in the phone book. She had already gone to two other doctors, both women, before seeing him. The two previous doctors, she felt, were unscrupulous in their desire for money; after learning what a good health insurance plan she had through her husband's job, they had immediately wanted to perform hysterectomies without even running a single test or analysis. As a rule she prefers women doctors, she says, because she's a Latina and finds it shameful to be examined by a man. But the doctor she found in the phone book impressed her enough that she put her trust in him. He's Cuban, she tells me, which I already know, cringing at the thought that Marta, in a subliminal way, may have put her trust in him because she's learned from me that Cubans are okay. I am holding the microphone that is taping nothing as she tells me that she wanted to have tests done, and the Cuban doctor did them. She wanted to be sure she needed this operation, and he convinced her she did. Her heavy menstrual bleeding had worried her since she was a young girl, but after giving birth, it had gotten worse. She had to rest during her periods and take iron; during those days, she fell behind on the cooking and cleaning, and she didn't like that, because if the house was going to be her only responsibility, she wanted to do it well. The doctor told her that if she went on bleeding so heavily, one day she'd have a hemorrhage. He also told her that she had a tumor in her uterus, but after removing the uterus he admitted there was no tumor. He claimed her uterus was abnormally enlarged, that it had not shrunk back to its proper size after pregnancy.

Marta is beginning to question her doctor's advice and motives. She's not so sure anymore that he wasn't out for the money too. And she recognizes that he's not so honest, perhaps, as she thought at first. When she tells him she's been gaining weight after the operation, he pretends it's her eating habits that are responsible; later she finds out that it's very common for women who lose their uterus to put on weight. But what matters is her health, she says. It's nice not to be worried about her periods anymore or about getting pregnant. She couldn't have gone on taking iron pills forever. And if she's not going to have any more children anyway, then she really doesn't need her uterus. She's lucky, she tells me, that Saúl is educated and accepts her in her new wombless state. In Mexico, she says, there are men who won't have a woman who's had a hysterectomy; they claim those women aren't women anymore.

Marta needs to affirm to herself that her decision was a wise one. She thought about it for a year, and she feels she explored her options by getting several medical opinions. She believes her health has improved, that she is really better, much better. But the loss of her uterus has made her aware of all her losses—of everything she has given up, everything she is giving up, to make a new life for herself and her family on this side of the border.

You know, Marta says to me, the last time she was in Mexico she and her mother were joking around and her mother called her a good-for-nothing. Those words—"*no sirves para nada*"—stung, and the pain was compounded when Saúl recently said the same thing to her, also as a joke. As she recounts this, Marta's eyes fill with tears. Marta was the second daughter; it was her sister, the eldest, who was always the smart one, always the favorite of her father. When she was in Mexico, her father told her how proud he was of her older unmarried sister for having gotten so far in her studies and achieving degrees in two fields. But he didn't say anything to Marta about being proud of her. She longs for greater affirmation from her parents, and yet her deepest wish is to someday bring them both to the United States and provide for them in their old age.

Marta left everything behind to come to the States with Saúl, but she didn't receive a very warm welcome from his family. When her mother-in-law suddenly developed an inexplicable illness, her father-in-law accused Marta of having used witchcraft to cause the illness; later he told Marta that Saúl didn't love her and that she was lucky he had paid any attention to her. One brother-in-law called her an Indian from the rancho because she refused to drink beer; another brother-in-law told her she was "*un perro entrenado*" (a trained dog), because she was so concerned to keep Saúl happy, having dinner on the table when he returned from work and setting his clothes out for him, neatly ironed, each morning.

She doesn't do those things for Saúl anymore, Marta says, because he never thanked her, never showed any appreciation. If Saúl thought he was bringing back a young and innocent Mexican wife to do all his housework for him, those days are over, she says, wiping her eyes, her face hardening.

As David and I drive back to Ann Arbor, I tell him about how Marta told me she often feels worthless, that her life isn't amounting to anything. Tears come into David's eyes; he says that's how he often feels.

In our relationship, the usual division of labor and power have been reversed. David has played the role of faculty wife, caring for our son, Gabriel, and doing the kind of secretarial work for me that male professors are always thanking their wives for in the acknowledgment section of their books. Most of the time, I am able to display gratitude for David's help on a more regular basis and to encourage him in his own work, but I have also been spoiled by the bargain prices he offers on his services; like my male counterparts, I've gotten into the habit of depending on certain unpaid labors from him. So, back at home, when I discover that the tape on which I am expecting to base my paper for the women's health conference hasn't come out, a paper that must be ready to present in a week, I break out in a merciless fury.

"Why did you give me that microphone in the first place? I've never used that silly thing before! How was I to know it needed its own battery? Aren't you the one who always handles that stuff? Now what am I going to do? I can't replicate the conversation I just had with Marta! I may as well forget about going to the conference. And my paper is one of the plenaries. Thanks to you, I won't be able to go!"

David's head sinks. "I'm sorry," he says. But I go on, repeating the litany of my complaints, even though I know I'll be able to piece my paper together from notes and memories. After a while he gets angry enough to say, "Well, next time, *you* get the tape recorder set up."

"That's very easy to say now, isn't it?"

"Look, if you don't like the way I do things, maybe I should just leave."

"You really love to press the anxiety button by threatening to leave just when I'm counting on you to take care of Gabriel. That's so cruel!"

In the afternoon the two of us go to our Yoga class, where we pretend not to recognize one another and occupy different parts of the room as though we were strangers.

Sometimes anthropology comes too close to home.

A few days later we return to Marta's house with a functioning tape recorder. David goes off to look at computers, and I stay with Marta and Eddy. Our conversation is not so intense this time because of Eddy's interruptions. At one point Marta takes Eddy in her arms and holds him tight. "I try to remember to do this at least once a day," she says. But later, he gets wilder and, trying to get her attention, he punches her in the belly. "I'll be right back," she says and goes into the bathroom with Eddy. I think I can hear her hitting him. Lisandra is back from school and comes in to entertain me. No, I can't believe she'd hit Eddy, her one and only. Would she?

Marta returns with Eddy, and I can't read any clues in his face or hers. From the closet she pulls out her photo album, and we slowly turn the pages, looking at the pictures of her as a student, eyes gleaming with promise. Eddy points to a picture of Marta and says, "Stupid!" Marta calmly says to him, "Don't say that. Say chicken." Eddy points to the picture again and says, "Stupid!" Marta takes a deep breath and repeats, "Say chicken, Eddy, okay?" Her eyes look as if they're starting to water. Finally, Eddy whispers "Chicken" and Marta says, "*Gracias*, that's better, Eddy."

Eddy soon tires of the pictures and rushes out to the living room to watch the cartoons on television. Lisandra, always good-natured, excuses herself and follows after him. Glad to be alone with me again, Marta returns to her closet and pulls out a stack of neatly folded, sparkling clean towels. "These are my towels," she says. "I don't let Saúl or Polo use them. Polo has pimples, and I don't want him staining my towels."

Then Marta pulls out a big plastic bag. It is full of letters, the love letters Saúl wrote to her from Minnesota, North Dakota, and Michigan in the two years of their romance. She reads from two of them: one letter is about his struggle to find work after deciding to leave Minnesota; the other is about how they should deal with the problem of getting married by the Catholic Church, given his family's conversion to Protestantism (but later, as Marta explains, it turns out that his grandmother had baptized him and there was no problem at all). He'd start his letters with *Amor mío* ("My love"), punctuating them constantly with those words. He wrote very lyrically and in correct Spanish. When he went to ask Marta's father if he'd let her marry him, Saúl announced, "I have a great weight upon my heart," and her father said, "Forget the poetry and get to the point."

Saúl saved all her letters, just as she saved all of his. But her letters are gone. Destroyed by her own hands. Why, I ask, unable to hide the disappointment in my voice. Marta says she just decided, one day, to tear them all up. She told Saúl she was going to do it. And all he said was, "Well, if that's what you want to do. . . ."

Back in a small town in Mexico, in the front room where her abuelitos sleep, Marta's wedding dress hangs from a nail in the wall. The dress remembers her body. Remembers how she danced before she said good-bye. Waits for her.

CLAIRE R. FARRER

TURNING THE STORM

Using the word *storm* as both an information term and a metaphor, Farrer allows glimpses of the ever-changing character of long-term fieldwork. She presents her interactions with her primary consultant, the late Bernard Second, through a dialogic framework. Second and Farrer were friends and partners in her anthropological and folkloristic work for almost fourteen years. It was the friendship more than the data that brought Farrer to her current level of understanding.

Here Farrer presents data Euroamerican cultures and people do not credit, such as witchcraft and the ability of one individual to change the weather. She also presents storms more easily understood by members of Western cultures, such as political storms and stormy interpersonal relationships. Each of the storms was turned into a positive experience, even if it took a bit of time and even if some of them still do not make sense to Euroamericans. It is the sense-making of the Other to Us that engages many in the anthropological enterprise.

Prologue

The majority of my adult life has been spent interacting, to a greater or lesser degree, with Mescalero Apaches of south-central New Mexico. From an initial social contact in 1964 through year-round fieldwork in 1974–75 and continuing with various intensities to the present, people from the Mescalero Apache Indian Reservation have been important in both my professional and personal lives.

The Mescalero Apache Indian Reservation covers about 720 square miles in south-central New Mexico. It is a high reservation, the lowest point being over 3,400 feet and the tallest mountain over 12,000 feet. Most of the reservation is well forested and cross-cut by deep, narrow canyons—it is no surprise that everyday directions are spoken of as being "up," "down," or "across."

The Tribal Council and people of the Reservation have several goals: to provide adequate housing for all, to provide jobs for all who are able to work, to manage carefully both natural and human resources, and to maintain and prolong their traditional way of life. Housing is always being built or remodeled at Mescalero, it seems. While there are many jobs—such as in forestry and wildlife— conservation, managing the communally owned Herefords, at the Inn of the Mountain Gods, in the recent gambling casino, in the sustained yield timber-cutting program and sawmill operation, in Tribal government, in small businesses, in law enforcement—there are not yet enough jobs for all. It is particularly difficult for young, well-educated people to find work at home. New plans are constantly under development to maximize both the natural resources and the vital people resources of the Reservation. Yet, despite all, people maintain that it is their traditions, and especially their religion, that is of primary importance. Indeed, although not so planned, it also became of primary importance to me.

No one was more important to me than the late Bernard Second, singer of ceremonies, as he preferred to be cailed rather than shaman, as most Euroamericans termed him. Bernard and I were fictive kin, at his instigation; we cooperated, fought, learned from each other, and loved each other as do most siblings whether they are born to a family or adopted into it, as were my daughter and I. It was he who taught me Apachean esoterica and about the everday, as well; and it was he who demanded the best of me from our initial meeting in February 1975 until his death in November 1988. It is his voice that I present here.

This essay assumed its shape after discussions with Bruce Grindal and his reading of some of my published and in-progress pieces. We agreed that a dialogic mode of presentation would be most effective for what I wished to communicate. Yet, the dialogic mode is not entirely satisfactory, either. A dialogue presupposes exchanges; in Euroamerican cultures it is usually of the I-talk/you-listen and I-listen/you-talk variety. Bernard did not often operate that way, especially after the first year or two we worked together. Our dialogues were almost always one-sided: he teaching me or me teaching him. We did occasionally have true dialogues and sometimes, as in Dialogue 1 below, they were about important subjects. Usually, however, our dialogues were of mundane subjects: the TV program we had just watched; arrangements for a forthcoming event; whether we should listen to Cajun, Indian, "chicken scratch," country, or popular music; whether to take a trip of long or short duration; who was going to dance with me at a local bar or powwow and what signal he wanted me to use to indicate he should rescue me from a partner I was not keen on; who was going to wash the dishes (and indeed whether anyone should bother since there were still some clean ones to use!).

My fieldnotes and tapes are full of talk, and occasional song, but little of it fits a proper dialogic mode. So when choosing the transcriptions of talk through the years that constitute this essay, I determined a thematic focus would best characterize the relationship Bernard and I shared. That theme is reflected in the title I chose.

Apaches in general and Mescalero Apaches in particular have faced many storms in their Anglo-recorded history. Some of the storms have been of a political nature; indeed, the Apaches are still fighting these, now inside courtrooms rather than outside on battlefields. Some storms are interpersonal but have had an effect on the tribal group as a whole. Some storms have been, and continue to be, of a social nature. And, of course, some storms are the physical ones that bring rain to parched desert land and snow to alpine altitudes or swirl about in dust devils, producing little of value to anyone. Here, I discuss four storms, each of which is preceded by a brief statement of setting, date, participants, general topic, and each of which is followed by an even more brief conclusion that I have placed in brackets to indicate that it was not part of the original conversation.

In each of the quotations, ellipses (. . .) indicate omissions of information while en-dashes (–) indicate pauses, with each dash approximating one second of time; brackets ([]) indicate editorial comments added by me. A slash (/) after an Apache word followed by an English word indicates the English translation of the Apache word. Apache uses sounds not common in English that I render as follows: 'n is a syllabic 'n' pronounced with a high tone; ' indicates a glottal stop; the slanted line over a vowel means it is pronounced with a high tone.

Dialogue 1–Social Storms

The third week of June 1975 was an exciting time on the Mescalero Apache Indian Reservation, for it was the first powwow in what became an annual event. In this dialogue, tape-recorded four months after Bernard and I began working together, I was trying to understand some of the parameters of Power and witchcraft, both of which can and do produce social storms. Power relates to the ability to influence others, whether animate or inanimate. Power has no valence; it is neither good nor bad but can be used for either purpose. Those who abuse Power are considered to be witches, those intent on doing harm to others for the betterment of themselves. Witches and witchcraft are known to exist in contemporary Apachean cultures and are forces to be reckoned with, whether or not one wishes to become involved in such nefarious business.

The following discussion took place after lunch and before the commencement of the afternoon's dancing. Bernard and I were in the family's camp-out home, a tipi made, and owned, by the women in the family. Intermittently, the tape has background music of people practicing, then performing, powwow music. Catherine, Bernard's oldest sister, and her children were also in the tipi, although Bernard and I were doing most of the talking (about what I had termed the "5,286 questions I have to ask").

    CRF: How do you ask somebody about witching, to begin with?
     BS: Let's start off, there are two categories. All right? The first one is the witchin' and it's called 'nt'i, the word, witchin' . . .
    CRF: . . . 'nt'i/witching? [Trying out the pronunciation of the term.]
     BS: Yeah ——————— And that is just the word, the word for the practice. —————————— opposite of that is called 'nt'inabiné.
    CRF: 'nt'inabiné.
     BS: An' 'nt'inabiné is the one that is . . . against the first.
    CRF: 'nt'i?
     BS: Yeah. . . . [Meaning you counteract witchcraft.]
    CRF: Would the person who does one do the other?
     BS: No——'Cause one is positive; one is negative, obviously.
    CRF: Yeah. [Although it was far from obvious to me at the time.]
     BS: Generally the people that you go to for 'nt'inabiné/counterwitchcraft are people that would know somethin' about, ah, ah, Ghost Medicine, because they see in the darkness when men are asleep 'n' when vicious people are alive. Not alive, but awake, you know, and actin' up.
    CRF: Like that lady that talks to them when they're in grief, would she be one? [That is, one who practices 'nt'inabiné.]
     BS: Umhum. And another place that you would find it is in, ahm, ——— in peyote.
    CRF: You find 'nt'inabiné/counterwitchcraft in peyote.
     BS: Umhum.

[The children interrupt here and require attention. After tending to them, Bernard continues as though there had been no break in our dialogue.]

     BS: See, peyote, peyote is for goodness; it is *eyes*; it is our eyes. It is our extra sense to see, to feel the things of the world that we do not normally see and feel. And through that medium we see 'nt'i/witchcraft and all other negative . . . thoughts.
    CRF: But you don't have to take peyote in order to see 'nt'i/witchcraft, do you?
     BS: Huh'uhn. Like a good person, who has never done anything wrong in this world, who always prays to, to The Ones Above, then they *see*; they see these things automatically.

[Visiting Anglos/white people interrupt looking for dinner; they are directed to the place where food is available to all. Bernard makes a joke of their mistaking our tipi for a food tent by saying, "We got no wood to cook here with." The Anglos and we laugh and thus diffuse a potentially embarrassing situation. No proper Apache embarrasses another adult publicly. Again, Bernard continues as though we had not been interrupted.]

> BS: And so good people can see that, because, ah, a lot of ways that bad people who do things like that give away themselves, so they can see it.

[The children interrupt again, purposefully talking close to the tape recorder. They are verbally ignored but gestured away by both their mother and Bernard, as he continues:]

> Now, we got those two [terms] figured out. Now what?
> CRF: Why would people want to harm other people? . . . Why would people witch people?
> BS: Now, let's get that straight! Today in Mescalero there are probably about only two people that have really *Power* to do that, to destroy the lives of people ———— and ——————
> Apaches are just conditioned to be suspicious of . . . people who act oddly: duu'ndéat'édaa ———— not in the way of The People . . .
> CRF: [Writing and pronouncing] Au/yes, duú'ndéat'édaa/not in the way of The People.
> BS: So, a person that is actin' crazy or in an odd way, he automatically comes under the suspicion of being either a goofball or –– witchin' . . . because Apaches, historically, and prehistorically, have, ah, people that were *really* like that, had put them to the fire.
> CRF: Really!? They've burned witches, too.
> BS: Yes!
> CRF: Like the Pilgrims used to do?
> BS: But ours has nothin' to do with the Puritan
> CRF: Right, right!
> BS: ethic, or anything. It has to do with that fire usually destroys things. And any sane person that knows that Power to destroy will *not* expose themself to that, because they know the consequences.
> CRF: Yeah. ———— The people who have that Power, do they have to do like in ———— well, do they haf'ta' sell their souls or some member of their family or somethin' like that?
> BS: In life, in life the Law of Nature, the law of our God, says, "Anything that you do has to be paid in life." Anything that takes great Power and emotional strain. Therefore, I sing over a girl; I have done my best; therefore, it is only befitting that they would pay me in a horse, which is alive and breathing. ———————— And so the opposite of that, the opposite of that is if you are goin' to destroy life, you are destroying life, something that is breathin', warm, feels, then you must pay in, ah, comparably.
> CRF: So you must pay with a death.

BS: Yes. And where does that payment come from? The payment comes from your blood ———— ones that you love the most; that's where . . . the payment comes from.

CRF: Why would anybody want to be a witch then, if they gotta pay with their own blood?

BS: Some people, some people, whiteman, Indian: same way. Some are motivated by

CRF: power, lust, and greed.

BS: Yes! So they'll do that. That's the natural order of things.

[The natural order of things: whether one is Anglo, Indian, or any other ethnicity, there is tension in social relationships. Witchcraft is one way of explaining and dealing with such social storms. Social storms can be handled through social sanctions, ritual, payment, and if all else fails, through execution.]

Dialogue 2–Political Storms

This dialogue is primary in the sense of chronology; it was the first in terms of history. The dialogue that produced it was initiated by Michael Barnes, a BBC producer/director who was at Mescalero in the summer of 1975 making a documentary film, inappropriately titled—I argued to no avail—"Geronimo's Children." The film was first aired in London on BBC's *Horizon* series and later shown in the United States on *Nova*. My role was that of ethnographic consultant and, when necessary, translator.

Barnes had a script he prepared in consultation with me, even if he seldom took my advice. Dialogue 2 came about because of that script. It took place, and was filmed and professionally recorded, on July 29, 1975, on a mountain summit of over 9,000 feet elevation.

In this dialogue, which was to form the continuity among scenes Barnes planned to use to illustrate points Bernard Second was making, Barnes asked questions off mike and off camera to which Bernard responded on mike and on camera. I sat on the ground off camera (with tape recorder and notebook) next to Bernard's elder brother, Cedric, who had driven the three of us to the mountaintop in a jeep while Barnes had brought in his crew and equipment by helicopter. Bernard, Cedric, and I later agreed that flying in by helicopter was certainly faster than the ride we took, since we seldom were on more than a trail that led to a fire lookout station at the summit of the mountain; we also agreed that our bottoms would have been much less sore had we been flown in rather than having bounced around in an open, uncomfortable jeep for over an hour up that mountain.

When reading through this dialogue, note the poetic structure of Bernard's words that is easily grasped by carefully following the punctuation and indication of pauses in speech. Although not set in poetic lines, much of Bernard's discourse is poetic.

MB: So what did it mean to you to have a fight and lose most of this land?

BS: Our first encounter with Europeans was in the 1500s, when we met the Spaniards. And our difficulties with them started right immediately afterwards, because they were starting to send out slave expeditions against us. So we, the Apaches, retaliated by raiding them. And for the next 300 years, we devastated the northern part of Mexico. We took everything that was in sight. We made sure that those people paid for every slave that they took from among our people. And it was a long and hard war. And then, but we stood on our own.

Then the Americans came in; the Americans came in from the east. And they, they wanted treaties with us. So we, we supposedly made peace with them. But then they kept encroaching on our land. And we had to fight *them* –– An' the Americans were a hard enemy, because they were determined. –– They were not out for slaves. They were out for land. And they were out for our . . . freedom. They were gonna *take* it. They did. From all this vast land that we had –– this little reservation is all that we have left.

And it did *some*thing to us. We were a proud, free, roving people on this land. We asked no one for handouts. We asked no one for *nothin'*! We were a proud people. We were a good people and our ways were holy. That was destroyed. We became a dependent –– on Washington. Our style of life came to an abrupt end.

There was no more game to hunt. There was no, our warpath was stopped. Our buffalo, buffalo plains were taken from us. ––– Our horses were taken from us. ––– And we became – A camp people, just stayed at one place ––– one time were a clean people; we became a dirty people. We had nothing clean to put on, no clean place to move to. We stayed in one place and lived in our filth. ––– And it's a, it's a hard thing we are still tryin' to recover from.

Because in our hearts, all the land that we lost is still ours. It will always be ours. And, hopefully, some day we will get a fraction of it back. But what little we have left means the world to us, for it *is* our world. It is everything to us.

And those who are, those who do not have long history do not know what I am talking about. But this land is a part of

our history. We are a part of it. We cannot be taken from it.
It cannot be taken from us, because when you take one from
the other, then you have destroyed that ---- situation. ----
And we, unlike many of our fellow tribes in the United
States, have the heart of our homeland—which – is a great
psychological help to us.

[Despite the centuries of protracted wars, storms whose
aftermath can still be felt and seen, there remains the land, the shelter
and point of contention in the storms brought by the Spaniards,
Mexicans, and Americans. Those storms turned many times, when the
fights were with Spaniards or Mexicans. The storms generated by the
Americans had their early turnings but eventually those storms turned
the Apaches into reservation Indians.]

Dialogue 3–Interpersonal Storms With Societal Consequences

I taught a summer field school in Santa Fe, New Mexico, in 1981; it
was the practicum and continuation of an ethnography course I taught
on campus at the University of Illinois at Urbana-Champaign, where
I was an assistant professor. We, the students and I, took time out from
fieldwork in Santa Fe and smaller, nearby communities to go to the
Mescalero Apache Indian Reservation for the annual early July girls'
puberty ceremonial, of which Bernard was the head singer, the one who
leads all the other singers in conducting the ritual. My fictive family
erected a tipi for us to live in during the ceremonial time. Since this
was also the tipi that Bernard used as his base while singing and
conducting the ceremonial, there was a great deal of interaction among
Bernard and my students. Bonds were formed that, for some of the
students, continued through the years.

My students and I left after the public aspects of the ceremonial.
Several days later, at the conclusion of his duties connected with the
ceremonial on the Reservation, Bernard joined us at St. John's College,
our Santa Fe headquarters.

I had expected Bernard to arrive in Santa Fe on July 17, but
we missed each other. I had received word of his coming to Santa Fe
by "moccasin telegraph," a system of communication whereby a
message is initiated by a person and designated for another specific
person who is not present; the message is passed from one to another
until it reaches the person for whom it is intended, sometimes covering
hundreds of miles in the process, as it did this time. Moccasin telegraph
can be amazingly fast or agonizingly slow. This particular message had
arrived, by personal messenger, very quickly—within a day of its

having been sent. But I assumed Bernard would arrive by bus; instead, he had found a ride. So while he was looking for St. John's on the 17th, I was in central Santa Fe hanging around the bus station looking for him. I gave up shortly after 5:00 P.M. and returned to St. John's in time for dinner, while Bernard continued his search for me. When he located St. John's, it was long past nightfall, so he bedded down on hay in the horse corral. As soon as it was light on the 18th, he found several of my students sleeping outdoors on a porch—these were the ones who had never camped out prior to their Mescalero experience. They liked it so much, they continued to sleep outside when we returned to St. John's. One of those students awakened me, and Bernard and I began working as the glorious colors of a new day began to spread out in a panorama before us.

As the ceremonial was still much on his mind, it was there that we began. Note that in this dialogue, my role is minimal. I was almost to the point of not asking any more questions. Our communication style, and its content, had changed.

> CRF: You were gonna tell me, or told me to remind you, about how Old Man C. almost corrupted the [girls'] ceremony.
> BS: He did in a way, but then, I told you: he put a *lot* of Christian elements in it.
> CRF: I thought [someone else] had done that.
> BS: Huh'uhn. . . . That Old Man C., he put a lot of English terms and Christian, you know,
> CRF: Hmmmm.
> BS: Christian ideology, I guess. . . . Christianity. He put it in there. Like he made a song that he would sing about a flood. . . . In Apache theology, we have nothin' about a flood or anything like that. And he tried to incorporate that. You *know* where that comes from.
> CRF: Sure. Sure. The biblical story
> BS: Yeah.
> CRF: of Noah.
> BS: He tried to incorporate that. . . . He made another song that . . . talks [about one of the Warrior Gods] and a cross [our Warrior God] hanging on a cross! You know where *that* comes from!
> CRF: Right.
> BS: So, so when I started singing [the girls' puberty ceremonial], all those ones that I was singing with [other singers], I said, "Don't sing those songs anymore. Those are not the Holy Lodge songs. Those are made-up songs."
>
> Each man that is the head [singer of the ceremonial] is entitled to, to incorporate one song that will be his. ------ So that, say like, ---- my grandfather [who was the singer who taught Bernard] didn't incorporate any songs. But, if he

did, since me and Willeto [another highly respected singer] are his two blood descendants, we could also sing those songs. [He meant here that the songs that are added, one each by each head singer, become a part of the ceremonial that is then passed down to future generations of singers.] And those who we teach, if they choose to, will also sing . . . that song. But my grandfather never did that.

But *I* did it. It's about the horse. –– But then, you know, it's the blessingway for the horse, because we are a horse people. And that's my *right* [as head singer for his generation]. . . . I have the right to do that. So I *did* it. So I made a song about a horse. –– And that is ––– to bless all our horses.

. . . Whereas he [Old Man C.] was just makin' up songs and with a Christian . . . motif!

CRF: Umhum.

BS: . . . like, I told you, when I made that song about the horse . . . when Apaches – sing horse songs, they're always to the beat of a horse. And that song –– ah, can you turn that [the tape recorder] off for a while?

[During the time the recorder was off, Bernard related an incident he did not want in a permanent record. It concerned a singer who transgressed and was punished with a stroke. People, like Old Man C. with his Christian influences, or the herein unnamed singer who committed a more serious transgression, must pay for their misdeeds. Old Man C. was chastised by a then very young Bernard, a state of affairs unusual in Apachean decorum. And the other singer had his very voice taken from him, for a time. After he related the incident about the stroke, its antecedents and consequences, he gestured for me to turn on the tape recorder once again.]

BS: Like I said, there are no accidents in this world. When [there are] people [like] that, they are just trying to cover up their own inadequacies, their own ignorance and their –––– inability to –– function. There's not place in this world for that kind of people. But it seems to me that there's a *lot* of them.

[The sun was fully up; my students were taking turns in the showers. It was time to dress and go to breakfast, all the while thinking of the long-term effects of such interpersonal storms. Some of Old Man C.'s relatives would not allow Bernard to sing for their daughters, remembering the embarrassing corrections a much-younger Bernard had made of their ancestor's singing. And, although the singer who had had a stroke had recovered even before I arrived for my year-round residence, many people still believed him to be a danger for his hubris.

Bad feelings in such a small community (there are fewer than 3,000 Mescalero Apaches) do not die a quick death. They linger to precipitate storms in the next generation, and the ones after that as well.]

Dialogue 4–Turning the Storm

By 1983, Bernard and I were communicating more and more through 'inch'in'di'/communication without words—a kind of mindspeak. It is not a mode of communication that has credence in Euroamerican parlance (other than in science fiction) but is, nonetheless, used in many places in the world by many cultures, including some of those in East India that, through various religious traditions, influenced Christianity. So I here stretch the term "dialogue" to include what I learned through observation and 'inch'in'di'.

Again, in 1983, I had field school students with me at Mescalero. They were all sleeping in the tipi, for they were subject to the Anglo midnight curfew. At Bernard's insistence, I, however, had been up all night, as had all the Apache participants in the girls' puberty ceremonial for this was the last, and most important, night of the ceremonial that extended on through morning (of July 6).

The following excerpt from my fieldnotes took place between 4:30 A.M. and 5:00 A.M. In the "dialogue" that follows, Bernard was first using 'inch'in'di' to communicate with me as he indicated how I was to dress him and then he used it with The Ones Above, with Wind, and finally with Storm itself. I was a "listening" observer.

> . . . I had just loaded pockets with gear and slung the two cameras around my shoulders when Bernard asked for help dressing. He'd put on his G-string while we [a student who had awakened and I] were gone [to the toilet]—looping the long, black cloth around a black cord he wore at his waist. Next he put on his moccasins, after I found them for him, left foot first. [Although one cannot understand it from the written text of my fieldnotes, I was dressing him, and putting on his jewelry, after he had put on his own G-string and moccasins. It is highly inappropriate for real or fictive siblings to see each other's genitals or bare feet.] Next came the white buckskin leggings, left then right, also tied to the G-string and waist cord. His beautiful, heavily fringed, new, white buckskin shirt came next. Then the earrings: two in his left ear and one in his right. The lower left one matched the right one; they were very long, hanging from hooks in his pierced earlobes down to the middle of his chest. (See photographs, this day.) The extra one in his left ear consisted of an old, short, bone bead, a long silver chain, ending in a small silver cross. Next came the shawl that was

pinned around his waist over the G-string and waist cord but under the shirt. [Here I stopped dressing him and merely handed him the next few items.] Then he put on the pewter and leather wide belt, his double stranded bandolier (from left shoulder to right waist), a black scarf at his neck, an eagle feather tied in his hair, and finally a man's (nonfringed) Pendleton blanket went over his left arm. An elegant figure indeed! He left the tipi with me in tow, looking for all the world like an inane, camera-happy tourist.

At [the camp of the family for whose girl he was singing the ceremony] all was calm and quite where just moments before it was hurry and bustle. He sat me down on a bench near the fire and someone handed me coffee with sugar—fantastic! . . . I watched a rain storm move toward the ceremonial mesa [where it must not rain on the last morning, for the full rays of the rising sun must "wash over" the girls who are having their ceremonial]. I moved to the edge of camp to watch the coming storm. Bernard came and stood beside me, praying [with his left arm extended—his left hand, palm outward and at shoulder level—facing the fast approaching storm]. He whispered, "It will turn now." And it did! Ninety degrees to the north. I could smell the rain and see it. But turn it did and go off [sic; my fieldnotes are not always in the best English] up Soldier Canyon. The ceremonial mesa stayed dry and the sky lightened.

[How can I comment upon what my own culture defines out of existence? In Euroamerican cultures, storms do not change direction at the instruction of anyone. But they do in Apachean culture. Perhaps we Euroamericans have forgotten how to command storm—wind and rain. Perhaps we never knew how to do it. But Apaches know. There are many stories from the last century of Geronimo (a Chiricahua Apache, one of those who are considered to be "cousins," that is, distant relatives, of the Mescalero); those stories often relate what is usually termed his "uncanny ability" to know the whereabouts and numbers of the enemy without being in their presence. And Apaches—whether Mescalero, Chiricahua, or from any of the other tribes—remember accounts from, or know personally, those who can stop bears from attacking, can bring rain when it is needed, can see far away while staying in one place, or who can reverse the directions of the natural elements—those who can turn storms of any variety away from The People.]

BRUCE T. GRINDAL

IMMORTALITY DENIED

The relationship between the anthropologist and a fellow human being in the field is many times problematic, involving contradictory feelings and the mutual and painful exchange of personhood and value. The anthropologist's understanding of that friendship is often not realized at the time but must await a later-life maturity that awakens the deeper revelations of a life lived.

Based upon his early field researches among the Sisala people of west Africa during the late 1960s, Grindal tells a story about the circumstances and life of one Sisala man who, by failing to attend his father's funeral and to go into the grave in order to hear his father's last words, disowned his family and thereby sealed his spiritual death. Grindal's life in the field became entangled in the events of his friend's tragedy over which he was powerless to change their course. From his Sisala friend, Grindal came to grips with his own parental feelings. Shedding tears enabled him to see more clearly. The blurring of his eyesight cleansed his soul.

Wandering between two worlds, one dead,
The other powerless to be born,
With nowhere yet to rest my head,
Like those, on earth I wait forlorn.
Their faith, my tears, the world deride—
I come to shed them at their side.
—Matthew Arnold, *Stanzas from the Grand Chartreuse*, 1855

I first met John Tia one afternoon in September of 1966. I was sitting on the screen porch outside my room at the Chalets, a student housing complex at the University of Ghana in Accra. The sea breezes were up, carrying the scents of papaya and the moist storm clouds.

John drove up on a black motorcycle. He was a lean, handsome man in his middle to late twenties, dressed in cotton pants, a loose-fitting cotton shirt open at the chest, and leather sandals. He parked his cycle about thirty feet away, got off and walked toward where I was sitting. He moved lightly, with an easy grace. As he approached, his face was smiling in the attitude of polite humility. There was a dignity and nobility in his bearing; his steps were even and deliberately measured.

An earlier version of this essay appeared in the *Anthropology and Humanism Quarterly*, vol. 17, no. 1 (1992): 23–32.

"Hello, Mr. Bruce. I understand you are looking for a Sisala man to teach you Sisala language and about Sisala people."

One week earlier I had arrived in West Africa via Ghana Airways from London. I was twenty-six years old, a neophyte anthropologist. I had come to Africa by way of Indiana University, where I was a Ph.D. candidate in anthropology. I never had a course in anthropological field methods. What I recall most from my education at that time was the sage advice of my major professor, Alan Merriam, about doing fieldwork in the tropics; don't drink; if you get bored or overwhelmed, take a vacation; and be wary of those who try to too easily befriend you.

I had come to Africa to study education and cultural change among the Sisala people of northern Ghana: a tribal people of the savannah grasslands—a people who lived by subsistence farming, who congregated and cooperated in extended families and villages, and who worshipped their ancestors and sacrificed animals. They were a recent entry into the "twentieth century," an ideal "laboratory" to look at how modern education affected traditional society. At the time, the subject of culture change was an important academic subject. I received a grant from the Foreign Area Fellowship Program to do field research for eighteen months. I subsequently wrote a book on my researches.

Two days after my arrival, I went to the administrative office at University of Ghana in order to gain advice about my researches and to solicit letters of introduction to certify my official importance for a trip north to Isala to meet the Sisala people. I met one civil servant named Danqua. He was sitting behind a desk piled with mildewed papers, stamping documents. I explained my proposed research of the Sisala. He grimaced with displeasure. I mentioned that I wanted a Sisala linguistic informant. He told me he had a "boy" in mind; his name was John Tia, a former university student, currently unemployed.

Thus I was both excited and curious that day when I met John. I invited him onto the screen porch in front of my room and offered him a seat. I then introduced myself and explained to him my desire to live and do research in Sisalaland. As I elaborated my plans and my interests about modern education and change in Africa, John patiently listened and nodded his assent, smiling. When I finished my more or less scholarly monologue, John leaned back in his chair and smiled. "So you want a Sisala man to teach you Sisala language."

"Yes," I replied. "If you are interested."

"You know anything about Sisala language?"

I had previously read a few Sisala linguistic studies and remembered one line from a text, "*Mi mu Isala*," which meant I am going to the village of Isala.

John became ecstatic. He bent forward and slapped his knee. "You see, you can speak Sisala." He paused briefly. "*N yara fiela.*" He nodded his head in expectation.

"I don't know what you are saying."

"*N yara fiela*. It means, How are you? And you say, '*O fiela*,' I am fine."

I repeated the phrase and again John expressed his pleasure. I then asked John what the separate words of the two phrases meant. N yara fiela meant, Is your body cool? O fiela meant, It is cool.

"Why cool?" I asked John.

"Why not? If you are cool, you are well. No? A man who is hot, he is always angry and abusing people. Nobody wants to be hot."

So it was that I came to know John. For two months, until I went north to live in Sisalaland, I learned from John the Sisala language. He was a good teacher, both intelligent and sympathetic. He knew what I wanted, and if I made a grammatical mistake, he would correct me without apology. If I became too serious or frustrated about some detail of the language, he would laugh gently. "Poor Bruce. This Sisala language is not easy, it is? I will come back tomorrow, and we will work some more."

John did not talk much about his past or his personal life. Usually he would deflect any such question, preferring instead to talk about Sisala people and customs on an abstract plane. For John, the Sisala people seemed a distant reality, and he spoke about them in a nostalgic and often condescending manner. He felt that the Sisala people had a provincial outlook on the world. If an elder man said something that was untrue, the younger person would accept it without question. As for himself, he had to discover the world by himself, the value of learning from other tribes and peoples.

What little I knew of John at the time sounded like an impersonal biography one might find in a resume. John was born in Isala, Ghana, in 1938 and went to Isala Primary School from 1945 to 1949. Then his family left Sisalaland and moved to the city of Tamale, where his father found employment as a bureaucrat with the colonial government. After attending middle and secondary school in Tamale, John entered the University in Kumasi, where he studied for an engineering degree. In 1962, he left the university in order to find work and did not complete his diploma. Since that time, he had worked many jobs.

One afternoon, while we were working together, I was particularly frustrated. Perhaps it was my mood or a particular difficulty in the language I could not comprehend. I became irritable and raised my voice. I told John that what he was telling me didn't make sense, that the Sisala language didn't make sense. He remained quite for a while, then got up and went to the refrigerator. Soon he came back with a beer and two glasses. He first poured my glass, to the rim, then his. We sat quietly for a while.

"N yara fiela," John said. He smiled.

"O fiela," I replied.

"Yes, yes. You begin to understand now, don't you? 'Be cool,' that's what you say in America, no? You are learning to be a Sisala man."

Toward November, I was preparing to leave for Sisalaland. My 1962 VW bug was stuffed with clothes, books, papers, first-aid kit, typewriter, and all the paraphernalia of an anthropologist trekking into the bush. That afternoon John dropped by.

"So you are really going?"

"Yes," I replied.

"You think you will like Sisala food?" John nodded his head in the direction where Ata, the caretaker, lived. "You think you could eat that old man's food? That's how Sisala people eat, with their fingers, sitting on the mud floor."

"I guess I will have to learn," I replied somewhat defiantly.

"Why do you want to go to Sisalaland? You know it is a hard life up there. The heat is so bad it can make a man crazy. And there are insects that bite you real bad. Many Sisala people are blind because of insects. And in the dry season, the people drink their water from mud holes. They are dying all the time. You won't like it . . ." John smiled. "Why don't you stay in Accra? I will teach you everything you need to know about Sisala people."

I continued to pack my car. "I understand that the chief of the Sisala is named Janduru Batong. Since you are from Isala, you must know him."

John stiffened, and his expression became defensive. "Yes, I know him."

"What kind of man is he? I would like to introduce myself to him when I arrive in Isala."

"You know, people say that Janduru has a lion under his garment. Nobody can see it, but you can hear it roar. You better be careful."

"That's magic, John," I said jokingly.

"He's no joke. You better watch out. He's a dangerous man."

"But how do you know these things?"

"I should know, he's my brother."

"You mean, your father, Tia, is also his father?" I asked, somewhat surprised by his revelation.

"No," John replied. "We are not brothers in that way." John glared at me. "Look, I don't like people poking their noses in my business. It makes me angry, you understand."

For a long time neither of us said a word. Then John broke the silence. "I am sorry. It used to be that life made me angry; now it only makes me sad."

"Why?" I asked.

John glared at me again. "What did I tell you, Mr. Bruce, I don't like people poking noses in my business."

The next morning as I was leaving, John came by. He brought with him a letter for his "brother" Bajo Batong. Proudly, he said that the letter would serve as an introduction to the Isala people. As he said this, he laughingly mocked his self-importance. "Bajo is a good man. You can trust him."

"What do you mean, trust him? Are there others whom I shouldn't trust?"

"You will find out," John laughed.

The trip to Isala in the north was 550 miles. It took me six days: from Accra to the rain-forest city of Kumasi; from there to Yedji and a two-day wait while the ferry boat, which would take me across Lake Volta, was being repaired; then on to Tamale and Bolgatanga in the tribal north; and finally eighty miles to Sisalaland, over treacherous dirt roads.

After I crossed Lake Volta, the paved roads quickly disappeared, and so did any semblance of the modern world. The primitive world of mud huts and women naked to the waist in corn fields began to dominate the landscape. When, on occasion, I would step out of my car to relieve myself in the bush, I would return with bleeding welts on my arms and legs; and before I drove off, I would have to pull the thorns out of my sandals. On the day before my trek into Sisalaland, I stayed in the rest house in Bolgatanga. The night was intensely dry and hot. Before going to bed that night, I chanced to spill a glass of water on the floor. All the flies and stinging insects that had been clinging to the mosquito netting over my bed suddenly descended to the wet spot and drank eagerly.

During the journey, I often thought about John and the things he said, particularly about the hardships of the northern bush country. Unlike the South, where the bustle and theater of humanity clung closely to the road, here the landscape had a humanly patterned geography, impervious to the design of some white man's road. John was of this world, but what did I really know about him? I was curious to meet his brothers: Bajo, for whom I had a letter and who was to be trusted, and Janduru, the chief of the Sisala, who had a lion under his garment.

I arrived in Isala on the evening of the sixth day. Tropical twilight had descended upon the town, and except for an occasional kerosene lantern in the doorway of a house, the place was dark. I walked through the meandering paths and passageways of the town, accompanied by a chorus of curious voices talking in the darkness. Finally I found the police station and secured a room for the night in one of the local rest houses.

The next morning, I went to meet Janduru Batong, the chief of the Sisala. When I arrived at his compound, a young man greeted me and escorted me to the chief's elevated balcony. I was seated, and within a few minutes Janduru made his appearance. He was dressed in a long, flowing light blue robe. His posture was erect and regal; the hand he offered me in greeting was soft and gentle. After we sat, I greeted him in Sisala. He asked me how I had learned the language. I told him that I knew John Tia and that he had taught me. At the mention of John's name, Janduru's face grew stern and defensive. Abruptly he got up, shook my hand, and welcomed me to Sisalaland.

That afternoon, I went to visit the district administrator of the Isala District in order to find a place to stay. He was a young Ashanti man, educated in England. When I arrived at his bungalow on the outskirts of town, he was talking with a group of men about an urgent governmental affair. He introduced himself and then introduced me to the others present, one of whom was Bajo Batong, the "brother" of John, for whom I had a letter. I remained while they talked, sometimes in English, sometimes in Sisala.

Bajo was a tall, well-built, handsome man. His manner was easygoing and friendly, given easily to laughter. What I recall most was that he stuttered. During the conversation, and particularly during moments of heated argument, he would stutter uncontrollably. When this happened, the others would wait patiently and respectfully until Bajo could articulate his words. When he finished, his eyes seemed to twinkle with a teary quality that portrayed a sense of happiness or relief.

Following the meeting, I had an opportunity to talk briefly with Bajo. I told him that I had a letter for him from John. He took the letter and read it immediately. His expression was intent. Occasionally he smiled, but more often he grimaced and shook his head in displeasure. When he finished, he put the letter in his pocket. Then, as though he had never read it, he turned to me and welcomed me to Sisalaland. He said he was busy then but that he would like to get together with me later that evening at the Moonlight Bar.

I met Bajo outside the bar, just as the sun was setting. We went in and sat at a table. The Moonlight Bar was located in the center of the Isala *zongo*, or market section, of the town. I had passed the bar the night before and had been impressed that it was the only place in town that had electric lights. Fluorescent lights of red, blue, and green adorned the entrance. Inside was a bar and two refrigerators. On the wall, across from the bar, was a mural painting of a young man, in coat and tie, holding a glass of beer in his hand. Out of his mouth came a cartoon bubble on which was printed, "When you are full of sadness and woe, come with your comrades and drink together at the Moonlight Bar." The bar then opened onto an open-air courtyard with metal tables and chairs, illuminated only by the stars and moon. Within minutes other people arrived, and soon there were eight people sitting around the table, drinking glasses of lager beer and engaged in animated discussion. Each time I took a drink from my glass, somebody at the table would fill it to the rim.

Toward the end of the evening, when the others had left, I asked Bajo about John. Bajo immediately became uncomfortable, then said, as if to change the subject, that John had said good things about me, that I was a good student of the Sisala language.

"Isn't John your brother?" I asked.

Bajo laughed, "You know we are not really brothers. My father, Batong, and his father, Tia, were brothers. So I guess that makes us clan brothers."

"Aren't you and Janduru Batong, the chief, brothers?"

"Yes," Bajo replied; then he laughed. "You know my father, Batong, was a very powerful man and he had many, many wives. So Janduru and I have many, many, many brothers." As Bajo spoke he indicated with his hands the manyness of Batongs in Isala.

"Why doesn't John ever come to Isala?" I said. I felt I was inquiring into a subject I shouldn't, but I was compelled to ask nonetheless.

Bajo stared at me. For a moment, he seemed defensive. He stuttered, then assuming a dignified composure of great seriousness. "You know, John is a careless young man. You know he drinks a lot, don't you?"

"No, I didn't know," I replied.

Bajo became very thoughtful. "John needs to come back to Isala. It is very important that he comes back."

"Why?" I asked.

Bajo shook his head sadly. Then, as though we had never talked about John, Bajo changed the subject with his same ever-present smile, and we talked about other things.

I remained in Sisalaland for five months. Soon after my arrival I arranged to stay at the old British District Commissioner's bungalow. Built in the 1930s of mud and thatch, it was both spacious and dilapidated. Rats, bats, and occasionally poisonous snakes infested the thatch roof and darker recesses of the structure. On most days I arose before dawn, ate breakfast, and began my work while the morning was still cool. Often I went to talk to old men in their homes. The thick mudbrick walls of their houses resisted the intense sun; inside the rooms were pleasant, cool, and sensuous with the odors of human living. We talked about traditions and olden times. Other days, I would attend the marketplace, the local magistrate court, or go to the farm and participate in the harvest. And more often than not, in the evening, I would visit with my friends, tipping a beer or two at the Moonlight Bar.

During this time, I saw how the Sisala people reacted to death.

The dry season, in which I arrived, was the dying season, as the Sisala called it. The dry air of the harmattan burned the nostrils and caused mucus and blood to form in the sinuses. Many coughed blood. The unsightly facts of Sisala life—the broken bones improperly mended, the milky cataracts of river blindness, the protruded swellings of quinea worm infection, and demented ravings or organic brain deterioration— the incidents of human wretchedness and misery became events to be both mourned and celebrated.

I spent many hours of many days in Sisala funeral places. I walked about in shorts and sandals, the dust caked to my feet. I talked with people, exchanged niceties, chewed kola nut, observed ceremonies, saw gifts exchanged and people mourning, animals sacrificed, and spirits released in drumming and dancing. All of this I religiously recorded in my fieldnotes. Nonetheless, I felt that much was hidden from me. Perhaps it was my inexperience, not knowing how to ask the right questions. Yet, I felt a secrecy, an unwillingness among those whom I knew, to talk about the things that I saw.

By April of 1967 the dry season was giving way to the hot season. The humidity rose to 90 percent and the nighttime temperatures did not drop below 80 degrees. One night a tornado came through Isala and took the roof off a house 100 yards from mine. That night the winds blew out my lantern. The moist electricity in the air signaled the nuptial flight of the termites buried in the woodwork and masonry of my house. I nearly choked to death in a swirl of dust and termite wings. The next day I resolved to leave Sisalaland for a few months until the hot season passed. The sea breezes of Accra beckoned to me.

Before I left Sisalaland, I went and visited Bajo. He expressed regret that the climate had become too burdensome for me. If he had a chance, he said laughingly, he would go with me to Accra. Then I asked whether he had a message I could give to John when I arrived in Accra. At my remark, Bajo became embarrassed. He told me that John's father had died about four months ago. There had been a church funeral in Kumasi, but afterward Tia's body had been brought to Isala for a proper burial and funeral. Somewhat angered, I demanded why I had not been told about it. Bajo apologized but was unwilling or unable to talk further.

"Did John come to Isala for his father's funeral?" I asked.

"No," Bajo replied. He sadly shook his head and said no more.

The trip back to Accra was easier and less eventful. The ferry boat across Lake Volta was in operation, and the 500-mile journey took only three days. Also I was less anxious. I was happy to take a vacation. I also wished, if but for a short time, to escape the relentless heat, the dust, the stinging insects and the ever-present evidence of hardship and physical suffering. I longed to sit on the patio of the Ambassador Hotel and enjoy a club sandwich and ice-cold beer.

When I arrived in Accra, I once again took up residence at the Chalets, and after a day on the beach and a festive Lebanese meal with my European friends, I went to look for John. I knew he lived in Mamobi, a migrant community on the outskirts of Accra. But I was not sure where, since he had always come to visit me at the Chalets.

That night I wandered along the dirt paths of Mamobi. How different from Sisalaland, I thought at the time. The evening sea breezes and the red cloudy sunset. Young men, dressed in shorts, leather sandals, and brightly colored shirts, sitting on benches, drinking palm wine, and telling jokes. Colored neon lights, high-life bands, shops, and cinemas. Commotion, street life. Riverlets of water running in the gullies, pregnant with the smells of orange peel, papaya, soap suds, and urine.

Finally, I was directed to a large rectangular compound in which John had rented a room. I knocked on the door. Shortly I heard a commotion inside, so I waited but there was no further response. I then tried to peer through the cracks of the shuttered window, but it was dark inside and I could see nothing. I waited for some time, then wrote a message and slipped it under the door.

Two days later I was sitting on my screened porch at the Chalets when John rode up on his motorcycle. He sped into the yard and came to a sudden halt in a cloud of dust. As he walked toward me, I could see that his white pants were smudged with red clay and motorcycle grease. His manner had the careless abandon of somebody stoned on marijuana, and when he greeted me, it was obvious that he had been drinking.

"Hello, Mr. Bruce." He paused—"How do like the Isala people?"

I didn't answer immediately, for I was shocked at his appearance and his careless demeanor. More than that, however, I was offended by his cool formality, about the way he said "Mr. Bruce." It was as though we had never met. His father had died, I thought to myself. How could he not acknowledge that fact? How could he be so impervious, so cool?

"Bajo says hello," I finally said, somewhat stiffly.

"You like Bajo?"

"Yes, he is a good man."

"You look well, Mr. Bruce. You like Sisala food?" John laughed, averting his eyes. "Mr. Bruce, can you lend me five cedi? There is this policeman I have to bribe. You know, give him a 'dash.' I was driving without my license and he stopped me."

"Will you pay me back?" I felt an edge of anger in my voice.

"Of course, Mr. Bruce. I get my pay in two days. I promise." As John spoke, he assumed a servile attitude.

"I'd like to come to Mamobi and talk with you sometime."

Assuming the same servile attitude, but this time more defense, he hurriedly replied, "Sure, sure, anytime."

Soon after our conversation, I went to Mamobi to search for John. The first two times I went to his room, he was not at home—or at least as far as I knew, for the shutters were closed, and I couldn't see in. The second time, I left a note under his door, saying I would come by on the following Saturday.

I arrived at nine o'clock Saturday morning. I knocked on John's door. Within a few moments, he opened it and in a very polite and formal manner invited me to enter. In comparison to most Mamobi dwellers John had a luxurious room. It was spacious and clean. Both the walls and concrete floor had been recently painted in combinations of soft blue and white, and brightly colored straw mats were neatly arranged on the floor. In one corner was a clothes rack, the kind one sees in department stores. On it were arrayed a considerable variety of trousers, shirts, dashikis, and a white dinner jacket with a starched white shirt and two ties. Next to it stood a bookshelf containing magazines, comic books, and an assortment of books with titles like *How to Improve the Power of Your Mind*. In another corner was a four-postered wooden bed with mattress, sheets, and mosquito netting. In the center of the room stood four rattan chairs with cushions, and two wicker end tables. Everything in the room seemed to have been recently purchased.

John was neatly dressed in white cotton trousers and a bright blue shirt, opened wide at the collar. He invited me to sit and asked if I would like a cup of coffee. I said yes. As he prepared the coffee on a hot plate, he asked whether I would like it with gin. I declined. John then proceeded to mix my coffee with canned milk; into his own cup, he poured about three ounces of gin. Offering me a cup, he sat across from me, crossed his legs, and took a long drink from his cup.

"Well, Mr. Bruce, what do want to know about Sisala people, as an anthropologist of course?" His tone of voice was haughty. His expansive self-confidence challenged and mocked me.

I wanted to ask him about his father and to offer my condolences, but I couldn't force my words against his hostility. Instead, I asked him a standard ethnographic question. "I understand from Bajo that you and he are first cousins, that your father Tia and Janduru's father, old chief Batong, were brothers."

John stiffened. "Yes, Bajo and I are first cousins. How would you say, anthropologically, we are father's brother's children. Am I right, Mr. Bruce?"

John stared at me, taking pleasure at my discomfort. As for myself I was at a loss for words. I was also getting angry, but I controlled myself.

"You know, John, I would really like to know more about you, about your life."

John laughed bitterly and took a long sip from his gin-laced coffee. "And why would you find my life interesting, anthropologically speaking? And would not your life, Mr. Bruce, be equally interesting, anthropologically?"

"We can talk about my life, if you wish," I replied.

John was at a loss for words. He slumped back in his chair, sullen. For a long time, neither of us spoke. Then I summoned my courage and said, "I am sorry to hear that your father died."

"Yes, Mr. Bruce, my father is dead." His words seemed hollow and wooden, and as he spoke he gazed intensely at the wall behind me. For a long time, neither of us spoke.

"How did your father die?" I finally asked.

John went rigid. He glared at me with unveiled hatred. "I tell you this, and you go back and tell the Isala people, yes?"

"No," I replied. "I wouldn't do that."

At this John could no longer control his rage. He pulled himself forward in his chair and pushed face into mine. "Tell me, Mr. Bruce, how did your father die?"

"My father isn't dead," I replied.

"Well, someday he will die. And when he dies, we can put our arms around each other and mourn our fathers. You think we can do that, Mr. Bruce?"

John leaned back in his chair, once again crossing his legs. He took a deep drink from his cup, and laying his head back on his shoulder, began to laugh. John continued to laugh, staring at the ceiling, oblivious of my presence. I got up from my chair and quietly left his room. As I walked into the yard with its commotion of people, I hid my face lest others could see my anger and humiliation.

For the next month, I spent most of my days and nights in Mamobi. Here Sisala migrants, along with other northern tribesmen, confused in the new world of the city, huddled together in rooms rented from strangers, sought work, and barely survived. I met many young men who, like John, had come to the city in search of fortune and adventure. Compared with life in the north, the city provided many comforts and distractions. Yet it was a harder life. The struggle to survive placed great burdens upon the individual's initiative and character. Many collapsed under those burdens and were reduced to a life of poverty and shame. Others survived and modestly prospered.

One night when I returned to the Chalets at the university, Ata, the caretaker, approached me. He said that a young man in an automobile had come to see me and had given him a message for me. By the expression on the caretaker's face I could tell that he disapproved of the young man; and before he gave me the message, he made me promise to tell that "careless young man" that he killed one of his chickens and that he owed him two cedi. The message was from John. He had to see me. It was urgent.

I went to see John at nine o'clock the next morning. After a few minutes, he came to the door. I could see that he was terribly hung over from the night before. At first he didn't recognize me as he opened the door in the glare of the morning light. When he did, he was overly happy and invited me in for coffee. As he stumbled around preparing the coffee, I could see that his room was a mess. Soiled clothing lay strewn across the floor, and in one corner lay the disassembled parts of a motorcycle engine. When we were seated, I sipping my coffee, John his gin, John said, "You know what Sisala people call gin? They call it 'kill me quick.'"

"Speaking of 'kill me quick,' I understand you ran over one of the caretaker's chickens. He says you owe him two cedi."

John laughed, "I bet the old chap has already cooked it for dinner." John then looked at me to see if I was still angry with him. I was. For some time neither of us spoke.

"I didn't know you owned a car," I finally asked.

My query caught John by surprise. Trying to shake off his hangover, he said, "Oh, that is not my car. It belongs to a friend." Nodding to the corner of his room, he said, "You see my bike. It will cost 200 cedi to fix it. Now I can't even go to work."

"So you want me to give you money, don't you?" I was still angry with John, and I wanted to inflict humiliation on him as he had done to me.

"No, no, I don't want money." He bent over, holding his hands over his face. "You know, I would like to believe in God. But I am always in agony." John's voice was incoherent, to the point of crying. Slowly he gathered himself together.

"I invited you because I want to tell you the truth about my father's death. You probably don't know it, but the Isala people are wicked. Sure, they are very nice to your face, but they are wicked, and they will work you with magic. Why? Because they are jealous of you. And Janduru, the chief, my brother—he was jealous of me and my father. You know about a year ago, my father's elder brother died, and it was Janduru who killed him. He was in Isala when he got in a very bad argument with Janduru. Soon after that argument, my senior father died. You know we believe that if a younger man abuses an older man, the older man will die. And my father and my father's brother were both uncles to Janduru, so he is the younger man. You know the history of Isala. Both my father and Batong were brothers with the same father. When Batong died, my father was asked to be chief. At that time, I was thirteen years old and was in the primary school. I told my father not to become chief. You know that my father was a senior veterinary assistant. He didn't think that being a chief meant that much. A white man, a District Commissioner, educated my father. So my father left Isala."

"But why didn't your father want to be chief? If he had been chief, you might be chief today."

John laughed. "Oh, Bruce, you don't understand things. As I told you, my father was educated by the white man. He was a white man's child. He had a different character from Sisala people. And me, I am the child of a white man's child. How could it be otherwise? Anyway, Janduru would have had us killed."

"But how could he do that?" I asked.

"Let me tell you. About a week before my father died, he received a letter from Janduru. It was a very unpleasant and wicked letter. My sisters saw it, but I didn't. After he received the letter, my father knew that he was going to die. So he told my sisters that they should rally around me. You know, my father was not so old, and he was a very strong man. He shouldn't have died."

"Did you return to Isala for your father's funeral?" I asked.

"You know, if I had returned to perform my father's funeral in Isala, I would have died. It is just superstition I guess, but I believe it. Now if I go to Isala and try to claim my father's car and my inheritance, Janduru will try to kill me in the customary way. I know these things, and Janduru knows that I am no fool. And if I die, my father's next son is in Isala, but he is uneducated. After him, there are only my sisters. Janduru could cheat them all. He wants my father's inheritance for himself."

A week later, I returned to Sisalaland and there remained for an entire year. The hot season, which I had sought to escape, was transformed upon my arrival into a lush, green landscape with cooling afternoon showers. The Sisala were busy toiling upon their farms. During the rainy summer I spent much of my time visiting with old men, since they were always at home. Oftentimes I would sit upon a cowskin on the mud floor and talk for hours while sharing millet beer, boiled peanuts, kola, and whatever other gift was brought in by some grandson or granddaughter. The conversation was always polite and never hurried.

The old men talked about traditions and olden times, about law and custom, about "what the ancestors brought down," about the ways and paths of right conduct. They talked of the times when men were masters, when they could kill their enemies without secrecy or a faint heart. They debated upon the disputes and quarrels of the day: the enmities between clans, enmities inherited by generations, enmities that caused wives to quarrel, children to fight, and women to miscarry. They talked about "today's people"—about how everybody is out after their own selfish ends. They remembered their childhoods, the joys of being "herd boys" and taking lovers to their flesh in the grass; of crazy youth, of quarrels, about witches who threw "killer bees" at their enemies in public places. Among some, the sadder ones, they talked about their drinking and their will to die. The modern world had taken away their sons and left them without immortality and purpose. As one said, "But for the singing of women, I am alone in this house."

From the mouths of old men I learned that things were not always as they appeared, that beneath the masks of politeness and charity often lie deceit, violent passions, and great suffering. These contradictions and passions became most obvious to me during times when Sisala both mourned and celebrated the death of family and kin. As the rainy season passed into the dry season, and as the roads became passable, I came to attend many funerals.

My understanding of the Sisala people deepened. What I saw touched and disturbed my soul. The questions I asked were more to the point. In response, what my Sisala friends told me was less embellished with propriety and more grounded in the harsh, passionate, and ambiguous realities in which they lived.

One night in early November, I was drinking beers with Bajo at the Moonlight Bar. It was sunset. The last clouds of the rainy season lingered in the cool dry air of the oncoming night. Above the courtyard the black vultures looked down from the trees. The sky was red. Bajo and I were alone. We talked about deep things.

We talked about a funeral we had both attended in a small village outside of Isala. A young man from the village had been attending the medical school at the University of Ghana when he was stricken with hepatitis and died. His body had been brought back to his village to be buried. On that day, I sat next to Bajo and his agemates. They had come to mourn the death of their close friend, a "star" as they saw him, a young man who had challenged the heights of the white man's world, only to be defeated by death. At a moment during the funeral, the xylophone player beat out a measure of song; in unison the young men joined arms and mourned. They danced together around the xylophone, wailing, tears flowing from their eyes.

"Why did such a young man die?" I asked. "He was a medical student; surely he shouldn't have died from hepatitis."

Bajo became grave. "You know, a young man's funeral is very sad. When the xylophone sounds, you know the corpse is being buried. When this happens, the brothers and agemates of the man must mourn and then be led away from the funeral place. The funeral of a young man is a thing of great agony. If we were to see the corpse of our friend, we would want to jump into the grave and say, 'I will go with you.'"

"But why did he die? He was too young," I persisted.

"You know my friend's father had educated all three of his sons, and two of them have died. He has a brother who is not married and is without children. His children always brought gifts for their father, but never to their father's brother. And the father's brother was the senior brother."

"Is that why your friend died?" I asked.

"Yes," Bajo replied. As he spoke, he averted his eyes. He did not want to talk further about his deep sadness. Also he didn't want to talk about the possibility of witchcraft.

After a long pause I asked, "Why didn't John come back to his father's funeral in Isala?"

Bajo became pensive and grave. "It is a bad omen to the family that John was not there when his father was buried. For he had to select the clothes in which to bury him. Also it is the first son who walks around proudly at the funeral place with a red hat on. But John was not there. He did not even try to come back to his father's funeral. When John came up to his father's church funeral in Kumasi, he was drunk, and only stayed a short while and did not greet anybody. He went back to Accra instead of coming home. In fact, he did not even help to raise money for his father's funeral. His sister had to do it all."

"John told me," I ventured timidly, "that he was afraid to come back to Isala."

Bajo became very serious. "The reason for John's behavior goes back to an argument between Tia and Batong—who you know were brothers. The argument was quite serious and led to a split between the two. John then listened too much to his father, and since John doesn't really understand the Sisala customs very well, he was probably afraid to come back to Isala. Also John flunked out of Kumasi, not because of any girl, but because he drank too much. This was because of the bad influence of his father."

"I understand that John and his father were quite close."

Bajo sighed. "You know that John and his father used to talk together as equals. This is bad. A son and his father cannot talk this way. John and his father would even drink together, and John would quarrel with his father when he was drunk." Bajo shook his head in dismay.

"But John told me," I repeated again, "that he was afraid to come to Isala."

"No, he's wrong," Bajo said emphatically. "Were he to bring his father's car to Isala and offer it to Janduru, he would allow him to keep it. But since he hasn't it is very bad."

"But I thought Janduru had the car."

"No," Bajo said in disbelief. "John has the car! He has all of his father's inheritance. The courts in Kumasi gave all of his father's wealth to him because he is a first son. The law in this country doesn't respect our Sisala law."

Bajo paused and reflected. "You know, sons should never get

involved in their father's quarrels as John has done. Often if two brothers quarrel and they say 'yours is yours and mine is mine,' their sons may later resolve the quarrel, by offering their father's inheritance to the elder of the household as a symbolic gesture. Therefore, John could have resolved the old quarrel between Tia and Batong by offering his father's property to his senior brother, Janduru. He could have then kept his property and maintained his family."

"And now?" I asked. "What is to become of John?"

"You know, when a man's father dies, the first son must go down into the grave and talk with his father for the last time. This is a wonderful thing. If he doesn't, there will never be peace in his house. His soul will never be cool." Bajo bowed his head; tears welled up in his eyes. "John has made a real break with his family. He can never come home again and ask for help if he needs it. Also, we can never ask him for help."

Before I left Sisalaland, I paid my respects to Janduru, chief of the Sisala. We sat on his veranda, and I offered him a carton of Rothman cigarettes and a bottle of Johnny Walker Black Label as a parting gift. He accepted my gift with a formal graciousness that bespoke no emotion. He then asked if I had learned what I had come to learn. With equal formality, I said "Yes."

He stared at me warily. "I hope you say the truth about Sisala people when you go back to America." Not anticipating my response, he started to get up and to excuse his absence as though the conversation had concluded.

On a sudden impulse, I said, "When I arrive in Accra, I shall see John Tia. May I take a message to him from you?"

Janduru stiffened. Slowly he turned his gaze toward me. It was one of thinly veiled hatred. It was the same gaze I had seen before in the eyes of John. "John is a careless boy. He drinks too much."

"Yes, I know," I replied. Janduru's gaze intimidated me. I now felt sorry that I had spoken.

"You don't trust him; he tells lies." Without so much as looking at me again, Janduru walked back into his room.

Life is a marketplace, the Sisala say. Sometimes we know what we have; sometimes we don't. Sometimes we give when we should take; other times we possess when we should be generous. Life is conflict. Over a life, a life with someone, in John's case, his father, there are conflicts, hurts, minsunderstandings. Pain is inflicted upon the soul that leaves doubt, unresolved questions, the absence of certitude and faith.

The last moments in the grave are magical moments. It is a private time in which confessions are made. Perhaps harsh words had been said. Perhaps secrets one had always longed to reveal remained sealed in the soul. And then, in a moment of magic, all truth is revealed. The son speaks to the father, and the father to his son. The tension of a life lived together is cooled. The life of the living is set right, the spirit and the flesh become one. The eldest son inherits, lives in peace, and worships his father, and by extension, establishes connection with eternity.

When John deliberately failed to return and perform the rites of a first son upon the grave of his father, he severed his connection with eternity. But why? What was the quarrel between John and Janduru? Of this I know nothing except that it was a quarrel inherited from their fathers, one of whom became chief of the Sisala and the other who became the first Western-educated Sisala man to leave his homeland in search of a new world. All I knew was Janduru's instant coldness to me when I mentioned John's name, the stare of thinly veiled hatred. Then there were Bajo's painful revelations about John. His words were deeply truthful, yet they contradicted those of John. Did Janduru really wish to kill John, or were John's suspicions merely intoxicated delusions? And who really had the father's car? What was the truth? What was the heart of the matter?

I left Sisalaland in April of 1968 and returned to the Chalets, where I remained for a few weeks before I left Africa. One afternoon while I was alone, John drove up on his motorcycle. I could see a trail of dust coming up the road, chickens and guinea fowl running, feathers flying. When John saw me, he stopped the bike suddenly, swerving into a hedge in front of my house and overturning his bike on the dirt. For a moment he lay in the dirt, trying to find his orientation. Slowly he got up, brushed himself off and walked toward me. His steps were careless and uneven. "Hello, Mr. Bruce," he began. "How are Isala people?"

I remained silent for a moment, aghast at his appearance. His clothes were stained with dirt and motorcycle grease, and pieces of straw and lint clung to his hair. His eyes were jaundiced and bloodshot, and his two front teeth were badly chipped, which gave to his speech a slight lisp.

"What has happened to you, John?" I exclaimed. "How did you break your teeth?"

"Oh man, you know this meat I eat has bones in it. I chopped too hard." He paused, trying to orient himself. "Mr. Bruce, by God above, I have met this woman. She is beautiful. She walks like a deer. I must have her. I need money to buy a gift for her father." He paused. "You don't understand, do you?"

"Understand what?"

"God's will," he replied. "This woman is the love of my life.

I will take her to the end of the world. I will take her to England, I will bring my family to England, and then we will see."

"See what?"

"What?" John staggered, and reached back trying to brace himself on his motorcycle, which lay on the ground. His posture was crooked, his expression, uncomprehending.

"John, please, come on the porch and have a seat."

"No, no." He staggered again. He brought his hands up over his face and averted his head. It seemed to me that he was crying, but I couldn't be sure.

"Bruce!" He suddenly exclaimed. "You put your arms around me, and we sing to our fathers who are dead. You think we can do that?"

I recoiled from his question and his outstretched hand. There were tears in his eyes; yet there was something malicious and hateful in his expression. My father was not dead. He was crazy. He was seeing a vision of the world that was beyond my eyes. I was afraid of him—no, better, I was terrified. Had I reached out to touch his hand, I would most surely have descended into the terrifying abyss of his madness.

"My father is not dead, John."

"One day," John said slowly, "Your father will die, and so will your world. Then we can put our arms around each other and sing a father's mourning. Yes, Mr. Bruce, you will see."

He walked to his motorcycle in the dust and righted it. Then I saw a piece of rope strapped on the carrier over the rear wheel. It was fashioned into a hangman's noose, a half-inch twined rope, twisted in exactly thirteen loops.

"What is that?" I asked, pointing to the back of his bike.

"That's my good luck," John exclaimed. He suddenly became excited. "You see, nobody can kill me. You see, it's my 'juju.' Nothing can kill me."

"I don't understand."

"Oh, Mr. Bruce, you don't know anything, do you? You see, nobody can kill me, because I'm already a dead man."

John laughed and his eyes became glassy. It was a laughter that defied my presence. It defied the presence of any human being, any creature. It was a laugh so cold that nothing could touch it. He murmured, "You will see. You will see."

John then got on his motorcycle and drove out of my life.

But did John really drive out of my life? Why, after nearly a quarter of a century, has John's story remained stuck in this middle-aged anthropologist's guts?

I see my father now, an old man in his late eighties. He gets up from bed late in the night and wanders around his house, lost in naive forgetfulness. He dreams about his boyhood in Sweden. At times he harkens to the voice of his mother or brother; at other times he looks for the maid hidden behind the wooden walls of the bath house. My father is senile. He has Alzheimer's disease.

On nights like these, my mother reaches across the bed and, feeling for his presence, discovers he's gone. Wearily, she gets up and searches for my father through the rooms of their south Florida home. When she finds him, perhaps in a guest room looking at old photographs, she pats him on the back and tells him softly that he has a home. Gently, she leads him back to bed.

I look now into my father's eyes, and I can see, no, remember, his always courteous old-world manner, his strength, his fortitude, his solid values. I also remember our quarrels, often bitter quarrels about politics and my personal self-determination. And I long to hear his words of advice and to feel the touch of his understanding of that which is in my heart.

And I remember occasions at Sisala funerals, when those whose fathers had died would join together—men among men and women among women—and place their arms about one another and weep the songs of their ancestors. And I long to reach across the years and put my arms about John and sing a father's mourning.

KIRIN NARAYAN

SHARED STORIES

Entering a complex arena of preexisting social relations, anthropologists going to the field tend to find their understanding shaped by those with whom they become aligned. So-called "informants" may actually end up being research directors. The pervasive influence of the people an anthropologist lives with or talks to is especially marked in the cases of friendship. The sharing of perspectives, the bestowing of privileged knowledge may lead to unexpected collaborative projects. At the same time, these close ties may work at cross-purposes to the anthropological mission, compelling an anthropologist to silently share confidences, shielding a friend from the probing eye of ethnography.

Narayan's field research in the Western Himalayan foothill region of Kangra was complicated by this also being the home of her American mother. Though Narayan went to Kangra intending to study women's songs, on her mother's urging, she also started to tape folktales from a village woman called Urmila Devi Sood. In the early 1990s, when television had increasingly come to dominate village social life, Urmila Devi felt herself marginalized as a storyteller. Sharing her knowledge with Narayan, Urmila Devi was not just recapturing an audience, but gaining a friend. In addition, Urmila Devi was bestowing her traditional stories into the written word, in trust for future, literate generations.

"Tears came into my eyes," my mother said over breakfast one September morning in 1990. "It was such a beautiful story, with such classic themes." We sat out on the porch with homemade muesli in bowls before us. Through the shiny dark leaves of mango trees, we could catch glimpses of the mountains. My mother had just retold a folktale she had hear from Urmila Devi Sood, a woman of the trader caste who lived at the other end of this village. In the story, a girl has the fate to never be married: it is predicted that her groom will drop dead during the marriage ceremony. The girl's mother is distressed and asks a holy man how this situation can be remedied. On his instructions, the girl and her brother cross the seven seas. They seek audience with a washerwoman who carries the secret of the nectar of immortality. Though the girl's husband does indeed drop dead during rounds of the wedding fire, the washerwoman appears and sprinkles him with this nectar. He comes to life, and the wedding proceeds.

This story, my mother said, was associated with the Hindu ritual performed on the occasional Mondays that fall on the Dark Night of the Moon. She had been overwhelmed with she heard Urmila Devi Sood tell this story on an actual Monday of this ritual's observance. "After all the years of reading you fairytales, I felt I was in the presence of the real thing," my mother said. "It took my breath away to watch the assurance and artistry with which she told that story. She's a gem, Kirin. You really must go talk to her."

87

Must go talk to her. Sitting across the table from my mother, I sulked. Who was the anthropologist here anyway? I knew my mother was trying to cheer me on to go out and throw myself energetically into fieldwork; along with a nourishing breakfast she was feeding me her choicest leads. After all, it was she who had lived in this ramshackle house on the hillside of a Kangra village for the last twelve years. It was she who had left Taos, New Mexico, to marry my father and move to India in 1950. It was she who had cheerfully declared, "If Margaret Mead can live in Samoa, I can live in a joint family." It was she who bought the anthropological paperbacks that sat beside the sea-mildewed murder mysteries on our bathroom shelves in Bombay: *Patterns of Culture, The Children of Sanchez, Male and Female, Sex and Temperament in a Savage Society.* After she and my father separated, and all my elder siblings had made use of their dual citizenship by going off to college in America, my mother and I had come to Kangra in the Himalayan foothills for a summer in 1975. Three years later, she had moved here. Through this time, it was she who kept up neighborly responsibilities by attending village rituals and feasts. Also, she had designed a solar oven that could be made with mud and old tin cans, an invention that took her to many remote parts of the valley and had made her a variety of friends.

The same twelve years that she had lived in Kangra, I had been in college, then graduate school, then teaching in the United States. I had visited her almost every year, and had even tried my hand at writing a campus proposal to do research in Kangra (partly so I could get a ticket home) during my first year of graduate school. The proposal had been funded, and I had spent the summer of 1982 taping wedding songs from a variety of my own and my mother's friends and acquaintances (Narayan 1986).

I had done my dissertation research on storytelling as a form of religious teaching in Nasik, my father's home town (Narayan 1989). Now, in 1990, with a dissertation and book behind me, I was back in Kangra for a full year of research. I had been here a few weeks, meaning to move out from my mother's house soon, but realizing too that if I did so, I would lose local credibility. Every day, I fought against a great desire to hide away indoors. Most of my closest friends had through the years been married away—the high-spirited camaraderie we had shared while I did my project on wedding songs (which are sung especially by groups of girlfriends) now seemed a matter of the past. Women my own age in the village were now those who had married in and who did not know me. I felt myself as a walking anomaly—a thirty-year-old "girl" who had not followed the right course of marrying, and who, regardless of Ph.D. and job abroad, was now back living with her mother. Every time I went bravely out to rekindle rapport for the new project, I felt lacerated by the well-meaning interrogations, "Not married? When will you get married?" And then aside, "How old is she? Whose agemate did you say? Poor thing! And she's so skinny. . . ."

When my mother advised me to go see Urmila Devi Sood, then, I hesitated. It wasn't that I didn't know who Urmila Devi was: after all, she and her two sisters had taped two of the longest and most lovely songs the summer of my wedding song research. A slide I had taken of them, clustered together around the sacred basil shrine at the center of the courtyard, had accompanied me to talks and to class presentations through the years. I had seen her at village events on my vacations when I cast an anthropological persona aside and was just a daughter visiting home. But I simply felt rebellious about following a research route that my mother laid out for me. I heard my mother's advice, but instead took off to visit a friend my own age who had been married into the next village over, across a boulder-strewn stream.

In November, the rice crop had grown golden and been harvested. Between the eleventh day of the lunar month and the full moon, the Five Days of Bhishma were being celebrated. In the courtyards of all upper-case households, the sacred basil plant, which is considered a goddess (*tulsi, saili*), was being dressed up in red cloth for her marriage. I came by to visit Urmila Devi's younger sister, Nirmala, who was a primary schoolteacher. Nirmala Sood spoke excellent Hindi and English, which at this point were still easier for me to follow than the local dialect of Pahari. But her door was shut: there was no response when I knocked.

"She's not home." Sello, Nirmala's niece and Urmila's youngest daughter, came out from the other wing of the house. She was a large-eyed girl in her early teens, wrapped now in a shawl. Her oiled braids were looped up with ribbons. She unlocked the door and sat me down. Then she proceeded to interrogate me: "Why did I want to talk to her aunt? What was I interested in? What did I mean by 'research' anyway?"

I shrank under this volley of questions. All the authority I once carried over not just fourteen-year-olds but full-grown graduate students had been stripped away from me. Feeling awkward, inadequate, I did my best at answering. When Sello gathered that I wanted to learn more about the plant's wedding in progress, she offered to help. "I'll take you to houses where they are worshipping," she said. She led me further up the cobbled path, under the plumed bamboo. We visited a mother and her three daughters who were engrossed in painting the cement base of their sacred basil plant with scenes from the wedding. We also visited an indoor shrine that had been set up for the sacred basil goddess, Saili, with folk art paintings on the wall and offerings of fruit.

"You don't need to wait for my aunt," Sello announced on our way back. "My mother will sing for you."

"Mother!" Sello called as we reached their courtyard. her mother, Urmila Devi, thrust her head out of the kitchen. She was a slim woman with graying hair and a shy, diffident manner. She joined her palms and greeted me, then withdrew.

"Sing for her!" Sello demanded. "Sing her the song for Saili."

"I'm cooking," pleaded her mother.

"I'll cook," said Sello. She led us into her aunt's quarters and sat us down on two of the folding aluminum chairs in the front room with the green walls festooned with cards and calendars. Then she disappeared off into the kitchen, leaving us together with an admonition that her mother "fill up my tape."

This was one of those moments that I felt I simply did not have the gall to be a good anthropologist. Already unsure of myself, I now felt sick with the sense that my presence was an imposition. Urmila Devi in turn seemed painfully shy. Both of us would probably have found an excuse to terminate this encounter at once, but there was Sello, toiling away in the kitchen on our behalf. After a few conversational dead ends, I reiterated the request that Urmila Devi sing the narrative that described the marriage of the sacred basil plant. Urmila Devi sat awkwardly in the chair, my recorder before her, singing in a soft, cracking voice:

o āi mālin	The female gardener came,
o āyā mālī	along with the male gardener.
hāth kadāri	With a spade in hand,
sire parakhāri	a basket on the head,
yamunā kināre	On the banks of the Yamuna river,
kitti kiyāri	they prepared a seed bed.

These were the first few verses; the song went on and on in a hypnotically repetitive melody as the plant grew, budded, blossomed, needed to be married. It told of how god after god was proposed for the plant-girl; yet each already had a wife. In the end, it was settled that she would be a co-wife. But at the time of the wedding, the first wife of her groom laced the feast with poison, and Saili wilted, withered, died. The song ended by extolling the fruits of singing the tale at all.

kanyā gāve	If an unmarried girl sings this,
changā bar pāve	she'll get a fine groom.
suhāgan gāve	If a married woman sings this,
putra khilāve	she'll feed sons.
vidhavā gāve	If a widow sings this,
vaikunthe jo jāve	she'll go to heaven.
suna diyo guna diyo	To listen to this and hear this

gangā dā nauna	is to bathe in the ganga.
gānde bajāndeyo	To sing this and play this
yamunā dā nauna	is to bathe in the Yamuna.

I was moved by the beauty and artistry in this song: like other songs I had taped from her eight years before, it seemed a clear indication of her enormous cultural knowledge. Yet, when the song was done, Urmila Devi fell silent. She drew her scarf over her mouth and regarded me. My Pahari was not yet fluent enough to engage her in easy conversation. Soon after, she muttered something about the kitchen, and I beat a hasty retreat.

My mother had tried to match me up with Urmila Devi; so had Sello. But it was not until March, when my speaking skills had significantly improved and I felt more confident in my role as researcher, that I returned to visit her. Most women, I had learned by now, were flattered and amused to be consulted—my bursting in upon them was not as dreadful an imposition as I had feared. Also, I had become more skilled at deflecting questions about my unmarried state. Thanks to my mother's dabbling in astrology, I now briskly replied, "I have bad transits for another two years: astrologers have told me I must not even think about marriage until then." This explanation seemed to make perfect sense to everyone I used it with. Though I remained an object of pity, I was not subject to such elaborate interrogations.

I visited Urmila Devi again one cool afternoon in March. The wheat crop was turning delicate shades of green, and the air was scented with blossoms. Urmila Devi sat out in her courtyard, her hair still damp after washing. When I found her reticent, I told her about what I was doing: the places I had gone, the people I had visited. She pricked up her ears when I said that I had spent that morning in a nearby village visiting with a Brahman priest and astrologer. I later learned that this charismatic man, with hooped gold earrings and a booming laugh, was also her family priest. She wanted to know what we had talked about: I said it was women's rituals, and we went over the material I'd learned, with her adding comments.

In this way began our exchange as friends who shared a fascination with local symbolic forms. Urmila Devi soon became "Urmilaji" to me—the "ji" being a form of respect. Her original reticence was flooded over by unexpected wellsprings of warmth, interest, generosity, and humor. The next time I came by, at my request, Urmilaji told me the story my mother had described over breakfast all those months ago. But then, as though some hidden spring had been released, she went on to tell me five other beautiful folktales. Between tales, she would pause and we would talk about them. Sello stopped in to lean against her mother, listening to parts of tales. We stopped only when it was time for her to prepare the evening meal. "Come back another day, though," she invited. "Whenever you have time, come back. I still haven't told you the story of the lion."

My work was ostensibly on women's songs, but of course I came back. Who could resist such an invitation? These afternoon sessions made me think of Victor Turner's (1960) description of his time spent discussing ritual with Muchona and Winston as "seminars." We shared all the seriousness of purpose and passion for the material that I have known in the most stimulating of university seminars. Some afternoons we would talk about songs. Urmilaji would put on her black glasses and leaf through my hand-written collection of songs taped in different villages. (She had studied to the fifth grade and could read, mouthing the words.) Sometimes she would tell me how the version she knew was different, adding or amending a verse as I taped. She would explain to me the narrative lines of particular songs. Also, she poured out story after story.

Urmilaji had learned her stories in settings of intimacy and goodwill: from her father during the winters, as his children huddled around a blazing fire; from a female neighbor in the tea garden where her father was employed; from her husband's saintly old aunt in her in-laws' house after she was married off at fifteen; among gatherings of related women participating in a ritual. Urmilaji had told these folktales through the years to her five children. Yet in 1991, her youngest daughter, Sello, was fourteen; two other daughters had been married away; and both sons, employed as tobacco salesmen, were working long and grueling hours. Times had changed to bring not just electricity (in the 1960s), but also television (in the 1980s) to her village. As she said during one of our first taping sessions, "We have so many stories. In the past, there was so much storytelling! The children would sit down together, 'Tell a story (*kathā sunā*), tell a story, tell a story.' Now we can't find the time to do it. These days, after we've eaten dinner we come in and the television is going, the drama is on. . . ." Shaking her head with a laugh, she said, "The pictures play; that's all."

Telling her repertoire of folktales to me, then, Urmilaji seemed to be recapturing a riveted faced-to-face audience. I was an eager listener. Each evening, when I went home to my mother, I would retell the same stories as I spooned up soup.

By the time I had to go off in April to three conferences in the United States, I had taped eleven stories. One of these conferences included A. K. Ramanujan, a scholar who had worked extensively with Indian folktales. Sitting in a Minneapolis hotel lobby, fixed under his intent gaze, I had shared some of the stories Urmilaji had already narrated. Ramanujan had listened avidly, sometimes countering with related folktales from other regions of India. "How many stories does this woman know?" he had inquired. "Do you think you might put them together in a book?"

"Do you think you might put them together in a book?" I repeated when I was back, sitting with Urmilaji, her sister Nirmalaji, and their children on a Sunday afternoon with the television going.

Nirmalaji's laughter was filled with pleasure: "*Le!* Look at this!" she said, turning to her sister. Urmilaji's grown sons focused their attention away from the television long enough to give me bemused looks. Raju, the older one with close-set eyes, teased his mother, "You can become famous in America!" Urmilaji covered her mouth with an end of the gauzy pink *dupatta* looped over her head. She clucked, shaking her head but smiling. "Of what value are these old stories?" her expression seemed to say. "Why so much attention?"

The electric current suddenly gave way, felicitously snapping the television off at a steamy romantic moment that had made the mix of generations squirm. In the startling silence, free from words streaming from the television set, Urmilaji led me to her own room next door. We sat down on the floor, and she took out her handiwork that she often did as we chatted. This time, it was fluffing and cleaning through white sheerings from her sheep. She asked me again in detail about my trip, saying her afternoons had seemed empty while I was gone. In my floundering Pahari/Hindi mix I repeated a story that Ramanujan had told at the conference, a Kannada tale from a southern region of India in which a girl is turned into a flowering tree. Urmilaji listened with interest, then said that she had remembered some more tales in my absence; she would tell them next time.

"These stories have wisdom in them," she observed. "They tell you about different kinds of love." Speaking the local Pahari dialect softly through the gaps where her front teeth had once been, she looked up through the glasses she wore for fine handiwork to instruct: "These stories are about love as deluded attraction (*moha*), as possessive attachment (*mamata*), and as affection (*prem*). Television can't teach you these things. Wisdom is ebbing with every generation."

Later that evening—crickets creaking, mosquitoes whining, and the faint sound of the nearby carpenter family's radio ringing merry advertisements—I typed the notes from which I reconstruct this encounter into my battery-run portable computer. It was settled that I would put together a book of her tales.

Urmilaji was one of the few Kangra women who did not at some point cross-examine me, particularly on the subject of why I had not married. I was grateful to Urmilaji for granting me this space to be different. Yet through the months I had, from time to time, urged Urmilaji to allow me to tape her life story. I knew—largely from my mother's awareness of village families—that she was a middle child among nine children. Through unusual circumstances in north Indian society, where village exogamy is valued, Urmilaji had been married into the village of her birth. She explained that this was partly due to her having grown up mostly outside the village, when her father worked in tea gardens, and partly because her husband's pious old aunt had come to request her from her father, and her father felt he could not refuse a saintly person. I knew that Urmilaji's husband worked in a distant village, and I rarely saw him. I learned from Urmilaji that she had five children, two daughters already married away. But these are just facts framing a life, not the lived experience that gives it shape.

One afternoon in the late summer, when everyone else in the family was off visiting or at weddings, Urmilaji and I found ourselves alone. I renewed my request for her life story. Urmilaji hedged. She dictated a few riddles into my notebook. Unexpectedly, she launched into an account of how she had been betrayed in her friendship with another older woman who, like me, was an infrequent visitor "from outside." In retrospect, looking over my notes, I see that in starting with the humiliation Urmilaji had felt with this severed friendship, she was imploring me not to betray her, too.

Wrapping up her depiction of this episode and the vulnerability she had felt, Urmilaji softly said, "I was going through my hard times." In a rush of friendship, I overlooked the standard anthropological practice oriented toward extracting material from others rather than revealing ourselves to them. I said, "I've had hard times too," and I confided to her some of them. Holding my hands, tears in both our eyes, Urmilaji began her own personal story. It was a story that left me reeling. As I typed in my field diary the next day:

> Couldn't bring myself to turn on the tape recorder as she spoke. Feeling so much it was an outpouring for me, her trusted friend, not a professional who was coldly appraising it as "rich data." Feeling anthropologists as vultures, preying on others' sufferings. I couldn't bring myself to write this out last night, I had a suffering [sic] of diarrhoea and headache, almost as though my mind could not digest all the pain, my body wanted to cast it off. All day I've been circling around the issue of writing this down, and recoiling a little.

Yet, dutiful fieldworker that I was, I wrote the story out after all, reconstructing her words while they still rang in my ears.

Why had this story left me so upset? It was partly because bonds of affection had tied me to Urmilaji through time, and I could not hear this tale without identifying with the teller. This was not just a story to me, it was real life, harshly lived amid gendered and economic constraints that were unlikely to soon change in this area.

This story was upsetting too on account of its blunt admission of personal suffering. Very few of the other life stories I had taped had this directness. In becoming Urmilaji's close friend, I had been taken backstage, entrusted with confidences not meant for public consumption. Later, when I had returned to Madison, one of Urmilaji's first letters to me said, "I gave you all my secrets to put into your shoulder bag and take away with you." She was reminding me, I thought, of the moral responsibility of being entrusted with these secrets. They make good anthropological data, yes: they would certainly enrich my book on her folktales by showing how the themes to which a teller is drawn may match events in their own lives. Yet, Urmilaji has emphatically stated that I should not put personal details that implicated others into my rendition of her life for my—our—book. A strong friendship, then, can lead an anthropologist toward an empathetic understanding of a culture from within; yet also, personal loyalty can seal off these insights, hiding them away from the project of anthropology.

Nonetheless, what cannot be directly expressed in one form of discourse can be said in another (Abu-Lughod 1986). In a sense, all twenty of the folktales and the sixty-odd songs I had taped from or discussed with Urmilaji were in some respects a commentary on her life experience. Urmilaji used these symbolic forms to give her life meaning—as she said, they now "sat inside" her heart. Simultaneously, drawing these songs and stories out of herself, she shaped them according to her own insights. As Sudha, a schoolteacher, had stated after watching me go about my collection of songs and stories: "Kirinji, the person who becomes a singer or a storyteller is one with a lot of pain. She wants a way to express this pain. There are some things you can't say directly, but you can say them in this form. Songs and folktales become a form of solace."

I left Kangra at the end of August, when rice shoots had been transplanted, and the corn crop was towering tall. Shortly before I departed, Urmilaji's eldest daughter, Rama, came to visit with her two sons. Rama was a bright-eyed woman of my own age, but as a wife and mother she had an edge of seniority. She reminded her mother of yet more stories she had once told but which were no longer actively part of her repertoire. Urmilaji was delighted to be reminded of these tales. As monsoon rain poured down off the eaves, we sat together in Nirmalaji's front room. Urmilaji and her daughter knitted in unison as Urmilaji contributed two more stories to my tapes.

When Urmilaji had finished up the second story about a brave young girl whose wicked sisters-in-law sent her off on seemingly impossible quests, she turned to more general reflections.

"If these stories weren't continuously told, would they still be with us today?'' she inquired, her voice strong. ''But these days, after eating and drinking, everyone wants to go sit elsewhere at once. When is a story to be told—?''

''Now everyone just watches television—'' Rama tried to get a word in edgewise.

''In the old days, what would happen is that we'd eat and then go lie down together. We'd all stay awake. 'Tell a story, tell a story': these kids really used to bother me. . . !'' Eyes narrowed a little, a smile puckered around her closed mouth, Urmilaji swiveled her head slowly from side to side.

''Really!'' I laughed, for though she said she was bothered, she seemed to be looking back into a circle of happy memories. ''And did children from other homes also come over sometimes?'' I asked, trying to imagine what these sessions were like. ''Your mother knows *so* many stories,'' I said to Rama.

''Oh yes,'' agreed Rama.

''Ummmmmm,'' Urmilaji affirmed with a nod. ''So many used to assemble! But it isn't just a matter of children. My sister from Pattiar, my elder sister—you met her the other day. When her husband was sick, he was unable to fall asleep. So he too requested: 'Now you must give me stories,' he said. I gave him many stories too.''

''Was it that you told your sister the stories and then she . . .'' I began.

''No-oo! We used to light a charcoal burner and sit together. It was winter then. And my brother-in-law would say, 'Tell us some stories.' So I would give stories.''

''I see,'' I said, moved that the stories I had heard had been able to divert someone who was in pain, delighted that I had testimony of this sort on tape.

Urmilaji continued, ''In the past, when the Five Days of Bhishma came around, women would get together and tell stories. Even now, when we go to float the lamps we walk together, and one woman says to another, 'Dear, let's hear a story.' When the Monday on the Dark Night of the Moon rolls around, even then it's the same, 'Dear, give us a story.'''

''They all know that you're the one who tells the stories,'' I said. ''And so it's 'give' and not just 'tell.'''

''Ummm . . .'' Urmilaji was still smiling to herself.

The following day, I broke the rhythm of packing and came to say my good-byes. Urmilaji was not in the now-familiar courtyard or in the outer rooms. ''She's in bed,'' murmured Sello, who came out when I called from the doorway. Urmilaji stood up when I arrived, her shoulders bent, her hair uncombed. She embraced me, tears glistening in her eyes. Then we sat side by side on the bed.

''I am going to be so sad when you are gone,'' she said, pressing my hand between her palms. ''It's already starting. We have told each other the innermost secrets in our hearts. To me, you're one in a million."

With her two daughters looking on, she presented me with a small package of *wadis*, a local specialty made from the dried stem of a large-leafed plant and coated with spiced flour from lentils. She had prepared these wadis herself, she said. They were for me to cook in America. "I've never cooked wadis," I confessed, and starting from the heating of oil and the chopping of onions, Urmilaji led me through a recipe.

Urmilaji also drew out a bulky, newspaper-wrapped package and put it in my hands. Sello and Rama looked on expectantly as I undid the package, embarrassed. It was a soft, white, unbleached shawl: woven by a local weaver from the wool Urmilaji had cleaned, carded and spun, afternoon upon afternoon, mostly from her own sheep's fleece. She had often told or talked about the stories with me as she had worked on this wool. Accepting this shawl, and with it the labor of uncountable hours, I felt as though I was being sent off in a mantle of care and goodwill.

Urmilaji and I changed each other in subtle ways. Listening to old tapes, I find my Pahari growing less broken as I talked to her and worked long hours on her stories. She in turn began to sprinkle her tales with Hindi expressions put in for my benefit as the months went by. My questioning her on meanings emphasized her already developed interpretive bent. She seemed to enjoy mulling over these stories, particularly those associated with women's rituals. Yet, she also saw the entire enterprise as a way of helping me. The following year when I was again visiting my mother—a further muddling of home and the field—I had a warm reunion with Urmilaji too. We had written to each other in the intervening months, and now I carried a very rough manuscript that brought the stories together. I read aloud translations from English for her comments.

In the course of these conversations, Urmilaji reminisced further about her husband's saintly old aunt. This old woman, whom she called Tayi Sas, had been a source of many of Urmilaji's stories. She had also instructed Urmilaji on the virtues of speaking good words and acting selflessly. Urmilaji elaborated, "For example, when I tell you these things, they are matters of interest (*matlab*) to you. This is work of your interest. So you feel enormously happy with me. You feel, 'This is meaningful. These are good words.' In this way, she [the aunt, Tayi Sas] would say, 'act toward others without selfishness.'"

Though Urmilaji told these stories to help me, through me it seemed she was also reaching out to a wider, literate audience. Early on in our friendship, after lamenting her rivalry with the television, she had said, "The only way that children might come to know these stories is if someone like you writes them down. Then they will read them." She paused, reflecting, then added with a rueful shake of her head, "But there's a big difference between reading something and hearing it told!"

Thinking of our relationship and also of my previous work with Swamiji, a storytelling holy man in Western India, I offered: "An affection grows between teller and listener."

"That's it," said Urmilaji, a hand on her heart and a smile warm on her face: "Affection!"

GREGORY G. RECK

OUT OF THE COLD INTO THE DARKNESS

SHADOWS OF FRIENDSHIP IN MEXICO

As Stanley Diamond (1974) has written, anthropology is the study of humans in crisis by humans in crisis. The problematic nature of friendship in the field in part revolves around these respective crises. Anthropologists, coming from the alienated world that is destroying the world of those who are studied, are bound to both worlds, unable to escape the instrumental motivations that bring them to the field and, yet, unable to live comfortably with those motivations. This tension is nowhere more manifest than in friendships forged in the field.

The story of friendship between Celistino de la Cruz Jimenez and Reck during Reck's 1969-70 fieldwork in the eastern Sierra Madre mountains of central Mexico is the story of how Celistino, devoid as he was of instrumental motivations, helped Reck resolve questions about his fieldwork and direct that research toward what Jules Henry (1964) has called passionate ethnography. Reck's surrender to the relationship and Celistino's genuineness lead, as any true friendship should, to the deepening of Reck's spirit, although the impact of the friendship on Celistino is never really known. This is the irony of many friendships in the field, a closeness in the shadow of separate paths.

Anthropology, abstractly conceived as the study of man, is actually the study of men in crisis by men in crisis.
—Stanley Diamond

1969. The full moon pierced the black August sky like a hole of white-hot light. I was careening down the road from College Park, Maryland, to my efficiency apartment in the Adams-Morgan area of D.C. The evening's conversation with a friend and fellow student flickered like a firefly before my eyes: Unamuno, socialism, Marcuse, Vietnam, Sartre, phenomenology, Lévi-Strauss, revolution. Heavy stuff that seemed to stick to my guts, weighing them down like wet cement drying into concrete. Outside, as U2 was later to sing, it's America. Fast food drive-ins with neon sign images of hamburgers, malts, and scantily clad carhops reflecting off my windshield. Funeral homes with Labor Day specials advertised in big black letters. Billboards showing blond, white families made happy by their new Fridgidaire and finding eternal youth in both liquid and cream form. Brightly lit shop windows filled with electronic kitchen fetishes. People—hippies, frats, suits, preps, druggies, jocks—placed strategically along sidewalks, staring with glued-on expressions, mannequins on parade. A tent revival promising eternal salvation, one soul for fifteen bucks and two for twenty-five. Automobiles that almost anyone could believe in. Triple-X movie houses with lines of men in felt hats and tan canvas raincoats. An occasional tree.

Then, just for a moment, America outside the windows of my little, red Fiat disappeared, and I was driving up into the sky and through that holelike moon, or was it a moonlike hole? An escape? My dry mouth tasted of cheap, Spanish red wine and grass. My head swirled like a merry-go-round on the wrong speed. The hole of white-hot light came closer and closer until I was surrounded by its brilliance.

Once there, surrounded by white light, I saw myself watching with tears from the rooftop of my apartment building as the fires consumed Georgia Avenue after the assassination of Martin Luther King. I saw myself dancing angry and trancelike for hours to Greek santuri music after I heard of Robert Kennedy's assassination. I watched as Black Panthers brought tears to stone-faced African-American soldiers guarding the Pentagon against antiwar demonstrators, imploring them to lay down their guns and stop fighting a racist, white man's war. I listened to the trembling voice of my high school friend as he spoke softly about shooting elderly Vietnamese women and the recurrent nightmares in which he is shooting his grandmother. I heard the screams from an apartment window at 18th Street and Columbia Road as a woman was beaten by her drunk boyfriend. I followed a homeless woman, dressed in August as if she were in the midst of a January blizzard, as she wandered up and down the aisles of the local Safeway pretending, perhaps dreaming, that she was filling her empty bag with groceries. I saw myself standing alone, surrounded by strangers who couldn't or wouldn't speak.

A chill crash-landed in my bones. A strange coldness on a hot, humid, dark August night. I looked from the bright light into the surrounding darkness, longing for something obscured by the light, something hidden in the dark night. But as I reached out the window for the darkness, my car and I tumbled end over end back to the road to D.C., where there was only America, outside my window and inside my chilled bones. The moon disappeared from the sky, hidden by the bright, cold lights of the city. Soon I was alone in my apartment, sleeping soundly behind the triple deadbolt locks on the door.

> *Let there be no purpose in friendship save*
> *the deepening of the spirit.*
> —Khalil Gibran

Exactly one week later, most everyone I knew was at Woodstock, and I was in Mexico. Armed with a research prospectus approved by my committee, a head full of anthropological constructs, an appropriate amount of angst, quite a bit of quiet bravado, and the parting advice from one of my committee members ("Don't forget your copy of *Notes and Queries* and remember to have a good time, but not *too* good of a time!"), I headed into the Sierra Norte of the state of Puebla. It wasn't Woodstock, but it seemed like the right place for an alienated member of my generation to be. While my brothers and sisters of the Woodstock generation celebrated their vision of a different world, I celebrated my vision by going to a different world.

Here in east-central Mexico, the green mountains, watered by the moist winds sweeping off the Gulf of Mexico, jutted skyward from deep valleys cut by water and time. Steep slopes were covered with dense vegetation spotted intermittently with fields of maize and coffee trees. Whitewashed buildings with red-tiled roofs dotted the countryside and clustered in small villages hidden in cracks and crevices of this ancient earth. Outside, America was nowhere in sight, and I secretly hoped that it had disappeared inside me as well.

Mexico and I were not complete strangers. Born in Hidalgo County, Texas, about ten miles from the border, I felt somehow connected to Mexico, about as strongly as I felt disconnected from my own country. Growing up in Houston, I lived in the same working-class neighborhood with Mexicans, and we all attended schools with names like William Travis and Jim Bowie Elementary, names which conjured up ten-gallon fantasies about tough Texans and reinforced deep-seated hate for Mexicans. For whatever reason, I never bought the fantasies nor the hate, but I never quite escaped them either. Adults wouldn't let me. In Texas, they really do remember the Alamo in their own distorted way.

Instead of hatred or fantasies, I had a few Mexican friends I remembered well. There was Domingo García, who claimed to be half Apache and half Mexican. Domingo always walked like he was riding tall in the saddle. He was proud of who he was before it was the cool thing to be. When we chose up sides to play cowboys and Indians, I was always happy when Domingo chose me to stand by his side and fight the hairy white invaders from the east. We usually won, too. And then there was Hector Velasquez, who was the best basketball player I had ever seen. The outdoor court at the old Methodist church was full of weed-filled cracks, but Hector could dribble over and around every last one of them. He was lean and quick, with radar like a bat. Embarrassed kids who had their hands deftly picked by Hector would cry out, "Just like a damn Mexican, always stealing something." Hector would just answer them with a lightening-quick drive and another bucket. Finally, there was Angela Lopez. I grew up with Angela, but I had never really noticed anything different about her except that she was an unusually good baseball player. But one day in fourth grade, while we were both trying to find Afghanistan on the large globe in the back of the classroom, our index fingers touched somewhere over the Indian Ocean, and I was in love. From then on, every time I saw her my stomach would fill with the nausea of adolescent love, and my skin would tingle like hot coals. But somehow I knew that my feelings were supposed to be directed at someone else, someone more like me. I tried to feel squirmy around Vicki Metzler, but it just wasn't the same. Several years later, I was in love with someone else, but every time I saw Angela I wondered what might have been, had the world been a different place.

Later, I traveled to Mexico with my family and with friends. When I discovered anthropology as a confused undergraduate sociology major, I knew that I would someday do my anthropology in Mexico. Mexico and me. It was a natural. And so here I was.

I was as prepared as I possibly could be. I had read all the right stuff, thought all the right thoughts, had the right discussions with faculty, and made contact with the *Instituto Indiginista* in Mexico City. Two years earlier, I had even spent three months in the village of Jonotla, conducting research for my M.A. thesis and scoping out the scene for my Ph.D. research. As a result of all this preparation, I was sure that initial adjustments would be easier and focused research would come more quickly. The groundwork was laid solidly, and I was convinced that despite the uncertainties of field research, in a year I would return to the United States with what I wanted: a reasonably good ethnographic study and interesting stories to tell. The next year seemed as certain as any of my somewhat uncertain years could be.

Although I hoped to conduct a study of the whole community, I planned to focus on the construction of ethnic identity, relationships between *mestizo* and Totonac and Nahuat-speaking *indio* residents of the village, and the disruption of "stabilized pluralism," resulting in the gradual disappearance of Indian identity. As a good anthropologist, I had a stringently conceived yet sufficiently open research design. I was far from being a naive empiricist. I was a 1960s rebel immersed in existentialism and Marxism. I had read Paul Feyerbend's work on science as anarchy. I had even started one of my undergraduate papers on the nature of anthropology with the e.e. cummings poem, "o sweet spontaneous earth." But behind this veneer of openness and nonconformity were my training and my research design, ready to make sense out of even the most slippery of experiences. My anthropological research was, I thought, basking under the noontime sun where there were no shadows.

My third day in Jonotla, I arrived at a relatively large two-story stone house near the center of the village where, I had been told, there were rooms for rent. The man who showed me the rooms that were available was short and round with a little wisp of hair growing crookedly above his mouth. His head was too large for his body, and his muscular arms were short and looked permanently crooked at the elbows. His light blue shirt would have fit him fifteen pounds earlier, and his little straw hat appeared to belong to the much smaller man whose head should have been attached to his body. Although he looked about the same age as me, something in his eyes and the corners of his mouth made him seem like a playful little boy. I liked him and, besides, the rooms were relatively large, private and filled with light, unlike the small, dark rooms I had looked at in other houses. So I agreed to rent them. The man explained to me that he and his wife and small daughter rented the downstairs rooms and that I would have to confirm the rental of the upstairs rooms with the owner, who lived twenty-five kilometers away in the town of Zacapoaxtla.

As we parted, he asked, "What are you doing here?" I told him that I was in Jonotla to learn about the way people lived. He laughed. "Why do you want to know that?" he continued.

I felt uneasy and I wasn't sure why. "I'm just interested," I lied.

The corners of his eyes and mouth smiled. He knew.

Within a few days all was settled with the landlord and I moved in. There was no sign of the family downstairs and, tired from the move, I went to sleep early. Around 10:00 P.M. that night, there was a knock on my door. "Señor, are you there? Are you all right? I'm sorry to disturb you."

I recognized the voice. It was the man who had shown me the rooms. I opened the door, and there he stood with the same knowing smile etched across his face, which was illuminated by an old smelly kerosene lantern. "Is there a problem?" I asked.

"Well, no, no, yes, yes. I mean there is, but not a big problem. I'm sorry to disturb you, don Gregorio." He spoke so fast that I wasn't sure I was following him. I was also surprised when he called me by my name, since I didn't remember his.

"I am Celistino. Celistino de la Cruz Jiminez." He seemed to read my mind. "Remember? I live below."

Before I could answer, he continued, "I thought you could help me, if you don't mind. My wife is afraid. Please, señor."

I was too groggy and too uncertain to ask normal questions like "What in the hell are you talking about?" So I just nodded my assent and off we went downstairs. We reached a room that was full of boxes, large burlap bags, and old furniture. In the next room, the dim light reflected off a woman and small child huddled together on a bed. The woman nodded and laughed nervously, and the little girl just stared through her oversized black eyes. Looking back at Celistino, I finally asked, "What are we doing?"

"The rats," he said dryly. "The rats. We're going to kill the rats." Handing the lantern to me, he picked up a large wool blanket and started to tiptoe around the room, peeking under, over and around the junk that filled it. I tried to act like somebody who had done this hundreds of times before. Every once in a while, I heard the sound of little feet scurrying for their life, and Celistino would squeal and leap into the darkness, knocking boxes and bags aside. I saw nothing but brief flickers in the shadows.

Finally, Celistino crept into a corner, signaling for me to bring the light closer, but not too close. In one graceful movement, he threw the blanket to the floor, stepped on its edges, and swept the corners upward to form an inescapable trap. I still had not seen anything, but now the shrieking of the animal inside the blanket left no doubt that Celistino's mission was accomplished. To my surprise, he peered down into the bottom of the blanket, moved one hand slowly over the opening, and reached suddenly down into the trap and pulled an eight-inch rat out by the tail. Then he let out a high-pitched yell and twirled the rat around and around and flung it forcefully onto the cement floor, sending small splatters of blood across it.

"Shit," I said in English. Celistino and his wife and daughter laughed and whooped it up like it was *El Cinco de Mayo*.

Their celebration and my shock were short-lived, however. The sudden death of their *compadre* panicked the other rats in the room, who came flying out from under junk, screeching and seeming to fly inches off the floor as they searched frantically for a means of escape. I froze. Celistino became as frantic as the rats, catching one after the other and flinging them all to the same fate. Moments later, five large rats lay motionless, their blood splattered across the floor like a Jackson Pollack canvas.

"Shit," I said in English again. Celistino was smiling, but he seemed exhausted by his short burst of exhilarating energy. I didn't know what more to say, and so we stood there in silence as he caught his breath. Were congratulations in order? I wondered to myself. Or perhaps that would be insensitive, kind of like congratulating a warrior too soon after the trauma of fighting and winning a violent battle. Maybe just a smile and a friendly shake of the head would do.

Celistino seemed to notice my hesitancy and motioned me into the small hallway where the stairs led up to my rooms. "Men who hunt and kill rats together should be friends," he said, smiling. "Friends should not be formal, so from now on you should call me 'Mincho,' which is my nickname and, with your permission, I shall call you 'Goyo,' which is the nickname for Gregorio. Is it alright?"

"Of course," I agreed, not necessarily with the premise that killing rats together was a basis for friendship, but with the name changes. After all, forming friendships would only serve to facilitate my research.

For the next several weeks, I spoke with Celistino every day and gradually started to get to know details of his past and present life. On the cover of a red spiral notebook that I brought from the States, I neatly printed the label "Celistino," and I began to fill its pages with our conversations.

By this time, I saw my rental of the space in the same house occupied by Celistino and his family as one of those remarkably fortunate events that melded perfectly with my research interests. Celistino seemed to be an ideal case study. Born into a Nahuat-speaking family from a nearby village, he had moved as a young boy with his family to Jonotla. His family had come to "look for *centavos*," as the saying went, after being evicted from the land they had sharecropped for decades. This event, along with the early death of his father and other family tragedies, had cut Celistino loose from his past, leaving him to drift in a mestizo world of competitive wage labor. As I talked more and more with him, I found him to be an individual manifestation of the cultural patterns I was beginning to abstract from the rest of my data with the aid of my research design: he was a man in crisis, an Indian who, through a series of life events related to the larger process of socioeconomic change in the region, was severed from his past and pushed hesitantly toward a new personal and cultural identity.

The work table in one corner of my room was starting to look impressive. Stacks of census cards, notebooks, papers, and maps cluttered its surface. An anthropologist I was. After only several months of research, I had completed a household census, recorded numerous formal and informal interviews, participated in a variety of formal and informal social interactions, mapped the village, and started to abstract patterns that seemed important to my research focus. In addition, I had started to collect several interesting life histories, but Celistino was still my star. His life as I was coming to know it was a perfect example of what I was studying. I called him my friend, referred to him as Mincho, and was happy to have him call me Goyo, all without the slightest sensation of insincerity. Yet, despite the external trappings of friendship, Celistino was not really my friend. Rather, he was the object of my friendship, an abstraction based on an instrumental relationship defined by my need for data. However, I remained oblivious to this distinction, preferring to believe that I was not only a reasonably good anthropologist, but a reasonably good friend as well.

Just at the time when my sense of satisfaction with my progress peaked, my life suddenly became shaky. I felt depressed and empty. The data scattered across my desk appeared meaningless. My abstractions felt trivial. My research stopped. When I wrote my mentor about the black hole that I seemed to have inexplicably entered, he responded by writing, "It's just culture shock, the inevitable consequence of field research. You'll get over it like the rest of us did." I resented his attempt to transform the deep feelings and anxieties that I was experiencing into a generalized abstraction, as if I had the same temporarily pesky, but harmless, virus that everyone else once had. At first, convinced that I was not just another case study illustrating the existence of an abstraction, I desperately tried to fight this unwelcome lethargy. I forced myself out into the village and sat for long hours at my desk trying to coerce my hands to record observations and conversations. I tried to draw on the strengths of my personality, preparation, and training. But after several weeks, I gave up the fight and surrendered to what I was experiencing. I continued to live in Jonotla, but I stopped collecting data. For more than two weeks, not a note was recorded, not a journal entry made, not a single thought of interpretation. Nothing.

Then, one day I was returning home after running some errands and chatting with people when I stopped to talk with Celistino, who was standing in front of our house enjoying a cigarette in the cool and damp morning air. As we talked, we were approached by a young man who had quite a local reputation as a *macho*. Although it was only noon, he was so drunk that he struggled with each step over the rough cobblestone street. Almost immediately, he tried to engage me in a verbal duel over what he saw as our respective masculine attributes, ranging from various anatomical features to the virtues of our mothers and even to the durability of our watches when smashed against the cobblestones.

Initially, I couldn't believe this was happening. One moment I felt like I was co-starring in a bad movie, and the next moment I was in a Timex commercial. I could only think of how I might extricate myself from this unwanted situation. Of course, I would have welcomed the opportunity to *observe* such a verbal duel and analyze it within the context of social channels of conflict and mestizo *machismo*, but personal involvement was quite another thing. I had neither desire nor need, I thought, to exchange subtle insults with anyone, much less a near stranger who meant nothing to me. My meager responses to the verbal jabs of the young man reflected my lack of enthusiasm.

Slowly and inexplicably this all changed. At some point—I could never remember precisely when—I started to take the encounter seriously. Alternately threatened, proud, angered, smug, and afraid, I had surrendered to the moment and entered some previously unknown place within me. Anthropology and my research design were nowhere in sight. But neither was my depression and withdrawal, which were nothing more than the negative extensions of my assumed role of anthropologist. The wall constructed out of the objectification of self and other had momentarily crumbled. Here, at this moment, there was no object of study, no professional who studied, no other who was studied. I could not hide and pretend there was no one here but an anthropologist.

Standing by my side throughout the encounter was Celistino. At first, he was concerned for me, but as time passed he egged me on, reinforcing my verbal insults with laughs, facial expressions, and body language. Under his breath, he even directed some insults of his own toward my opponent. I felt a strong connection with him, like that of two old friends sharing some important secret.

After almost an hour, which seemed like only minutes to me, the young, drunk man in front of me tired of subtlety and harmless threats. He began to talk about *la buena pistola* which he claimed to be carrying in his belt under his *sarape*. Patting his waistline and lifting one side of the sarape to peer at the handgun that he said was there, he sneered, "Don Gringo, would you like to see it?" As he lifted his sarape one more time, I looked at Celistino, who was standing to the young man's side at an appropriate angle to see whether there really was a buena pistola in his belt. Celistino shifted his head ever so slightly, straining to get a better look, then gazed forcefully up into my eyes and almost imperceptibly shook his head back and forth.

There is no gun, I thought. Smiling, I turned my eyes back to the young man in front of me. "Yes, certainly, I want to see your buena pistola," I challenged him. My opponent backed down, mumbling something that no one could hear. There was no gun.

Celistino gently pulled me by the elbow and motioned with his head that I should follow him. It was an acceptable time for me to exist, since I had called my opponent's final bluff. Only then did I notice that a group of twenty or so people had been listening to the verbal duel. As the two of us entered through the front door of our house, I felt exhilarated until Celistino barred the door behind us. Seeing him lock the door in the middle of the day and noticing the anxiety on his face, I returned from that place inside—or was it outside?—me where I had been.

"Why are you locking the door?" I asked, already fearing the reply.

"Because he will return," Celistino replied, as if he were talking to an idiot. "With the pistol."

Within minutes, there was a fierce pounding at the door. The young man shouted for the blood of the gringo, declaring that if I was a real man I'd open the door and accept my fate with honor. Celistino and I stood quietly in the next room away from the door. Minutes seemed like hours. Then there was silence.

Later, over a lunch of beans and tortillas, Celistino asked how I knew that there was no gun. "You told me," I said. "You looked under his sarape and there was no gun. Then you told me with your head." And I mimicked his head moving slightly back and forth.

Celistino laughed and slapped his leg. "Goyo," he said, "I was trying to tell you that I didn't know if he had a gun. I couldn't see. With that shake of my head, I was trying to say 'Don't do anything foolish, he may really have a gun.'" He laughed again. "My friend, you are very lucky!"

I suddenly lost my appetite.

That night I wrote the first fieldnotes that I had written in over two weeks. Paradoxically, now that I wanted desperately to record something, I had difficulty remembering many details. The experience was like a nighttime dream recorded on chalkboard, erased by the consciousness of a new day, leaving little more than white chalk dust spread across my memory.

As I struggled to write, I realized that not only had I been momentarily in Celistino's world, but he had seen me in it. I had forgotten who I was and Celistino had as well, briefly erasing my personal history as an anthropologist, a gringo, a stranger. As he egged me on, laughing in support at my verbal jabs, wincing when those jabs were returned with greater force, as he feared for my safety when we both waited for bullets to fly through our front door, and as he laughed at my near fatal misinterpretation of his gesture, Celistino had seen me only as a friend. I was not an object to him, and now he could no longer be an object to me.

When I woke the next morning, nothing looked the same. It was almost as if my previous months in the village hadn't occurred. Whatever else might have happened the preceding day, it was clear that the experience and Celistino's involvement in it had neatly carved away the facade of anthropologist and informant to reveal the persons beneath. I had never been an abstraction to him. A novelty and oddity, perhaps, but never an abstraction, and he had quietly resisted my efforts to turn him into one. I remembered how I had resented my mentor's attempt to dilute the experience that I was struggling with into just another case of culture shock, and I wondered how I ever could have felt comfortable with transforming Celistino into just another identity crisis. In fact, I now realized that the lethargy that had enveloped me for the past several weeks was a response to the growing recognition that the lives of Celistino and others constituted consistent challenges to my attempts to turn them into ethnographic examples or case studies.

As a result, my research turned more and more toward the struggle to understand and depict the lived passion of those who were sharing their lives with me. I had come to realize that the idealized features that had guided my research, those same general features typically valued as evidence of a mature social science, are in fact reflections of our crisis as voyagers within contemporary civilization. The notions of objectivity and detachment, power and control, precision and efficiency, bureaucracy and standardization which explicitly and implicitly guide the practice of social science are indications of our alienation. But rather than authentically experiencing our alienation, we have tried to make a profession of sorts out of it. And just as surely as we have created an image of humans through a detached language and objectified research, we have transformed our own lives into the mirror image of that creation, reaffirming the prophecy of industrial civilization that we are all nothing but objects and that life is best understood as an efficient equation.

Somehow, Celistino had taught all of this to me. Of course, I was somehow ripe to learn, but, nevertheless, he had been my teacher, leading me as a friend to the threshold of my own mind. No other person had as significant an impact on my thinking as an anthropologist, and few other people have had such an impact on me personally. Despite my original instrumental motives, my spirit was deepened in ways that my words and work can only hope to approximate.

One of the final entries in my notebooks on Celistino de la Cruz Jiminez is a description of a night that we sat at a wobbly table in don Vicente's store, drinking small shots of *aguardiente* and chasing it with Orange Crush. The room was filled with men, most of whom had spent the day working in someone else's mud. Outside, several men sat on the cobblestones alone, their solitude intensified by the alcohol pumping through their bodies.

As we chatted, a man named Silvano entered the store and without looking at anyone else purchased a small shot glass of aguardiente and went back through the darkness into the street. Celistino explained to me that Silvano had only last week been humiliated by the son of one of the wealthy coffee growers for whom they both had worked. Silvano was a frail man, and when the boss's son had questioned his ability to pick coffee beans fast enough, Silvano had tried to lie about how much he had picked. But the son could clearly see that it was a lie, and he made sure that all the other workers heard his verbal insults. Silvano had been stupid to lie, but nothing could justify his humiliation.

Celistino excused himself, and when I asked if I could come, he nodded his assent. We went into the darkness together, finding Silvano propped against the wall of the store, his muddy legs stretched out in front of him. We greeted one another. Silvano smiled and motioned for us to join him on the ground. We were all silent for a moment. The full moon sat just above the red-tiled roofline of the village, once again like a white-hot hole in the black night sky. This time I felt no urge to flee toward it.

Silvano finally explained how the son had talked to his father, telling him that Silvano was too weak and tired to be of much help picking coffee beans. The next day, Silvano was informed that his labor would no longer be needed. "I told him how much I needed the money, but all he would say is 'maybe next week.'"

Celistino collected our glasses and went into the store for another round. I didn't know Silvano very well, and so I didn't know what to say. But I had lived long enough in Jonotla to know that both Celistino and Silvano struggled in a world where someone else, someone more powerful and wealthier, judged their right to exist and where their worth was measured in terms of how much coffee they could pick or how many sacks of coffee beans they could carry. They labored in someone else's mud and had little hope of ever working in their own. Unlike their parents, they had no refuge. They had no Indian community, no identity, to insulate them from the mestizo world. And yet they held onto something, something inside that they would not sell. They struggled not only to survive, but to thrive, to perform that impossible task of being fully human. They struggled in their world, just as I did in mine. I looked at Silvano, and he seemed to be reading my mind. We both smiled and shook our heads.

Celistino returned and we downed the aguardiente in three quick jerks. Wiping his mouth, Silvano continued."Well, this morning, Rafael, the son, came pounding on my door and asked whether I wanted to earn some centavos. 'Of course,' I said. He smiled and patted me on the shoulder and told me to bring my strong back to the plaza." Silvano went on to explain how he had spent the day carrying 100-pound sacks of coffee beans from a storehouse to the plaza, where they were loaded on a truck bound for the regional market in Zacapoaxtla. At the end of the day, Rafael paid Silvano almost nothing and invited him to work again tomorrow. "I told him I was not a burro," Silvano concluded. "And he said that I was right—a burro is worth more."

Celistino was quiet. "Shit," I said in English.

Finally, Celistino leaned close to Silvano and said, "This afternoon you may have been worth less than a burro, Silvano, but remember that tonight and tomorrow, when Andres and Rafael Ortuño are not using you, then you are a man!" We stared at one another, recognizing something shared, until we burst into a laughter that split the black night all the way to the moon.

We die of cold and not of darkness.

—Céline

When I left Jonotla several months later, I didn't realize that I would never see Celistino again. We bade good-bye with exuberant promises to write. I did. He never did. A year or so later, one of my letters came back stamped *domocilio no conocido*, address unknown. Later, I learned that Celistino had left Jonotla with his family in search of work and a better life. The next time I was in Mexico, I tried to pick up his trail, but it disappeared in the labyrinth of Mexico City, a yawning chasm of hope and despair expanded by hundreds of thousands of immigrants each year.

I would never see him again, but he wasn't gone from my life. Not really. He was there all the time. I talked about him in chandeliered ballrooms filled with anthropologists. I wrote a book and several articles about him. He came to my classes, and I introduced him to my students. I told stories about him, about us, to friends. But most of all, I thought about him. On late-night winter walks, in the middle of dinner, while reading a book, or sitting in the doctor's office, at the strangest of times, Celistino would simply appear in my head. He still does.

But I often wonder whether he ever thinks of me. Does he break up his friends with funny stories of the crazy gringo who fumbled through a year of Mexican village life? Does he remember the rats we hunted? Does he recall our long conversations? Does he know what he taught me? Does he know that he took me out of the cold of my alienation and into the darkness, the mystery, of attempting to fathom the depths of the human spirit? Does he remember what I look like?

At times, I think he must. But at others, I realize that it's not likely. For a friendship forged in the field is most often colored by an indelible kind of shadow, an irony, a deceit, a closeness hounded by the reality of separate paths. This is the joy, and this is the sadness. Celistino, my friend, gave me so much, but I will never know what, if anything, I gave to him.

ROBERT ROY REED

REMEMBERING CINITA

The dilemma for social scientists is how to apply the precision of science to the ambiguity of human relationships. The particular problem for anthropologists is how to do this among people who live in social worlds created by different assumptions about reality. It is no doubt a comment on the human condition (or nature, if you will) that this cultural abyss is regularly bridged. Scientist and native, self and Other, subject and object become friends, sometimes more.

Reed's story has all the ambiguity typical of any romance. He is not sure of what he feels and is totally in the dark about Cinita's feelings. Ambiguity is further heightened because of cultural differences, the very reason he is in Portugal. Thus the object of his scientific research, cultural difference, becomes an additional source of personal distress. In the face of all this uncertainty, and the certainties of his kibitzing friends, he dithers, until it is too late. But his relationship with Cinita does not end. It is picked up by villagers who embellish and embroider it until it becomes a tale that fulfills their desires . . . and maybe his too.

Anything could be true or false,
depending on whether one believed it.
    —Laura Esquivel, *Like Water for Chocolate*

Four days after I arrived in the foothills of Portugal's Serra de Estrela mountains, I feared I was going to be abandoned in the middle of the night. It was the fall of 1982, and I was in Belmonte, a village of 1,200 people, to do dissertation research. On arriving in the village I arranged for a room at the only lodgings available, the Pensão Altitude: a combination café, tavern, and rooming house. Four days later, the Altitude's middle-aged owners, José Manuel and his wife, Dona Maria, invited me to a birthday party in a nearby village. I was grateful for their attention.

    We left at ten o'clock, after the café closed and the tavern's business had slowed. Leaving the dim lights of Belmonte, we drove through silent countryside and shuttered hamlets. We turned regularly onto ever more narrow and rural roads. José Manuel and Dona Maria were silent. I began to wonder if the party was actually some traditional prank played on gullible foreigners. I nervously peered into the darkness, making plans about what to do if I was deserted on some country lane at midnight.

    Finally we stopped beside a group of houses crowding a narrow, twisting road. We stepped from the car into the moonlit stillness. We were miles from the main road or the nearest village. The stone walls of the buildings were heavy and rough and had narrow, deeply recessed windows. Everything looked long abandoned. Suddenly a heavy wooden door slammed open. Flashing colored lights and the sound of Duran Duran's "Hungry Like A Wolf" flooded out. We had arrived at the party.

The next day I wrote in my diary: "Went to some village near here. Some disco there. Bar, mirrored globe, disco lights and music. Everything but John Travolta. Woman—young, short hair, striking—who is dying of some disease? cancer? gave party." The woman was Cinita, and it was her birthday. She was slim and high-breasted and wore a chic black outfit. Her thick black hair and deep-set eyes contrasted with her pallid complexion. She was beautiful and surrounded by admiring men. José Manuel introduced us. Then, before I could stammer little more than hello, other guests took me aside wanting to know who I was, why I was in Portugal, and why soccer was not popular in America. I only caught glimpses of her again that night.

After the party I thought little of Cinita as I grappled with my research. Portugal had had a thoroughgoing revolution in 1974, and when I arrived it was still suffering aftershocks. Despite the drama of the revolution and the upheavals still unsettling Belmonte, I was determined to study local religious traditions. My meticulous methodology, however, was undone by villagers' indifference. No one—not even the village priest—wanted to talk about religion. Instead everyone talked about local politics, local scandal, and national soccer. Reluctantly and over many months, I slowly surrendered to village concerns and began, grudgingly, to study Belmonte's postrevolutionary political life.

From the start my new investigation went well. Villagers were interested in this research and even began to volunteer information freely. Although I was pleased by my mounting pile of fieldnotes, I was uncomfortable with how ad hoc my study had become. I felt I was not advancing deliberately toward a considered goal, but improvising furiously with each new day.

Villagers had not yet fully converted me to their concerns when, late one afternoon a week before Christmas, I found Cinita sitting alone in the Pensão Altitude. It was a blustery winter day, but the sunlight coming in the tavern's large windows warmed the tables along the wall where Cinita was sitting. The tavern was empty except for Cinita, Dona Maria, and two men talking quietly in a far corner.

In the three months since Cinita's party I had seen her often, but we had only exchanged vague pleasantries. She came to Belmonte regularly because she had many friends there and because the next largest market town, Covilhã, was an hour away. Since the party I had learned more about her from villagers' passing remarks. She had lived in France most of her life and spoke French better than Portuguese. She and her family now lived a half hour from Belmonte in Trigeis, a hamlet of less than a hundred people, mostly elderly farmers. With her younger sister, Odélia, and Odélia's fiancé, José, she ran a moderately successful small bar and discothéque. Everyone considered her very worldly. She was only twenty-three. She had *cancro de sangue*, blood cancer, leukemia.

"Olá, Cinita. How are you today? May I sit here?" (The dialogue I report, though based on fieldnotes and diary entries, is a resurrection in English of my own faltering Portuguese and Cinita's Gallo-Portuguese voice.)

"Olá, Roberto. Of course, please sit."

"What are you doing in Belmonte today?" I asked while I signaled Dona Maria for two espressos.

"Oh," she said, "I'm not feeling well. I'm getting the bus to Lisbon to have my medication changed. Then I can enjoy Christmas at home. Dona Maria is keeping me company while I wait." Dona Maria brought the coffees, greeted me, but instead of sitting with us, withdrew to the counter across the room.

Cinita and I sipped coffee, smoked cigarettes, and talked. She told me how, when she was four, her family moved to France, where her father could earn more at factory work than he could farming the few hectares the family owned in Trigeis. Although he earned good wages abroad, he always talked of returning to farm in Trigeis.

"Then, when I was nineteen, my father came home one day and announced that we were moving back to Trigeis. The factory offered early retirement, and he was one of the first to accept. I couldn't believe it. Trigeis was just this small village we visited on vacation every August. I liked it when I was a little girl. Running in the fields, playing with the animals. But to live there?

"Anyway, in one week we went from a Paris apartment to a old farmhouse in the middle of Portugal. I had almost finished school in France, but here I was put back because I couldn't speak Portuguese well. I still can't write it easily, and so I don't pass the tests. But I must finish my education, so I can enter a professional school and get a good job."

"Would you look for a job around here?" I asked. I could not imagine her working in Belmonte. The only local work for young women was as housemaids or sewing machine operators. Belmonte's eleven locally owned clothing factories were the county's only industry and the reason for its thriving economy. The work, however, was mind-numbing, sweatshop labor. Young women usually worked for only the few years between their quitting school and getting married.

Cinita paused to light a cigarette. "I would like to move to France or Switzerland. I don't like it here. There is no one to talk to. Not real talk. There is no *movimento*, no life. And no real jobs. This place is not good for me." She paused again. "But I have to take care of my illness before I do anything.

"What I really miss here," she said, looking out the window, "is freedom. When I first arrived, you never saw girls in taverns. Things are better today, some girls come here, but only in groups. Girls are still afraid to go to a tavern alone." She went on to tell how when she first arrived, people were so shocked that she smoked that she hid in the restroom to have a cigarette. "But," she laughed, "only a small group of my friends in France smoked marijuana. Here most of the kids do it, even young ones, and their parents don't even know."

That afternoon our conversation wandered from local personalities to international politics and back. Like me, she admitted that though she didn't like Lisbon—it was too dirty and hard to get around—she did enjoy the anonymity, if only for a few days.

"I know," I said. "Here I am in Belmonte wandering around with a limp, a cane, and a bad accent. People stop in the street to look at me. And they are not shy. They stare right at you. I didn't know that this part would be so hard. Always being looked at."

"Oh, the Portuguese will stare if anyone is different," Cinita remarked. "I've seen people in Lisbon inspecting a beggar's sores to see if they are real. Here in Belmonte, people first stared at me because I was different, *uma Francêsa*. Now they stare because I'm sick. But no one will talk openly or seriously about it. There is just this pity I feel from everyone. But no one ever talks about it."

"I know," I said. "People are anxious to know what happened to me in Vietnam. I know that some people know I have wooden legs, but, of course, no one would ever mention it. No one sober, at least. But they stare, all right. Stop dead right in the street and stare." Laughing, Cinita agreed and patted her hair, thinning from chemotherapy.

For the first time since arriving in Belmonte, I just talked. I forgot about my work. I had no agenda. I just wanted to enjoy Cinita's company and discover what we had in common. Sitting together in the sunlit tavern while the winter wind swept the streets outside, we let our talk go where it would.

Although the tavern remained quiet, Dona Maria never joined us. She brought coffee but would always withdraw behind the counter. I noticed her, however, with her back turned away, discreetly watching us in the mirrors behind the tavern's dusty display of exotic liqueurs. Once when she brought more coffee she asked what we were talking about. Cinita laughed and said, "Just those things *estrangeiros* talk about." I laughed loudly. Estrangeiro means foreigner or stranger, and most of our talk that afternoon had been about how we were both. She was right, what we had in common was that we were estrangeiros. Not only were we foreigners in Portugal, but also strangers to each other and the people of Belmonte. Being estrangeiros was our bond. Dona Maria cocked her head at my laughter but then smiled and returned to her counter.

That was my longest private conversation with Cinita. Over the next year we ran into each other regularly, either when she came to Belmonte to see friends or when some of us would go to her discothéque in Trigeis. In my fieldnotes, but mostly in my private diary, are passing references to her:

Cinita straightened out those weird government stats about Trigeis. Said no one was sure whether the hamlet belonged to the *concelho* [county] of Belmonte or Sabugal. The government counted it one way, then another, and occasionally both ways." (January)

Cinita was at the pensão last night talking to Dona Maria about Latino husbands. Said they were fine, but only after they got through sleeping around. Marry them before that and there would be trouble." (February)

This morning Dona Maria told me Cinita was so ill last night that an ambulance had to rush her to a cancer specialist in Lisbon, six hours away." (April)

Cinita and Odélia stopped at the pensão late last night as José Manuel, Dona Maria, Amaral, Alexandre and me were cleaning up before closing. Everyone was glad to see her and she got embarrassed about the fuss we were making. This hospital stay must have been hard, though she shrugged it off. But her eyes were bruised and she was bald from the chemotherapy. José Manuel closed the bar so he wouldn't have to serve anyone else. Then we all went to the back and drank beer, joked, and laughed. Cinita laughed a lot when everyone took turns modeling her new wig. José Manuel and Cinita couldn't believe it when I told them I once had hair that long. Wanted to hear all about being a "ippi" [hippie]. Had a good time. Got to bed about three." (June)

I saw Cinita every few weeks, but she appears in my fieldnotes and diary less often. She became such a regular part of my life that her presence was no longer noteworthy. When something special happened, or when she gave me new information, I noted it. But increasingly, references to her in my notes were perfunctory: "Went to Cinita's last night with Alexandre, Bela, and Luis. Talked to some farmers about . . ." As my fieldwork progressed, I became more comfortable in Belmonte and began to count a few friends among my informants. I counted Cinita.

Everyone liked Cinita and admired how she confronted her illness. Talking about her, villagers always recounted her first "episode" with leukemia. She had become very ill so quickly and mysteriously that no one believed she would survive. Her parents were so terrified that without hesitation they agreed to her demand that if she lived, she could live as she wanted. Who could say no? Who could bargain? She was dying.

I never heard her parents, a silent, haunted-looking couple, or Cinita, mention such an agreement. But I also never knew any Portuguese daughter who was allowed the freedom Cinita had or, if allowed it, who took such advantage of it. People frowned at Cinita's manner (her public smoking, her forthright opinions, her late nights), but they did not openly censure. Even people who sternly disapproved of what she did said they sympathized with why she did it.

I suspected that villagers also gave her dispensation because she created delicious scandal for them to share. It was rumored that when she was healthy, Cinita had slept with several local men. These men, however, though they often bragged of their sexual exploits, hotly denied ever having slept with her. But there was no denying that wherever she was, men surrounded her. When a group of us, males and females, would go somewhere, we always got better service if Cinita was with us. Often the male owner of the establishment appeared to serve us, or rather her, personally.

Sometimes Cinita encouraged men's attention, and, along the way, shocked even her friends. Once she came into the Pensão Altitude wearing a fish-net blouse and no bra. Within fifteen minutes most of the men in the café, including myself, left, because we could not stop staring at her breasts. Despite these occasions, which became local benchmarks of social daring, Cinita most often did nothing special. Yet her combination of fragile health, robust beauty, and irreverent spirit drew men.

One afternoon, one year after I met her, Cinita appeared at the café. It was her birthday and, following custom, she was buying drinks for everyone. She then invited me, my best friend, Alexandre, and his wife, Bela, to join her and her sister Odélia and Odélia's fiancé, José, for a birthday dinner at her home. Today, I know that invitations to dine at somebody's home are often overtures to move from casual acquaintanceship to a more intimate friendship. At that time, I was simply happy to be with Cinita and friends and to eat somewhere besides the café.

On our way to Cinita's everyone began talking about food and cooking. Cinita and the others were surprised when I said that I missed having a kitchen because I enjoyed cooking. This, they told me, was a rare skill—and admission—for a man in Portugal. But I persisted and volunteered to help prepare the meal. Cinita accepted my offer, and once we reached her home we set to work while the others went next door to the bar.

Together Cinita and I went through the larder to see what was available. In the end we created a simple meal of stuffed peppers and poached flounder with herbs. When we served it, the other guests raved, claiming they had never had a meal like it. Cinita surprised everyone further, especially the women, when she announced that I actually did know my way around a kitchen. After dinner Cinita and I amused everyone as we imagined the restaurant we would open in Trigeis. We agreed it should be an intimate place, serving only the freshest local food prepared in a simple manner. Soon Cinita was arguing for Provencal cooking techniques, if not cuisine, while I praised the merits of American sweet corn. We became so absurdly emphatic about what our restaurant would be like that the others were laughing and joining in. Even Cinita's father, who had sat silently throughout the evening, voiced strong opinions when we began arguing about what to feed pigs to get the sweetest pork.

I had been in the field for a year when I began wondering if I should ever leave. After the frenzy of graduate school, the thought of spending the rest of my life in rural Portugal was appealing. And as I thought about staying in Portugal, I wondered if Cinita could be more than a friend. I was, in fact, mulling over the Portuguese proverb, *Quem casa, quer casa* (Whoever marries, wants a home). I knew I wanted a home, and if it was in Portugal, then . . .

I was attracted to Cinita, but I was not sure what I was attracted to: her wit, vivacity, beauty, or what. And for all my attraction, I clearly heard cool voices in me resisting. She was seriously ill and could die soon. I hardly knew her; in a year we had had one private conversation. I imagined the voices of my academic advisers: Don't sleep with the natives. I heard my own professional conscience: Get your data, get home, and get your degree.

On the rare occasions when I felt sure of my attraction, I was at a loss about what to do next. Traditional courting customs were battered by postrevolutionary freedoms, but not all the customs were dead or despised. Villagers seemed as confused as me about how to court now. Moreover I wondered if I should court the untraditional Cinita traditionally? But I had also heard that she had never had a real boyfriend, just hangers-on. Maybe she wanted a traditional courtship and the public respect from having a serious suitor. But to me traditional Portuguese courtship, even in those postrevolutionary times, seemed to vault from being the most casual of acquaintances to being *namorados*: just short of a formal engagement.

I thought I had hidden my concerns and confusion, but friends began making probing comments and sly asides. Because I had no transportation, I had to find rides with people already going to Trigeis if I wanted to visit Cinita. My closest friends took to pointedly asking me if I wanted to go anywhere. If, after some embarrassed hesitation, I mentioned Trigeis, they gave a loud "Ah-ha" and grinned broadly. My best male friend, Alexandre, began casually, but comprehensively, to tell me what being namorados meant. Feigning only academic interest, I took scrupulous notes.

But while some friends were edging me toward declaring myself to Cinita, others were adamantly giving contrary advice. Senhor Jorge, an older man whose friendship and advice I valued, warned me against Cinita, saying she had only a *sentimento metálico*—an affection for metal [coins]—and rubbed his thumb and forefinger together, gesturing money. "If you need sex," he continued, "go to Lisbon," and offered me the name of an honest whorehouse. Other friends also took me aside to pass on rumors about Cinita's loose morals and "foreign" ways.

The one thing I knew for sure was that if I did court Cinita, it would be a more public and serious courtship than I was accustomed to—uncomfortably more. Imagining scenarios and consequences, I twisted myself into ever tighter knots of indecision. Finally, I postponed making any decision by immersing myself in fieldwork.

I did not see Cinita again after the birthday meal we had prepared. Then months later, one Sunday morning in January, I entered the café and Paula, Dona Maria's ten-year-old daughter, ran to me. "Did you hear? Cinita died last night!" she said breathlessly.

"It's true?" I asked, turning to Dona Maria.

"Yes. She died sometime last night," Dona Maria answered quietly. "Her sister, Odélia, said that Cinita did not feel well the last few weeks and stayed home. Odélia talked to her in her room yesterday afternoon, and when she returned that evening, Cinita was dead." Dona Maria said she had visited Cinita a few days before. Cinita had not left her bed in over a week, and Dona Maria was shocked to see the bedside table covered with medicines. "She told me that it took her over an hour each morning to swallow all her pills." Dona Maria hugged her daughter. "*Coitadinha*, poor thing," she said.

I stood stupidly in front of them. I felt ashamed. I had never fantasized about saving Cinita from her illness. I knew she was going to die. But I always felt I had time, time to discover how I felt, time to decide what to do. Now, there was no more time.

For all my indecision, I knew that I cared for Cinita. About that I was certain. I was not sure about how seriously I cared; what I was willing to go through for her. But I did care, and now I could not tell her even that. Before it never felt like it was enough to say; there should be more. I stood there stunned by the certainty that nothing could be said now, nothing could change.

I felt very much the estrangeiro that Sunday morning in Portugal at the Pensão Altitude. Whatever Portuguese custom was, I should have told her I cared.

Sunday afternoons were always busy for the pensão. Soon after lunch, villagers began arriving and claiming seats, until all the tables were filled. They stayed the entire afternoon, moving between groups, drinking coffee, and gossiping until it was time to go home for dinner. On that Sunday, all talk was at first about Cinita's death. But she was dead; there was little left to say. People moved to other topics. I wandered aimlessly and chatted.

That evening José Manuel and I shared dinner and talked about the day. He mentioned that he and Dona Maria had gone to view Cinita's body and there had been quite a crowd at her house.

"Is that where she is, at home?" I asked.

"Yes. She will remain there until the funeral tomorrow."

"Who is supposed to do that?" I asked. "Go to her house and view the body."

"Anyone who was family, a friend. When did you go?"

"I didn't know anything about it! Why didn't anyone tell me?"

José Manuel shrugged ignorance. "You should have gone, you know."

Somebody ordered a beer and José Manuel left to tend bar. I sat alone in the café. Why didn't anyone tell me what to do?

Monday afternoon was the funeral. Dona Maria was already at Cinita's house helping to prepare. I was going to ride to Trigeis with José Manuel and Amaral, a waiter who was also attending the funeral. When I met them in front of the pensão, they looked critically at my clothes. I was wearing my darkest pants and a tweed jacket. I wore my only tie, gray with red stripes. Finally José Manuel shook his head and said, "Since you are part of the family, you should dress properly."

"I don't have anything darker," I explained. "This is all I have."

"Well, use this one," he said, taking a cheap black tie off a coat hook in the café. The tie had hung there since I had first moved into the pensão. The waiters used it when they forgot theirs at home. It was fairly clean.

I put it on. I felt honored to be called "one of the family" and ashamed at lacking something every local boy gets with his first suit. Then I felt ashamed for feeling ashamed about a stupid tie. This is Cinita's funeral, I told myself. That is what is important.

On the way to Trigeis, José Manuel and Amaral talked about the customs for mourning dress. I took notes. It steadied me to do something familiar, and I started to feel better. After a while José and

Amaral stopped talking, and I watched the scenery going past the car's windows. I felt very still and very observant, as if I were hiding, waiting for something to happen.

When we got to Cinita's there was a crowd of fifty to seventy-five people waiting outside. José Manuel said he would not go inside again. I went in. Cinita lay in a coffin in the front parlor. The coffin stood alone in the middle of the room. Women dressed in black, many of them elderly, wept in the chairs which lined the walls.

I stood and looked at Cinita. She had the same waxy off-white color I had seen in the dead in Vietnam. She wore a white dress. I wondered if she had picked it out. Was it her wedding dress? I thought that was the custom for unmarried women. Or was that Greece? I stopped. Why was I wondering about customs? Cinita was dead. I tried to concentrate on Cinita's death but found myself wondering about her dress. I left the room.

Back outside with the men, I smoked cigarettes and stood in the sunshine. The local men were mostly elderly farmers with large hands; they fidgeted in their dark suits and tight collars. A sheep escaped a nearby pen, and the men herded it back, glad for the refuge of routine.

Cinita's sister, Odélia, wore a long black dress. José, her fiancé, was also all in black. He was supporting her as she went to each knot of people. I wondered where everyone had gotten their mourning clothes so quickly. Did they have them stored away for today? I tugged at my tie.

Odélia alternated between hysterical crying and sober efforts to comfort the people trying to comfort her. In my head I reviewed the grammar of the consoling words I had chosen. When she got to me, I mumbled about being sorry, if there was anything I could do, please. She thanked me for coming and embraced me. I felt stiff and unyielding.

A few minutes after three o'clock, some men brought out the coffin. It was loaded onto a two-wheeled cart, and people started to push it toward the cemetery in Bendada, a village five kilometers away in the county of Sabugal. Many people said it was too far to walk and went to their cars.

January is cold and raw in the hills around Belmonte, but that Monday was sunny and soft, and the hills were green. I felt comfortable in my suit and the pensão's tie. It felt good to be outside. I walked with the coffin. My friend Alexandre stayed with me. Occasionally cars stopped next to us, and people offered rides. Carefully not looking at my legs and cane, they said it was too far to walk and beckoned me in. I thanked them but said I wanted to walk. I did not say more.

Odélia and José stopped in a long black car I did not recognize. She had tried to walk, but she was crying too hard. Cinita's mother was in the car also. She had fainted so often she could not walk anymore. They were insistent that I join them, but I smiled, asked if Cinita's mother was feeling better, and continued walking. They pulled Alexandre aside to argue with him. "He says he wants to walk," Alexandre said, shrugging his shoulders. Finally the car pulled away and Alexandre rejoined me. I knew I was causing trouble, but I pretended not to notice the pointed looks and Alexandre's hushed explanations. I did not worry about what was culturally correct, what people thought, or doing the right thing. Walking next to Cinita felt right. So I walked.

After a while, all the cars had passed us and continued up the road to Bendada. There were perhaps twenty of us left on the road. As I walked next to the coffin, Alexandre absently began explaining things. It was our routine. He told me how Cinita's body had been washed by neighbor women who then dressed her. After this, he explained, there was the *rezada*, when the body was placed in the coffin and the women remained around it to pray and wait for the burial.

He told me how everyone was speculating about a young man who stayed throughout the rezada Sunday night. No one knew why. It was very unusual for a man, especially a young man, to do so. It was a woman's task. As far as everyone knew, he was just a neighbor boy and nothing special to Cinita. But everyone was moved by his devotion, even if they did not understand it.

"Of course," Alexandre continued, "Jorge is very sad." Jorge was a handsome young man and the local motorcycle daredevil. Although his family was undistinguished, he managed to marry into one of Belmonte's richest families. I had seen him at Cinita's this morning but hadn't seen his wife. I asked why he should be especially upset about Cinita's death.

"They were namorados for a long time," Alexandre said. "Then they broke up and he married O Rico's daughter. Didn't you know?"

"No. I thought she never had a namorado."

"Oh, no. Jorge and she were together for a long time. I thought you knew. Maybe someone told you and you didn't understand."

"Maybe you're right. Maybe I didn't understand."

We walked and Alexandre talked. He thought it was a scandal that there was no local mortician so that bodies could be prepared professionally. "And look at this," he said. "We're hauling her like a load of potatoes. There ought to be a hearse so she could travel with dignity." He complained that local politicians should do something. "This is too far for people to walk," he grumbled.

I listened absently. Again, I felt still and observant. I walked, using my cane lightly. It took over an hour to get to Bendada. The sun was warm.

When we arrived, I stood in front of the cemetery with several other men as the coffin was taken to a nearby church for the final services. Alexandre had to go back to work. After I assured him I would find a ride to Belmonte, he left to find a lift back to his car. I waited with the others for the service to finish and the burial to begin.

Jorge pulled up in his car, got out, and waited with us. Everyone was quiet, smoking cigarettes, and staring at the hills. Jorge said he used to ride his motorcycle around there a lot. It was a good place to ride. The others agreed. We stared at the hills.

Finally, the funeral procession returned from the church. A bent old man unlocked the graveyard gates. The priest led the procession, followed by two teenaged acolytes with bad complexions, the pallbearers, and the rest of us. We stood around the grave as the priest droned about "our sister," which showed how little he knew of Cinita's thoughts about religion—and priests. Everyone was subdued.

The bearers had placed the coffin at the foot of the grave and leaned it forward until it was almost completely upright. As the priest finished, a man stepped forward and threw open the coffin lid. Screams ripped the air. People were fainting all around me. Jorge stepped in to support Cinita's father, who was tearing at his face and wailing, "My daughter, my daughter." The priest and the acolytes left quickly.

The glossy white satin of Cinita's dress highlighted the dead pallor of her face. She looked wrong in the sunlight. I turned away as the wailing and screaming went on and on. Cinita's father tore away from Jorge and threw himself at Cinita's feet, kissing her shoes. Odélia buried herself in José's arms. I was supporting Dona Maria and Alexandre's wife, Bela. Finally the old man closed the lid and secured it. Four men with ropes grunted and heaved, lowering the coffin into the ground. Then they began shoveling in the loose soil.

The wailing subsided into low moans as people stumbled out of the cemetery. Jorge offered Dona Maria and Bela a ride back to their car next to the church. Afterward I rode with him to Belmonte.

"Odélia told me that I should have married Cinita," he said quietly, looking far down the road. "She is right. But after we separated, Cinita and I became true friends. Real friends." He drove silently before he continued. "I never thought she would die, though." For the rest of the trip he kept repeating, "I don't believe it. I don't believe it."

I watched him. Cinita's namorado. I wondered if his wife knew where he was. The question brought me upright. This was Cinita's funeral, I reminded myself again. But this time the charge echoed in me. I felt too battered to feel more and too worn for more questions.

When Jorge dropped me at the pensão, I went straight to my room. Without thinking, I put a carbon between two sheets of paper and loaded my typewriter. As I sat writing late into the evening, I relived the day.

Rereading my notes the next morning, I discovered they were detailed and evocative. It disturbed me how good they were.

I got little work done the next week as I sat in my room confronting the questions that crowded in on me. Why had no one told me about viewing the body, or about Jorge? Because, I finally answered myself, they thought I already knew, or they didn't think to tell me, or they were simply tired of explaining things. How could I have written such detailed fieldnotes about Cinita's funeral; did that mean I never had deeper feelings for her? Perhaps, but maybe they were my refuge in routine. Was all this what participant observation was really about? Yes, I decided. All this was real: Cinita, me, the people of Belmonte, the funeral, everything had happened. This is what I study because this is what I need to understand.

As I struggled with these questions, I began to feel the year and a half I had been working in Belmonte settle heavily on me. I felt sore, as if I had been beaten. I was tired of Portugal and fieldwork. I remained in Belmonte three more months, but I began leaving that day.

Seven years later, I was back in Belmonte, sharing a beer with Alexandre. I had returned for a summer to see friends and do more work. It felt good to be in Belmonte with Alexandre again, and as we talked people stopped to welcome me back. Alexandre talked about his daughters, Vania and Tania, and his struggles establishing his small clothing factory. I showed him pictures of my wife and eight-month-old son and talked about how hard it was to find a university job today.

Suddenly, Alexandre became serious. "I've never gone back to Cinita's grave," he said softly, "but when you want to go, just tell me and I'll give you a ride." I thanked him, unnerved by his offer and uncharacteristic gravity. I had a wife and child I loved. Cinita was gone, seven years gone.

Later that day at the Pensão Altitude, its new owner, Senhor Amandio, came around the counter to greet me personally. "It is good to have you here," he said shaking my hand. "Alexandre told me you were coming. While this is mine," he said indicating the pensão, "think of it as your home." Then he embraced me and said, "It is good to have you back." I was nonplussed; I did not know this man.

"I am Cinita's uncle," he continued, patting the back of my hand. "If you need anything—anything at all—just ask me." The next day, he extended his welcome by taking the entire afternoon to drive me throughout the countryside, introducing me to his many friends, telling them about my work, and saying that he personally would appreciate any help they could give me.

Although Alexandre's and Senhor Amandio's open reference to Cinita was uncommon, I soon learned that their sentiments were not. Cinita and I had become a minor, though definite, part of village folklore. There was a "Cinita and the American" story. We were public domain.

I cannot say how widespread the story was. I cannot even give a complete version of it: people were too embarrassed to tell me all, and I was too uncomfortable to pursue it. I assembled the story from hints, significant looks, things left unsaid, and topics suddenly changed. The story concerns an American professor who falls desperately in love with a beautiful Portuguese woman. He remains in Portugal to court her. But before the courtship can begin, she dies. At the funeral he cannot bear to say good-bye and, though crippled from a foreign war, struggles—kilometer after kilometer—alongside her coffin, all the way to the graveyard. Immediately afterward he leaves Belmonte brokenhearted.

That summer I became increasingly aware of villagers, such as Senhor Amandio, who related to me exclusively through Cinita or, more precisely, through the "Cinita and the American" story. Few mentioned her name, and no one openly extended condolences. Instead they offered ethnographic miscellanea and introductions to people "who know old things." They were trying to help me.

I was torn. Their concern was so heartfelt that my own indecision seven years ago now felt like betrayal. They remembered Cinita and me as lovers, though we never courted, kissed, or even held hands. But I also felt trapped in the melodrama they had scripted. No photographs of a wife and son or testimonies from me could dissuade villagers from the fantasy of "Cinita and the American."

The dishonesty upset me. But villagers love sentimental romances with melancholy endings. After all, the folk song of Portugal is called *fado*, fate, and people sing it to evoke *saudade*, the sorrow of irredeemable loss. Perhaps villagers have created a fado out of Cinita and me. Today, ten years after her death, I don't recognize the couple. But neither can I rely on my own memories. I love fados too.

ROBIN RIDINGTON

BRAIDED STORIES

ENCOUNTERS WITH "THE REAL OMAHA"

In 1962, Ridington encountered the Sacred Pole of the Omaha tribe in a glass case in Harvard's Peabody Museum. Twenty years later, he wrote a paper about the Pole that combined his reading of a classic 1911 ethnography by Alice C. Fletcher and Francis La Flesche with his recollections of the Pole. When he sent a copy of that paper to Dennis Hastings, the Omaha tribal historian, Dennis replied with an invitation to visit the tribe in person. That visit led to Ridington's collaboration with the tribe in their efforts to bring the Sacred Pole back to the reservation. In 1989 the tribe repatriated their Sacred Pole. Ridington was asked to speak to the tribe on that occasion. Through his experience of working with the tribe, he came to understand the Sacred Pole as a living person.

"Braided Stories" combines the text of Ridington's original paper with his narrative of how the Sacred Pole came back to the Omaha tribe. It represents the texts of Ridington's talks to the tribe and discusses issues of shared ethnographic authority. The paper concludes that reading a text can also be an act of shared authorship. Through his encounters with "The Real Omaha," Ridington came to participate in an ongoing shared narrative.

In his invitation to contribute to this volume, Bruce Grindal said that the papers "should flat out tell a story—an interesting and compelling story about another person, living in another culture, and the anthropologist's relationship with that person or people." Stories are central to the thoughtworlds of Native Americans and to those who document their history. Stories make the connection between thought and substance. Stories carry messages between cultures and between generations. Anthropologists record stories, but they also tell them and enact them. Anthropologists have been characters in Native American history as much as Native Americans have been the subjects of our ethnographic narratives. This interdependence has been particularly strong in anthropology's relationship to the Omaha Tribe of Nebraska. Omaha ethnographer Francis La Flesche was one of the first Native American anthropologists. Through him, the Sacred Pole of the tribe came to reside in the Peabody Museum of Harvard University in 1888.

My story continues the one he began. It tells about my relationship with a person of the Omaha tribe. That person is Umo^n'ho^n'ti, "The Venerable Man" or "The Real Omaha," known in English as the Sacred Pole of the Omaha tribe. He is a physical object, a cottonwood pole, but he is also a person. His life cannot be separated from that of the Omaha people. He is alive as the Omahas are alive. My story touches on his long and venerable life among his own people, on his more recent century of living in the care and custody of anthropology, and on my own witness to his return to the tribe in 1989.

I first met Umon'hon'ti in 1962, when I began graduate studies at Harvard's Peabody Museum. The Sacred Pole was on public display in a glass case there. I had no idea then that he might be something other than a physical object, although I did understand that the Pole had been sacred to the people who once cared for him. I visited the glass case often and wondered what stories this object could tell if it could speak. Then, in 1984, I was asked to review a new edition of Omaha stories edited by Roger Welch. I decided, instead, to write about the Sacred Pole, as Alice C. Fletcher and Francis La Flesche had described him in their classic 1911 ethnography *The Omaha Tribe*. I remembered having read this 660-page book with amazement during my days as a graduate student.

Each reading of a text brings it into a different context. I was in school when I first read Fletcher and La Flesche in 1964. Twenty years later, I had done fieldwork with a subarctic hunting people, the Dunne-za, and had written extensively about what I had learned from them. As an author of ethnographic texts, I had a different understanding about reading them than before. It seemed to me that reading is also an act of authorship in that it enacts a shared story. Reading brings a text into the story of a reader's life. When I read Fletcher and La Flesche for the second time, I guided my reading by writing about the book and recalling my earlier encounters with the text and with the Sacred Pole himself. I called the paper I wrote in 1984 "Mottled as by Shadows: The Life and Death of a Sacred Symbol."

According to Fletcher and La Flesche, the Sacred Pole's traditional name, Waxthe'xe, refers to something sacred that is "mottled as by shadows." The word "has also the idea of bringing into prominence to be seen by all the people as something distinctive" (Fletcher and La Flesche 1911:219). When I wrote the paper, I had no idea how, or even whether, the Omahas continued to exist as a tribal culture. Margaret Mead had described them as a "broken culture" in her 1965 introduction to *The Changing Culture of An Indian Tribe* (Mead 1965:xiii). She had given the entire tribe a pseudonym, the Antlers. My paper focused on the Sacred Pole as he had functioned during the tribe's buffalo-hunting days. I assumed that he and Omaha culture had lost contact with one another in the years that followed. As far as I knew, the Pole was still on display in the Peabody Museum. As far as I knew, it was no longer alive as a sacred symbol of the Omaha tribe.

The paper I wrote in 1984 reflected an understanding of Omaha history based on my reading of Fletcher and La Flesche. Since I wrote it, I have become directly involved in the life of the tribe. To my amazement, I discovered that an ongoing chapter in the story was still being written. In this narrative, an anthropologist (myself) who knew the Pole during my graduate studies began thinking about what the Pole as a sacred object means. The anthropologist put his thoughts into writing. His exercise of thought about the Sacred Pole literally wrote him into the ongoing story of the Pole's life. In Omaha tradition, as in that of many Native Americans, an integral relationship exists between thought and substance. Thought is a property of substance, although not necessarily its cause. Thought indwells within substance.

I cannot separate my thinking and writing about the Sacred Pole from the movement that subsequently took place in the story of his life. Following my writing about him, I found myself involved in his actual return to the care and keeping of contemporary Omahas. I came to understand that thinking and writing about him are storymaking as well as storytelling. The story of his origin is now part of the story of his return. According to Fletcher and La Flesche:

> Every acquisition that bettered the condition of the people was the result of the exercise of the mind. "And the people thought" is the preamble to every change; every new acquirement, every arrangement devised to foster tribal unity and to promote tribal strength, was the outcome of thought . . . So, too, was the tribal organization itself, which was based on certain ideas evolved from thinking over natural processes that were ever before their observation. The Sacred Legend speaks truly when it says "And the people thought." (608–609)

In thinking about the Sacred Pole, I found myself drawn into a story I had previously observed only from a distance. The paper I wrote led me to a relationship first with contemporary Omahas and later with Umon'hon'ti himself. When I sent what I had written to Dennis Hastings, the Omaha tribal historian, he reacted by inviting me to visit the tribe in person; and I did so in 1985. In the narrative that follows, I have blended passages from my 1984 text with an ongoing story of the Pole's return.

A Braiding of Stories

The text I wrote in 1984 reflected my reading of Fletcher and La Flesche and my recollection of having encountered the Sacred Pole as a graduate student. The text that follows is a reading of my 1984 paper in light of my subsequent involvement in the Sacred Pole's life. My story is relevant to literature as well as to ethnography. The integrity of a text exists both in relation to the conditions of its production and to the conditions of subsequent readings. When I wrote "Mottled as by Shadows," I assumed that the symbolic life of the Sacred Pole had died and become entombed by anthropology. I am now convinced that anthropology's responsibility to the Pole is to discover how he is alive with meaning.

My reprise of material from "Mottled as by Shadows" is simultaneously a new reading and a new writing. It reveals a renewal of my own experience of anthropology. Beginning with the original text gives the view of hindsight, but it also recognizes that the text itself looked forward to a potential relationship of which I was as yet unaware. Umon'hon'ti, I came to know, is a person. He is alive. He is a metonym, a person of the people. In contemporary Omaha speech, he is The Real Omaha. Neither he nor his symbolic meaning are dead, as I originally supposed them to be. I don't attribute some mystical prescience to my text or to the others that define Umon'hon'ti as a person, but I do honor the larger story of which both have now shown themselves to be parts.

The meaning of a story changes with each telling. The meaning of a text is similarly the product of each reading it receives. The anthropologist's reading of a text from an oral tradition inevitably differs from the way it is experienced orally within its own community. An ongoing story that moves between oral and written media is multiply reflexive. Its telling by people of one time is changed by the perspective of later tellings. The written document of a single telling must also change its point of reference with the passage of time. My encounters with Umon'hon'ti, The Real Omaha, began as a reading of the Pole himself (Ridington 1993). Later, I discovered the story of the Pole's origin as texts recorded by Alice Fletcher and Francis La Flesche from Yellow Smoke, the Pole's last keeper. When the Omaha tribe invited me to visit them, I spoke to them by braiding the story of my first encounters with the Sacred Pole with a telling of the texts from Fletcher and La Flesche.

"Braided Stories: Encounters with 'The Real Omaha'" tells an ongoing story of the Pole's relationship to his people and to the anthropologists in whose custody he rested for just over a century. Some of the texts appear in more than one context as the story of Umon'hon'ti and my encounters with him progresses. This repetition is intentional. In an oral tradition, the same story is told on multiple occasions. Each telling has its distinctively reflexive signature. In a story that is ongoing, each previous telling takes on additional meaning from the new context in which it finds itself. The Sacred Pole appeared to be a lifeless object in a glass case when I first encountered him. The story of his origin seemed to exist only as the textual artifact of a tribe that had become, in the words or Margaret Mead, "culturally deprived" (1965:xi).

Now, the Pole and his story have returned to the life of contemporary Omahas. That story also touches the lives of contemporary anthropologists. "Braided Stories: Encounters with 'The Real Omaha'" is just another chapter in the braided story that Omahas, anthropologists, and Umon'hon'ti himself continue to realize. In the following pages, I present passages from "Mottled as by Shadows" as indented text. My commentary on that text and transcriptions of talks I gave to the tribe alternate as full paragraphs.

Beginning

> When I first began graduate work in anthropology at the Peabody Museum of Harvard University, the "Sacred Objects of the Omaha tribe" were displayed in glass cases close to where I studied.

With these words I began a paper I called "Mottled as by Shadows: The Life and Death of a Sacred Symbol."

> The objects fascinated me but they were also dry, lifeless and largely incomprehensible.

In 1984 I was asked to review Roger Welch's new edition of Omaha stories originally collected by James Owen Dorsey (Welch 1981). The stories reminded me that twenty-two years before, as a graduate student at Harvard University, I had encountered the Sacred Pole of the Omaha tribe, an ethnological specimen on public view in a glass case.

> It took a great leap of imagination to put them back into the lives and minds of real people. Sacred Bundles lay open to view but remained opaque to my understanding. I remember dry birds, themselves bundles of enigma, their flight converted into symbols not revealed by their exposure in the glass cases. I remember animal furs and a human scalp.

I remember wondering whether the Omaha tribe still existed and, if so, what they might think of what I had written. Margaret Mead had described them as "culturally deprived" in her 1965 introduction to *The Changing Culture of an Indian Tribe* (1965:xi).

> Many years had passed since these objects were animated by wind, reflected firelight or even moved from one place to another. Once they were tribal emblems. In the museum they were merely objects of curiosity from a past "once so full of human activity and hope" (Fletcher and La Flesche 1911:224). Another order must have prevailed when these objects were alive with meaning. Then, they would have been opened only in ceremony by knowledgeable Keepers. Once, they represented Omaha tribal knowledge. In the glass cases they were reduced to being ethnological specimens. As I passed by them nearly every day, I came to wonder about the meaning and value of ethnological specimens. They seemed to be a category of our own creation.

In 1985, the answer to my question began to resolve itself. I learned from Joan Mark, who was then writing Alice Fletcher's biography (Mark 1988), that a contemporary Omaha anthropologist, Dennis Hastings, was tribal historian on the reservation at Macy, Nebraska. I sent him a copy of the paper. He responded by phoning me to say, "If you want to write about us, you should come and visit us in person." So it was that in 1985, Jillian Ridington and I attended the 155th annual Omaha tribal powwow in Macy and came face to face with real Omahas.

> One case contained the Sacred Pole of the Omaha Tribe. It was a dark, deeply stained shaft of great antiquity. At mid-point it was wrapped with a dark bundle above which was attached a smooth slender baton that served as a single supporting strut. The upper shaft was crusted with the remains of ancient anointings and carved like a phallus at the tip. A dark ragged scalplock hung from this part of the pole. I thought, "This was once a young man's pride, hot with sun-sheen and promises of dreams." I thought, "Someone kept this pole and carried it from camp to camp, year to year, generation to generation."

On the third day of the powwow, as the tribe gathered in the dance arena within a circle of oak trees open to the East, I spoke, at their request, about what I had learned.

> I was a young man then, new to the folklore of anthropology. I was fascinated with age and with changes. The Pole and bundles in their cases were artifacts of a past order. They did not reveal the stories that were once their animation, but mutely they spoke to me of stories and secrets that must have been real to a buffalo hunting people. I strained to know these objects by making them my familiars, not in the occult sense, but rather as stations in my daily rounds.

Talk to the Omaha Tribe, August 1985

Thank you. I'd like to share a few of the thoughts I've had during the days I've been here at this beautiful 155th annual Powwow. The journey that my wife and I took to get here from Vancouver, Canada, only took us a few hours, less than a day, but for me this journey began twenty years ago when I started school at the Peabody Museum of Harvard University.

> When reading cramps and the desire for open spaces, for lovers, for warm wind and for growing things, conspired to animate the young man within my scholarly facade, I found myself returning

to the Omaha cases. I sensed that in a different time they had represented powers for which my culture had no easy translation.

When I went to school there, one of the first things that I saw when I went through the doors of that great big brick building on Divinity Avenue was a glass case; and in that glass case was something that was labeled "The Sacred Pole of the Omaha Tribe," and I didn't know what that meant. There were a lot of other things in that big building, but somehow I was drawn to that one place, that one object, and every day I went past it and it was like there was something there, some hidden secret, some power there that I didn't understand.

Inevitably, during the course of my first year in anthropology, I discovered the Bureau of American Ethnology Annual Reports. Physically, the books are large and substantial. They are bound in olive green covers, embossed in gold with the bust of an Indian man wearing a pendant, elaborate neck piece, and turban or headband tied at one side and surmounted by a halo of feathers. Inside each volume are beautifully printed texts, plates and drawings documenting the arts, languages and accomplishments of various American Indian tribes.

And eventually I found out there was a book called *The Omaha Tribe*, published by the Bureau of American Ethnology, and I looked up in that book and I found that the name for the pole is Waxthe'xe. And in that book it said that means, "the power of motion and the power of life, the power of *Wakon'da*." And it also said, that that means, "mottled, as by shadows." Mottled means like a balance of light and dark.

The 27th Annual Report, a thick and lavishly illustrated volume of 672 pages, is called *The Omaha Tribe*. Its authors are Alice C. Fletcher, "Holder of the Thaw Fellowship, Peabody Museum, Harvard University," and Francis La Flesche, "A Member of the Omaha Tribe." The volume appeared in 1911. Chapter VI of the book describes and illustrates the Sacred Pole that I had come to know through the walls of a glass box in a brick building on Divinity Avenue devoted to the purposes of anthropology.

And I thought about that as I was watching this powwow for the last few days, and I noticed how the sky changes. Sometimes it's light and sometimes it's dark, and sometimes right here in the center of this arena, there was a balance of light and dark. And then I thought about—that name also refers to the balance of people that make up this Tribe, the Omaha People. There's a balance of earth people and sky people. And so that name seems to me to refer to something that is the life at the heart of this tribe.

I came to the brick building daily to assimilate these purposes as my own. I was there physically as were the Pole and the book. As I made my rounds from home to desk to book to museum case, I knew that my task was to discover some connection between the purposes of anthropology and those of the people who once kept the Pole. I knew that any such connection would also have to engage my own purposes. I knew that my fascination with age and with changes would lead me toward a center common to all these purposes. The facts I accumulated would turn around that center, in the same way that all other stars of the night sky turn around the fixed star Polaris. I knew that the Sacred Pole centered my interest in age and change.

And then there's one other thing that that book said Waxthe'xe means, and that is, "bringing that power into view to be seen by all the people," and that's what I've seen over here for the last few days, that in the center of this arena there's that life, that power of motion that is being brought into view to be seen by all the people, by all the Omaha people, and by all their guests and visitors. And I really count myself privileged and fortunate to be among those guests and visitors and to see this.

When I opened *The Omaha Tribe*, I found myself looking at Chapter VI, "The Sacred Pole." Plate 38 and Figure 51 of this chapter illustrate the Pole itself (224–225). Under the chapter title is the heading, "Origin." The Pole, they said, "should symbolize the unity of the tribe and of its governing power—something which should appeal to the people, an object they could all behold and around which they could gather to manifest their loyalty to the idea it represented" (217). The chapter thus begins by proclaiming that beyond its objective existence as an artifact in the Peabody Museum, the Pole represents an idea of the Omaha Tribe's identity. This idea, they said, could be discovered by reference to the story of the Pole's origin. The story began, "A great council was being held to devise some means by which the bands of the tribe might be kept together and the tribe itself saved from extinction" (217). In this book, I found the beginning of a story that could lead me toward an understanding of purposes common to both the Omaha and to anthropology. Francis La Flesche, according to the book's title page, was both an anthropologist and a member of the Omaha Tribe. He seemed to bridge the two worlds.

I'd like to thank Dennis Hastings for inviting me here. I wrote to him and told him that I'd been thinking about *The Omaha Tribe* and he said, "Well, you've got to come down here and see the powwow." I look forward to working with Dennis on some of the projects that he is doing.

Return

One of the projects Dennis worked on was the Sacred Pole's return to the tribe. On July 12, 1989, Tribal chairman Doran Morris brought Umo^n'ho^n'ti home to his people in Macy, Nebraska. Elder Lawrence Gilpin spoke to Umo^n'ho^n'ti in the Omaha language. His sister, Elsie Morris, translated his words into English. This is an excerpt from his prayer:

Aho! Umo^n'ho^n'ti!
We're humble people, the Omaha village
that you have come home to.
Today you have come home.
There's a few words I want to say to Wakon'da.
Umo^n'ho^n'ti,
you have come back to the Omaha camp.
I am very happy that you have come home.
Umo^n'ho^n'ti,
I am very happy that you have come home today
to our poor, humble reservation.
And towards Wakon'da, I'm going to say a few words.
Today, we are just pitiful [deserving of love]
and yet today we are celebrating.
All the Omahas have come home together happy,
feeling happy, good of heart.
Our relatives have gathered.
They have entered the doorway, the entry,
and we are seated together.
From way back, our forefathers, there was a tree.
There was a tree that grew from the earth.
From way back they used him for our lives.
It's been over a hundred years, past a hundred years,
in a strange place with strange people.
Dadeho, Wakon'da Xube. [Father, Most Holy Spirit.]
Today the head of the people, [the council]
have brought him home,
brought him home.
Dadeho, Wakon'da Xube.
Umo^n'ho^n'ti, they made him holy.
From way back in our camp he was the center,
lived in the center of the people.
And whatever they did, how they lived,
they did it with him, through Wakon'da.
Wakon'da made life in that tree from the earth.
Dadeho, Wakon'da Xube.
From God's power (Wakon'da Xube) he gave that tree.
Father, you made that tree, you gave it life,
You gave it life from the earth.
And that was through your goodness,
your power from the earth.
Dadeho, Wakon'da Xube.

You are the only one that has the power to do and give life.
It is yours.
Those, our elders, have brought him from way back,
and they have received nothing but good from him.
Whatever good that you have made, you have made for
  them.
Dadeho, Wakon'da Xube.
Our people carried you from way back,
and good things came from you.
And whatever you have made, you have made everything
  good,
Dadeho, Wakon'da Xube, Most Holy Spirit, you sit.
You do everything right.
You never make any mistakes.
Aho you singers, you drummers, that was my prayer.

At the Omaha Tribal powwow the following month, the tribe again brought Umon'hon'ti "into view to be seen by all the people." Tribal chairman Doran Morris invited me to speak to the tribe again. This time, I stood facing Umon'hon'ti himself. The following are some of my words:

Thank you, Doran. Thank you, members of the Tribal Council and everyone. Today is a very special occasion for me personally as I know it is for you, In'stashunda, you Hon'gashenu, you people who together, are the Omaha tribe. Twenty-seven years ago I first laid eyes on Umon'hon'ti, The Real Omaha, who is your Sacred Pole. He was resting in a glass case in the Peabody museum at Harvard University. He was motionless physically but when I was in his presence I could feel a power of life, a power of motion within me and all around me and extending out to wherever it was that his people, you people, were living. At that time I didn't know where the Omaha people were or how they were living. I began to study their traditions from what was written down by James Dorsey and Alice Fletcher and Francis La Flesche, who was the first Native American anthropologist.

Although he has been away from you physically, the spirit of the Sacred Pole has never left you. The people who went before you would be proud of this moment in the ongoing history of the Omaha tribe. They would be proud to share the Pole's blessing with you, just as you will be proud to pass on blessings that you are receiving today and have been receiving from your Sacred Pole now and in the times to come.

The Pole stands for the authority of your ancestral ways. The spirit of these ways remains strong within you. That spirit does not depend upon particular material things from the past like hunting buffalo or living in earth lodges as your ancestors did. It lives on in the generosity with which you live your lives. It lives in the help and respect that you give to one another. It lives in the blessings you pass on to those who come after you. In the old days, the chiefs told people:

Whenever we meet with troubles
we shall bring all our troubles to Him,
Umo^n'ho^n'ti
We shall make offerings and requests.
And all our prayers must be accompanied by gifts.

The chiefs said that the Pole belongs to all the people. The Pole and his teachings are gifts they have passed on to people of the present generation, to you. Your responsibility is to make these teachings your own and to pass them on with your prayers to those who come after you. Some of the teachings about the Pole are contained in a story of its origin that Yellow Smoke told to Alice Fletcher and Francis La Flesche in 1888. And I'll just give you a few excerpts from that story. Many of you already know the details of it. It's part of tribal history. It says:

A long time ago, there was a young man, the son of a chief, who went out hunting during a time when the elders of the tribe, the chiefs, were in council trying to deal with a problem just like the problems that the tribe has today and it's always had, that is, to keep itself together, to keep you together, to keep your traditions and your families together, living in the proper way. And this young man got lost when he was out at night. And for a moment he didn't know his direction. And then he remembered there is one star, the motionless star, right up there. You'll see it tonight if it's clear. And he found that star, the star around which all the other stars of the heavens turn. That star is the North Star. It gave him his direction. And then he looked down from beneath that star, and I'm going to read you the description of what he saw.

He saw a light.
He saw that it was a tree that sent forth light.
He went up to it
and found that the whole tree,
its trunk, branches, and leaves, were alight,
yet remained unconsumed.
The young man watched
until with the rising of the sun
the tree with its foliage
resumed its natural appearance.
He remained by it throughout the day.
As twilight came on it began to be luminous

and continued so until the sun rose again.
When the young man returned home
he told his father of the wonder.
Together they went to see the tree.
They saw it as it was before,
but the father observed something
that had escaped the notice of the young man.
This was that four animal paths led to it.
These paths were well beaten
and as the two men examined the paths and the tree,
it was clear to them that the animals came to the tree
and had rubbed against it
and polished its bark by doing so.

The young man and his father returned to where the chiefs were still in council. The father explained to them and to his son the meaning of what the young man had seen, this visionary experience. He told the chiefs:

My son has seen a wonderful tree.
The Thunder birds come and go upon this tree,
Making a trail of fire
that leaves four paths on the burnt grass
that stretch toward the Four Winds.
When the Thunder birds alight on the tree
it bursts into flame
and the fire mounts to the top.
But tree stands burning,
and no one can see the fire except at night.

They made a tent for the tree and set it up within the circle of lodges. They placed a large scalp lock on top of the Pole for hair.

And then they painted the Pole
and set it up before the tent,
leaning it on a crotched stick [just as you see today]
which they called "imongthe" [a staff].

When the people were gathered, the chiefs stood up and said:

You now see before you a mystery.
Whenever we meet with troubles
we shall bring all our troubles to Him.
This belongs to all the people.

And when all was finished, the people said:

Let us appoint a time
when we shall again paint him
and act before him
the battles we have fought.

This was the beginning of the ceremony called Waxthe'xe xigithe, which means "to paint, to anoint, to grease the Sacred Pole with red." Although that old ceremony of renewal was part of your buffalo hunting way of life and is no longer practiced, the spirit of renewal remains very much alive among you today. The old renewal ceremony took place in a Sacred Lodge made from tipi poles contributed by each family of the tribe. Today's renewal of your Sacred Pole is possible because each family and each clan continues to contribute its spiritual gifts to the tribe as a whole. The Pole is a person who stands for all of you together. His return to you today is a celebration of your survival during the past century and a promise that you will continue to honor the spirit of your traditions throughout the centuries to come.

I thank you for allowing me to speak to you. I thank you for allowing me to stand before Umon'hon'ti, your Sacred Pole. I thank you all. All My Relations.

I first read Umon'hon'ti as a physical object contextualized in a glass case in the Peabody Museum. Next, I read him in the pages of a classic ethnographic text. In my second reading of that book, I assumed the role of author. Writing about him had the effect of bringing his life closer to my own. That reading and writing became a discourse of shared ethnographic authority. In 1985 I found myself speaking to the Omaha tribe. Four years later, I spoke directly to Umon'hon'ti himself. What had begun as a distant reflection on cultural texts had grown into a shared story. I have come to know Umon'hon'ti as a real person, a "real Omaha." Already, he has generated many stories beyond the one I have told above.

Omahas themselves have many, sometimes conflicting, stories about how Umon'hon'ti fits into their lives together as a tribe. They are divided about how they should relate to him now. Factions within the tribe have different opinions about him (Ridington 1994ms). In time, they may come to some resolution, and once again have what Lawrence Gilpin called "an undivided interest" in him. I am thankful to have been both witness to and participant in the story of Umon'hon'ti's return. I trust that the words I am writing here will generate other stories in the lives of those who read them. Meanwhile, the story continues. All My Relations.

FRANK A. SALAMONE

HE SANG AWAY MY BLUES

Frank Salamone reveals the bitter loneliness that often accompanies fieldwork. His family's plans for a 1989-90 "family Fulbright" fell apart in spite of meticulous planning. He had traveled to Nigeria during the summer of 1989 to firm up plans for a house and transportation, as well as schooling for his children. When, in spite of these plans, no house or transportation was ready, his family had to leave Nigeria and return to the United States. Salamone was plunged into black despair. His friendship with Joseph, a Nigerian driver for the Dominican sisters, brought him back into the human comedy. Their shared love of the blues cleansed both of their private demons. Through his friendship with Joseph, Salamone gained deeper understanding of his own human situation.

Human companionship makes more of an impact on my spirit than mere theoretical conclusions. In my seven trips to Nigeria, Joseph Nathaniel Manga is the best and clearest example of a friend in the field who took me in the right direction, demonstrating to me once again that cross-cultural friendships are possible and even common. Periodically, it is necessary to recall the satisfaction and joy of discovering common humanity in diverse settings.

In retrospect it now strikes me as unusual that Joseph and I became close friends in Nigeria. At first, the odds appeared strongly against such an experience. Joseph was as formidable-looking a young man as I have ever seen. He was about twenty-five. He comes from an ethnic group, the Dakarkari, celebrated for its fierceness and pride. When I met him, he appeared every bit as forbidding as his Dakarkari reputation would have him. Even without their famous facial tattoos and without the slightest hint of tribal marks under his eyes, he was a man I would normally have avoided. He appeared rather fearsome and self-contained, not eager for human contact. He was sitting quietly on the Catholic mission veranda, more formally the Hall of Martyrs, reading the local Ibadan newspapers.

Ibadan is a town in Western Nigeria of rather indeterminate size. It has somewhere between 2 and 4 million people arranged in a series of sprawling villages connected by now-decaying asphalt roads.

149

It lies in the tropical rain forest and would soon return to it if left alone. It ranges in temperature from hot to hotter to hottest.

I had gone to the Dominican House of Studies seeking a ride and the companionship of my old friend Father Peter. I reasoned that if I could manage to appear sufficiently pathetic, Pete would take me shopping, and we'd indulge our mutual love for chocolate bars washed down with ice-cold Dr. Peppers—something neither of us truly needed, as our ever-expanding waistlines attested. With weighty anticipation, then, I approached the House of Studies. Pete, however, was teaching his class on the role of the missionary in a post–Vatican II world. My feet dragged as I shuffled out to sit and think on the veranda.

I was in a deep funk. My wife and kids had left Nigeria. It was supposed to be our "family Fulbright year," but the house that was supposed to be ready in September was still not ready when the family left in January. Our own alternate arrangements for living at the International Institute for Tropical Agriculture, where Virginia, my wife, had secured her own teaching job, had been vetoed through the efforts of the Fulbright representative. A brush with snakes in the kids' beds at our campus housing, lack of promised and contractual transportation, and a look at the unrepaired water cistern convinced my wife that she would leave me to my work alone in Nigeria.

My gloomy thoughts so preoccupied me that when Brother Henry, a close friend, excitedly approached me, I was startled.

"Dr. Frank (he pronounced it Fraank), would it be OK for that man," pointing to Joseph, "to take you to town?" My face screwed up. Sadly, it never can hide my emotions; hence I usually lose at poker. Quickly, Henry added, "He works for the Dominican sisters in Gusau, up North. He's free for a week because the sisters are at a conference up North. They don't need that man for a week since they have no use for their Peugeot. Get close to him, Dr. Frank. He'll take you wherever you want to go!"

Henry explained that during that week Joseph, their driver, had use of their car. Although slightly reluctant because of his forebidding appearance, I agreed. My desire for a change of scene and some movement overcame any lingering trepidation. I expected, at most, a quiet ride to town and back. What I got, however, was an anthropologist's dream, namely, a friend who loved fieldwork and could explain clearly what he knew.

Louis Armstrong singing "Basin Street Blues" greeted me as I entered the car.

"Armstrong!" I exclaimed with intense surprise in my voice. "I expected to hear some reggae."

"Oh, no, Dr. Frank. I always listen to Satchmo. I love the way he sings blues. When I am the least bit depressed, he sings away my blues."

I had been preparing to go through a protocol of questions on music and its meaning to him, tracing modern music choices to traditional preferences. Instead, when I heard Louis's "Basin Street Blues," all thought of conducting field research fled. It was really Louis! For jazz fans like me, there is only one Louis, Louis Armstrong. I suppose it was hearing Louis Armstrong on his car's tape deck that sealed our relationship, for nothing else can pick me up from the depths of depression like Louis. No matter how "progressive" my tastes in music become, Satchmo reaches something inside me no other musician can.

But Louis was only the beginning. I rifled through his tapes, asking him what was in his collection.

"Dr. Frank," he asserted, "I love all kinds of music. Look, I have Pavarotti here."

At that he burst into a perfectly sung aria in the original Italian from *Tosca*. He followed that up with more arias, most from operas I couldn't quite recognize.

"I have country and western music, too. I love Gentleman Jim Reeves and other old-timers. I have soul music and pop."

My rifling expedition verified that his collection was truly eclectic. I was amazed to find that he had managed to gather such a range of diverse material. It was almost a history of Western music.

"You know, Dr. Frank," he said, breaking into my revery, "I spent some time working for Filipinos in the south. They were very good to me and one of them gave me music lessons. She was a music teacher at a school there. She said I had a good voice and should get some training since I enjoyed singing too much."

It was one of the few times he had slipped into a Nigerian idiom. Too much—meaning "very much," not, as it does in standard English, "excessively"—did fit Joseph's enthusiasm for music. Come to think of it, it fit mine as well.

I learned a good deal about Joseph that day.

"Joseph, tell me about your background. Where were you born?"

"I am 'born Catholic.' I am a Northerner but not a Hausa. The North, you know, Dr. Frank, is not Hausa or Muslim property. They would like you to believe that. Oh, yes. I was born in the Northern area of Nigeria. I'm a Dakarkari."

"The Dakakari? Aren't they related to the Dukawa?" I inquired. I have often worked among the Dukawa, and my interest increased.

"Oh, yes. We are very close. Some people say we are the same people. We intermarry with them and in the old days of tribal warfare, they were our allies. My father, you know, was in the Nigerian army. We lived with his family in the east. You know, the Igbo are Christians, like me. But they make a mistake when they try to tell you that the

North is Muslim. They don't distinguish between Muslims and others there.'' He uttered this last shaking his head in surprised disgust.

I had found something else that bound me to Joseph, and he no longer appeared strange nor ferocious.

"Where did you go to school?" I persisted.

"I went to school in eastern Nigeria where my father was stationed. I loved school, Dr. Frank. I studied with Filipino teachers and other expatriates who were too nice to me. I learned my English from them. They encouraged me to go to school and helped me with my English and my music. They got me voice lessons, so I learned to love all good music, as I've already told you. When they left, they helped me find work with other expatriates. I still write to them."

Given Joseph's penchant for working with expatriates, his English was almost idiomatic American, for his ears and curiosity were indeed sharp.

Joseph's memory so dominates that day that I am not quite sure where we wound up. I do know that we discussed ideas until late at night. I found myself agreeing with Joseph's statement "Northerners *are* different from Southerners. No Northern Nigerian would leave a stranger alone at night. Dr. Frank, I worry about you all alone here in a strange country. You seem sad. You miss your children and your wife. It's not good for you to be alone. Let me stay a bit and keep you company."

"Yes, Joseph, I do miss my wife and kids. I'm still angry that they weren't able to stay, and I feel betrayed that my government did nothing to help them stay here. But your friendship helps me chase away my blues."

"Well, our people believe that a stranger is a sacred trust. Don't yours? You are my guest and my friend. I'm glad my tapes soothe your sorrow. It's quite unfortunate that your CD player has broken, but use my tapes all you wish."

By this time, he had lent me some tapes, which I used for the remainder of my stay to put me to sleep. My fancy CD player had blown a tube within a month of my arrival in Nigeria. We talked enthusiastically late into the night about many things.

"Joseph," I tentatively put forward, "do your people still believe in witches?"

Joseph swore. "It is still potent even though Christianity and Islam fight it vehemently. You know that people tell their priests and mallams what they want to hear. But at night, they *know*. Witches do come and work their evil."

"Yes," I mused, mumbling half to myself, "we do tell our priests and superiors what they wish to hear. It's rare that anyone tells it like it really is. Maybe that's why I like the blues so much—and Louis. I always feel that Louis sings straight to the heart."

"Oh, yes, Dr. Frank. It is good to be direct. Our people teach us to be honest at all times and not to be afraid of the truth. Isn't that what Christianity teaches you, too?"

"Yes, it is," was all I managed to say aloud, but my inner thoughts were much more complicated indeed.

And on and on our conversations went, as if we were still both young boys sitting up late in a college bull session. The eagerness of those discussions continues to live on in my tapes, and I marvel to hear my enthusiasm burst through.

"Dr. Frank," Joseph began one night as we were viewing some James Bond tapes, "is your country really so violent?

What could I say? For all my various official bureaucratic problems, I never felt physically threatened in Nigeria. No one appeared to be about to strike me. I was the one who generally lost his temper with official idiocy, American and Nigerian. So, I thought, how do I answer Joseph?

"Well," I stalled, "yes, there is far too much violence in America, but these movies do exaggerate it. People don't normally leap from helicopters onto bridges, and the villains don't usually go running down the street shooting at those who pass. I personally have never seen any of these things except in movies."

Even to me, my speech sounded pompous and weak, but Joseph was too polite to call me on it. Instead, he moved on to another topic.

"Tell me about your own people. Where did your father and his father come from?"

"They were born in a small town called Monta d'Ora, meaning the Golden Mountain."

"But that's beautiful! How lyrical," he exclaimed.

"Yes, Joseph. It *is* beautiful. But as my Grandfather said to one of his *paisani*—that means 'countrymen,'" I explained, "You can't eat beauty. I visited the town once and tried to picture myself living there, but it was hard for me to imagine. What about your father and his father?" I inquired. "What were their towns, and what were their early lives like?"

Joseph explained the child-rearing patterns of the Zuru people, of whom the Dakakari formed but one tribe. We delved into their kinship system and other points of interest. It seemed a fair bargain to each of us although I once remarked, "Joseph, I somehow don't feel that James Bond is a fair exchange for your information."

"But why not?" he returned. "I enjoy the action, and you explain things to me that the camera does not show. We drink beer together and spend our time in peace together. Don't worry so much, Dr. Frank. I'm fine!"

When he left at night, he stopped in the door of my apartment and turned to me. "Well, I can go in peace now. Your spirits seem lifted a bit. I am glad that I have been a true friend to you and you to me. It is not good for a visitor to be so depressed. *Sai anjuma.*"

"Sai anjuma [See you later]," I replied.

Joseph quickly ascertained that although I was in western Nigeria, my true interest remained in the Hausa and the rest of the northern community. It had, in fact, not taken him much time to delve into the workings of the Hausa community within Ibadan. Within a few days he had discovered the sources of power at the core of the Hausa community in Ibadan and had become friendly with its second-ranking figure, the *waziri* or prime minister.

That first week together we spent mostly planning future fieldwork and discussing the Zuru people of Joseph's home area. We did, however, explore the Hausa area of the *Katako* (wood) market. Joseph's initial reason for attending the market had been to frequent movies there. For a naira, at that time about seven cents, he could see a videotape of a movie in a concrete hut. Subsequently, he became familiar with all the habitués of the Hausa area of the market. During that first week together we simply explored one or two areas of the market together.

Joseph knew that I was interested in Hausa wrestling and that I had written a few articles on it. He exploded into the Dominican Hall of Martyrs one day.

"Dr. Frank, I have found Hausa wrestling here in Ibadan. It takes place every Friday afternoon in the Katako market. Bring your camera so you can tape it."

I turned to Father Peter. "What do you say, Pete? Are you up for it?"

Pete shrugged his shoulders. "No, you and Joseph go. I'll look at the tapes. I've seen plenty of Hausa wrestling in my time."

I looked at Joseph, nodding that we were on. That's how it came to pass that he took me to the Friday afternoon matches there. I expected to have problems bringing in my camcorder, and I was not disappointed. But Joseph simply pointed out to people that I was with him.

"Leave my friend alone," he commanded in Hausa. "He is a big doctor from a big school in America. He is interested in our culture and has written about Nigerian wrestling. Remember he is a guest. Let us show him how Northerners act toward a guest."

Joseph led us through the crowd with little incident and much good humor. We sat on a kitchen chair in the shade.

"Dr. Frank, you should give these men twenty naira," he said, indicating the praise singers who were in front of me. "That will make them feel good, and others will leave you alone."

"OK, but what are they saying?" I muttered.

"They are saying that you are a powerful man who loves the Hausa. The Hausa love you, for you are big," here he pointed to my ample belly. "The Hausa love stout men," he declared with typical candor.

I laughed and asked him questions about the wrestlers who were preparing themselves on the sidelines.

"These young men are not professionals. They are boys from the town—Hausas who wish to show themselves off and remember who they are. They work at offices or attend the university here. These are friendly matches, so no magic is practiced. Look!" he cried. "Notice how they adorn themselves. These boys want the ladies to notice them," he chuckled.

The *sarkin sabo*, chief of the Hausa of Ibadan and nearby areas, appeared and presented a significant short speech.

"What's he saying, Joseph?" I didn't trust my rusty Hausa on such an important occasion.

"He is talking about the role of the games in preserving and maintaining Hausa ethnic identity. He says that the Yoruba are watching them. They must behave themselves. If they do, they will be allowed to have more ethnic celebrations. You know, Doctor Frank," he interrupted himself, "this sarkin sabo is chief of all the Hausa outside the North. He paid for all this wrestling and this arena. These Hausa are his subjects, and he is responsible for them. He wants them to prosper. This wrestling reminds them of home and gives them the chance to come together. But more than wrestling is happening here." He winked as he uttered this last remark.

As the wrestling progressed, Joseph not only provided a running commentary but also ensured I was seated where he knew I would have a clear view of the proceedings. Additionally, he directed my actions so that I would present myself in the best manner possible to a Hausa audience.

"Dr. Frank," he whispered delicately, "the Hausa expect an important man like you to sit straight up and look comfortable."

Thus, I sat in a manner both comfortable and straight, not an easy thing for an inveterate sloucher to do. I also kept a controlled but pleasant face, with a slight smile playing on my lips.

As a result of Joseph's guidance, there was little that I did miss. The video of that event is rich in detail, and Joseph's prompting of my responses ensured that I shared in the good humor of fortune-tellers, musicians, wrestlers and others and was not simply the butt of their jokes.

We began one other piece of joint research that week, and it also proved gratifying. In his amblings through the market, Joseph had befriended a healer from one of the eastern states. As the herbalist's rather graphic sign proclaimed, he specialized in curing venereal diseases but also had cures for headaches, impotence, sores, cancer, leprosy, and whatever else might ail a person. All this he did from a small, neat, whitewashed hut.

"Hello, my friends. My name is Dr. Lawrence. I saw you approaching and have come to welcome you." Lawrence was dressed in a white shirt and impeccably creased trousers. He wore black European-style shoes rather than sandals.

"Hello," I replied, taking his proffered hand and shaking it. "My name is Frank. My friend, Joseph, and I saw your sign and were interested in finding out more about you and your work." Joseph extended his hand, and he and Lawrence shook hands companionably.

"Well, my friends. What can I tell you about my work?" Lawrence was a short, very dark Igbo from Anambra State in Nigeria's east. He assured us, "It is God who cures, not me. There is no magic in my cures. My father was a traditional healer. *He* used supernatural power, sometimes, my friend, for what we Christians," indicating Joseph, me, and himself, whispering this last statement, almost hissing it, "call the devil."

Lawrence insisted, perhaps too much, that he used only natural healing with the help of "the true Christian God." Joseph's familiarity with Igbo culture guided my probing. Joseph's father had been an officer in the Nigerian army, and Joseph had grown up in eastern Nigeria, the home of the Igbo people. In a sense, we were much like the "good cop, bad cop" that actors portray in "B" movies.

"What do you mean," I pressed Lawrence, "that you use only natural cures? Don't you wrap up your herbs in pages of the Bible? Isn't that similar to using magic?"

"Dr. Frank," Joseph smoothly intervened, "our Zuru doctors regard things as natural that work with what is best in human nature." Turning to Lawrence, he continued, "Isn't that how you Igbo doctors view 'natural,' too?"

Obviously relieved, Lawrence mopped his brow and responded, "Yes, indeed, my friend. And God is nature itself, for He is the king of nature. So using His Book is part of nature, an extension of nature."

Clearly, this white man among them did not understand the simplest facts about reality! Before Lawrence could become too relaxed, however, Joseph continued sweetly, "Then it is not just the herbs alone that cure. You are using a type of countermagic to those who use black magic, isn't it?"

Sly old Joseph was not taken in for a second, but he taught me how to slip questions in past a cultural guard. And I had prided myself above all on my interviewing ability! I realized, somewhat surprised, that he was no less persistent than I. In fact, if anything, he was more so. His persistence, however, was simply more culturally acceptable.

"Look," pointed Lawrence, indicating some roots. "I use these roots to cure ulcers. "What," he asked Joseph, "do your Zuru healers use for that?" Joseph's informed interest had elicited this response from Lawrence, taking me into areas I had not anticipated when we began our discussion.

When Joseph left in January to return to his permanent job with the Dominican mission sisters in Gusau in the North, it was the second traumatic parting of the month. Certainly, I had friends in Ibadan. No one, however, measured up to Joseph, who, I now realized, had become a surrogate son to me.

"What's up?" Pete probed one day.

"Nothing," I shrugged.

Ignoring my response, Pete continued, "You miss Joseph, don't you?"

"Yea, I do. I could really get some work done if I had Joseph with me. He really knows his way around and learns fast. Say, Pete, you don't suppose . . ."

"Now, wait a minute, Frank. We've been friends a long time, but Joseph doesn't work for me."

I didn't say anything. I had learned that sometimes silence is more eloquent than speech.

"Now, don't pout, Frank. We're both too old for this cat-and-mouse routine. What do you really want? Convince me."

"All right, Pete. I'll pay for Joseph's transportation and his wages. It'll cost the sisters nothing. I'll make sure Joseph eats, too. He'll gain financially from the deal. I'll have a friend and fellow worker. *My* research will benefit. *You'll* have me off your back. *We'll* all come out ahead. I'm assuming, of course, that Joseph will want to come."

"Oh, he'll come. He's been asking the good sisters at Gusau if he can be 'borrowed' to you. Did you two cook this whole scheme up?"

"No," I answered honestly, somewhat amused. "But I wish we had."

Pete laughed and announced, "I think it would be a good thing to have Joseph come to Ibadan for a time. If nothing else, it might end your growing funk and brighten your increasingly sour mood. I'll work on it."

From time to time, I delicately raised the issue, walking a tightrope between perseverance and badgering. Pete is a very accommodating soul, but one who wishes to do things in his own way and in his own time. That time is a cross between New Orleans and Nigerian time, a time zone my New York personality finds incompatible. Therefore, although he was in favor of the arrangement, he could not be rushed.

In late February, a set of circumstances converged that led to Joseph's being allowed to work with me in Ibadan. Pete had been talking about a vacation trip to the North, ultimately to Yauri, where I had done my initial fieldwork. One day, he broached the subject to me.

"Frank, would it be possible for you to get some time to travel to the North? I know," he stated, with a twinkle in his eye, "that you are terribly busy at the university, but maybe you just might be able to get away for a week."

Of course, Pete knew that I had wanted to get back for even a brief time to see the area. He also knew that my schedule at the university was an on-again, off-again matter, a source of great amusement for my old friend from New Orleans, at that time prior of the Dominican House of Studies in Ibadan and overdue for local leave. In his usual fashion Pete had been waiting for just the right moment to take it.

I again met Joseph, who was working at the mission station in Gusau.

"How are you, Joseph? How goes the building of the new church?"

"Well, it is going fine. We hope to finish soon, but I'm not happy about the way some of these beams are put up. I've told the sisters that they have to watch these contractors more carefully."

Pete eyed me with a hidden smile. Joseph had not changed. Pete had once remarked to me, "I like Joseph, Frank. I don't know how to describe it. He moves right in and joins every conversation. He isn't pushy but he has a—what?—a presence about him. He does his work and never complains, but he mixes with his bosses with an ease I've rarely seen."

Pete now turned to Joseph. "How is your brother? You know we have accepted him at the Dominican House of Studies."

"That's very good, Father. Is it all right for me to tell him?"

"Sure!"

Our stop at the church in Gusau and the consequent discussion prodded Pete's memory. "Oh, Frank, weren't you asking something about Joseph coming to Ibadan to work with you? Maybe we might ask the sisters at our next stop. Joseph, would you like to come to Ibadan?"

"Yes," Joseph said. He would like to come to Ibadan.

When we paused again, this time at the site of a conference that the sisters from Gusau were attending in Malumfashi, Pete asked that Joseph be "seconded" to Ibadan for two weeks. The sisters agreed to allow Joseph to join me in Ibadan on the condition that I pay his salary, transportation, and housing.

Sister Laurena, one of the sisters for whom Joseph worked stated, with a twinkle in her eye, "We have heard nothing from Joseph for some time except his adventures in Ibadan. Perhaps a trip back will get it out of his system. You know," she continued, "you're not what I expected. I expected, I don't know, an anthropologist to be more distant, more formidable. You're a regular person, so easy to talk to."

Evidently, I passed their inspection. Many of the sisters, in any case, knew me from my previous trips. Those who did not know me personally knew of me, for better or worse, because of my contacts over twenty years with the Dominicans.

I had decided that it would be best for Joseph to have his own place to live. Somewhat irritably, Father Peter asked, "Why can't Joseph live in your apartment? You've spent most of this trip in Nigeria asking for him to come to Ibadan, and now you want to find him somewhere else to live."

"Pete, I know I'm imposing on you. I'll pay his rent and provide his food. I'm not the Salamone of twenty years ago who bummed cigarettes from your partner at the mission in Yauri. Look, Pete, even though Joseph and I are good friends, even good friends can irritate each other if confined to a small apartment too long. Both of us will need some private space, and I find it difficult to write if someone else is nearby."

"OK, Frank, that makes sense. I know I get tired of you from time to time," he remarked with a twinkle in his eye.

The arrangement, in fact, worked out quite satisfactorily. Quite soon, Joseph and I had worked out a basic course of work. We would meet for breakfast about 7:30 and plan our day's research. Joseph would go his way armed with a camera, tape recorder, and notebook to look into some aspect of Hausa life in Ibadan. I would tell him what it was that interested me. We would meet in the evening to go over what he had discovered. That would lead to further discussion of where he would go from there. Then we would discuss the ethnography of his area, Zuru, in detail, view a movie, discuss that, and plan our next day.

Over the course of our work, I learned a great deal about Joseph's dreams.

"You know, Dr. Frank, I enjoy your university lectures, too much." Joseph put forth one night over a cold Star beer.

"Do you, Joseph?" I sleepily replied. "Well, why don't you apply to the university? Is there anything Father Peter or I can do to help you?"

"I don't know, Dr. Frank. I have to support my brother at the seminary. I give what I can, and I have other brothers and sisters, too. My father is retired, and I have to try to help out at home. And," he began shyly, "I am engaged to be married."

This last bit of news surprised me. I knew Joseph had an eye for a pretty face, but he seemed so young. But, of course, he would be eager to establish his own family, adding more burdens to those he already carried on his broad shoulders. I mused over his possibilities.

Finally, after a few more gulps of Star beer and a yawn or two, I looked at Joseph and said, "What are you going to do about your hope of going to the university?"

"Well, I will start at the polytech and learn a profession to pay me better. That will help me save money. I'm not in a hurry, Dr. Frank. Someday God will provide. Meanwhile I have the books you've given me. I can slip into lectures and talk with students and profs. People are good to me."

"What about your singing, Joseph?"

His eyes lit up and he exclaimed, "Oh, yes, someday I'll sing professionally. You know, I sang for the seminarians."

He looked rather self-satisfied. He had been undergoing a quiet struggle with one of the missionaries about being allowed to sing while at the House of Studies. Finally, Father Peter intervened, and he sang for breakfast. Evidently, he had been a hit. I was not surprised but asked him to describe his triumph.

"Well, you know that other Father—not Father Peter, but the other American, the one who shares my name, Father Joseph—and how he can be?"

I nodded.

"Well, he said that I couldn't really know the Latin hymns. He has been rather nasty. But Father Peter invited me to sing one song. The seminarians cheered me and begged me to sing more. After *five* songs, I finally sat down. Now," he stated in a manner that, for him, was fairly smug, "Father Joseph has asked me to sing at Mass on Sunday! Will you be there?"

I could and I was. He was quite good. His voice training had paid off, and he even sang a capella easily. After his success at Mass, I invited him to come to breakfast, and we videotaped him singing various songs, including a folk song about a pretty lady named Ladi for whose favors men would kill.

Joseph's singing often raised my spirits. He sang everywhere, usually under his breath. When we went to clubs to hear my friend's band play, he learned the lyrics of their songs and sang them faultlessly after one hearing. His taste in music equally demonstrated syncretistic tendencies. Easily switching from an operatic aria to a Dakakari folk tune, he provided each with the appropriate interpretation.

Time after time, Joseph self-assuredly put himself forward without undue pride, but with great assurance. He could walk into any setting, that of a Yoruba prince's court, a Hausa waziri's audience, or a cheap movie theater with the same self-possession and equanimity.

Joseph frequently accompanied me to class. He sat in the front row and took copious notes. After class, he politely sought permission to ask me a question.

"Sure, Joseph. What's troubling you?"

"Oh, it's no trouble. You were talking today about Northern kinship systems. My people's system is similar to what your were discussing. Would you be interested in my telling you how we Zuru people reckon relationships? We differ a bit from the Dukawa, but I think you could understand it if I took my time explaining it to you."

I laughed and nodded. "Yes, Joseph, I think you might *just* be able to explain it to me in a way I just *might* understand."

And he did.

Each night we would meet for two or three hours to go over the day's work. I found Joseph's notes to be precise and meticulous and filled with humor. One night he came in more excited than usual.

"What happened today, Joseph? You appear rather agitated."

"Well," he whispered, shyly but intently. "I went to the bar where prostitutes congregate."

We had been taking some notes on the market and Hausa prostitutes there, and I had asked Joseph to find out about their recruitment, work patterns, who organized them, and so forth. He had done so rather quickly. But he was still rather boyish about them and struck up conversations with bartenders who acted as their pimps.

Earlier that evening he had witnessed a brawl. To my quick question he answered, "No, I wasn't involved. I wasn't hurt—or arrested. But I never saw women so angry! They were fighting over a man—a customer. One woman said she had found him first. The other said she had him last—and best! My God, the language they used. You don't know *those* Hausa words!"

Nor could I ever persuade him to teach them to me.

Our routine varied, of course. Some days we would go out together. On one such day, we went to Sabo, the Hausa area of Ibadan, to see the waziri, an Islamic official second in authority only to the emir.

"You know the waziri?" he queried.

"Yes. At least I know what a waziri is and does," I replied, not sure where our conversation was headed.

It was about 11:00 P.M., and yet another of my James Bond movies had ended. James had once again bedded the heroines and slayed the evil villains. Once again, I was downing an ice-cold Star beer from my refrigerator and half-drowsing in my chair. I swear that Joseph waited for such moments to spring his biggest news on me.

"Well, Prof," he continued. He had taken to calling me Prof from time to time in imitation of other Nigerians who had become part of my entourage.

"Yes, Joseph," I mumbled.

"Well, I am friends with the waziri," he proceeded blandly. "And he wants to meet you and take us to his gold mine."

Visions of Snow White and the seven dwarfs came unbidden into my mind. I knew that they mined diamonds but, I reasoned, a mine is a mine. I grew excited and even opened my eyes.

"Sure. I'll meet him. When do we go? Where do we meet him? What do we bring?" The questions gushed from me, and I reverted to what some Nigerians termed my New York mode of speech.

"We meet him at Sabo, tomorrow, at 7:00 A.M. You can bring whatever you like. You won't need any food or drink. The waziri will supply them. He is a nice man and, you know, Dr. Frank, how courteous and gentle our Northern leaders can be. Relax! Enjoy!"

We arrived at Sabo by 7:00 A.M., having taken a cab and survived the always exciting ride through Ibadan's teeming streets. We sat at the edge of Sabo awaiting the arrival of the waziri and fended off a young Hausa who wanted to know why I was there. He addressed Joseph, not realizing that I understood Hausa.

"Why is this Bature here, bothering our people in Sabo?" he snapped out in Hausa.

"I am here," I started to snap back. However, I got no further. Joseph intervened, "The prof is here at the waziri's invitation. He is an important scholar who loves the Hausa people and all Northern people. The waziri, himself, invited Dr. Frank to come with him on a trip. Do you want to explain that you drove away the waziri's guest?"

Evidently, the young man did not. Before he could make his getaway, the waziri appeared and simply gazed at him. Then he approached me with a grace that I never have seen in men except for the men of the Hausa royalty.

"Is this young fool bothering you?" he inquired. Without waiting for my reply, he continued, "You are welcome, my friend. I am sorry to keep you waiting. My younger brother needed my car, and we'll have to hire a taxi to go to my mines. Unfortunately, the taxi will not be air-conditioned, but I'll try to make you comfortable, Prof, and I have a few drinks for you."

Joseph, as expected, joined right into the conversation. He was never one to be a shrinking violet, and he guided me toward asking the right questions.

"You know, Waziri," he began in Hausa, "the prof is interested in the history of Sabo. We have received two very different stories from people. I was telling him what you told me. Could you add to that?"

And the waziri did. Quite gladly, I would add. Soon I had a detailed history of the Sabo section, the emir's family lineage as well as the waziri's autobiography. We stopped periodically to buy Cokes and other cold "minerals." Before reaching the mines, we stopped in a restaurant to eat some fish. I politely tried to refuse the fish.

I said, attempting to use a culturally approved formula for refusal, "This is too generous," then, touching my stomach, "but I am filled with your generosity," referring to the snack we had devoured along the way.

Joseph quickly interjected and related the true version for my reluctance to eat fish. "Waziri, the prof fears fish bones since he almost choked to death on fish bones as a young child."

When I saw the hurt in the waziri's face, I relented to my gain.

He said, "I will tell them to be extra careful in deboning the fish, Sule," the nickname by which prestigious Hausa addressed me.

The waziri saw to it that the fish was expertly filleted and was essentially boneless. He insisted on buying me a large quantity of the fish for me to cook later. Joseph profited most from that transaction.

Shortly after, we arrived at the site of the mines, where we had a tour of the new Hausa settlement then still under construction. There were neat houses, a school, shops, government offices—in sum, the framework for a prosperous colony. We visited the mines, which looked nothing like those of the Seven Dwarfs.

We returned to the new town. While there, the waziri introduced me to his brother, who happened to be the town head. Unfortunately, not all was well in his brother's family, a situation leading to the waziri's discomfort in front of strangers such as Joseph and me. I turned to Joseph, not trusting my Hausa.

"What's happening?"

"This man, the waziri's brother, and his son, the waziri's nephew, are disputing about his nephew's marriage to a lady who just wants his money. She is *banza* (worthless)! This woman bothers her husband to seek more of his inheritance from his father. His father does not agree because his son has already wasted thousands of naira and is useless in numerous business enterprises. The son and daughter-in-law are both useless. The waziri, as head of the family, as well as the community here, has been appealed to. He must try to solve the problem. Put your camera away, Dr. Frank, it will embarrass your host."

"Of course, Joseph, of course," I muttered, engrossed in the soap opera that unfolded before me.

Open disputes broke out, and the waziri begged my indulgence as he separated father and son before physical violence erupted. Joseph kept me informed of the salient points of the arguments as we watched matters develop from a safe distance. He translated the more colorful words that hadn't entered my vocabulary.

"*Ka gani* (you see)," Joseph began again, "The waziri has been called in to mediate the dispute. The marriage is a bad marriage. Although the son is banza (literally, a worthless bastard), still he is a son and in need of redemption. Look (*Ga*) how the community prevents violence and restores civility to the proceedings."

I looked and noted that the community did so, first through placing themselves between the combatants, allowing them to express themselves verbally but not to strike one another. Next they continued to speak quietly to the combatants, reminding them of the Hausa values of civility and dignity. Eventually, these reminders shamed the antagonists into more appropriate behavior. After a time, we left, with the waziri blaming himself for failing to restore good relations within his brother's family.

Composing himself as best he could, the Waziri looked at me.
"You know, Sule, it's easier to rule a town than a family! I'm sorry.
These things happen in families, but I'm sorry you had to see it. It
spoiled your impression of the town and my family. It's my fault. I lack
the necessary skills to solve this problem."

We ate again, and plenty of cold drinks were available to ward
off the enervating heat and humidity, for "the rains were late again"
that year. His conversation regained its urbane equanimity, and soon
we put the unpleasantness behind us.

Throughout our work, the friendship between Joseph and me
grew, and I could speak openly with him about my family. He was
interested in American family life and my background, and in
answering his questions, I learned more about myself.

In late March 1990, I began to prepare for my return to the
United States. Joseph had already stayed with me far longer than he
was supposed to. The good sisters in Gusau were requesting his return.
Pete ran interference for us and told them that all was well. He only
half-jokingly told them, "Joseph has no ticket for the United States,
so everything is still OK. Frank doesn't have any large suitcases, so
I think Joseph just wants to stay with a friend until he leaves."

As my closest friend, Joseph accompanied me to my final round
of "good-bye" parties. He came to the home of Ibadan's USIS (United
States Information Service) director, to night clubs, to the mission
station, and to other parties. Finally, he hoped to give me his own going-
away party. He had already given me his company. He spent much
time shopping and fussing about the kitchen, insisting I relax and have
a drink. He sought to rush to avoid the crowds of people who had begun
pouring into my apartment now that it was time for me to leave. Joseph
was angry with these visitors.

"You know, Dr. Frank, people have not treated you right here
in Ibadan. You were left alone too often. Now that you are leaving, they
are coming by to ask favors. They are attempting to leave a favorable
impression. You know these Yoruba don't treat you the way we
Northerners would. You would never be alone. We would feed you all
the time and take care of your needs. We know how to treat a respected
visitor!"

He rushed around the kitchen, and once again I heard him
singing selections from his repertoire. There was "Basin Street Blues."
Could that be "Sunny Side of the Street?" Yes, it was. I had told Joseph
that when my kids were babies I put them to sleep singing it. He had
learned it for me! Arias from his Pavarotti collection followed until I
had listened to a rather eclectic concert.

All Joseph's efforts to hurry before the crowd arrived, however,
did not succeed in preparing the meal soon enough. The first of our

"guests" arrived before we had an opportunity to put the first spoonful of stew in our mouths. Since each guest felt honor-bound to take a taste of the stew and have some beer, Joseph and I found that we were the only people who had not had a chance to eat much that night. People were very kind in making sure that no food was left to spoil overnight.

"So, Prof, you travel tomorrow," began one young man. "Can you get my way paid to an archaeological convention? You know, we are a poor country and have no money for travel. You people from wealthy countries owe us the fare for all the exploitation you have carried on since colonial time! And before!"

Joseph glared at the man. I had never seen him so enraged. Steam still filled the apartment, but I wasn't sure whether it came from the boiling pots or from him. Before I could signal him to hold his peace, he erupted.

"You people have left the prof alone night after night. Until he came, he never knew if anyone would be here to talk to. You are Nigerians! You know how important it is for men to talk to other men, to share their dreams and plans, to drink together. Some of the people here did come to see him from time to time but *you*," he menaced, turning on the man who had requested aid to travel to an archaeology conference, "*you* once invited the prof to dinner and then canceled at the last moment. You have a car and never—even one time—offered him a ride."

Joseph strode from the room and stopped serving anyone, except me. Did I hear him humming "Take This Job and Shove It?" At least, it wasn't directed at me, for he winked at me and pointedly turned his back on the crowd. His outburst hadn't really stopped the flow of requests, but it had given me perspective on it.

"That's a fierce friend you have there, Prof." Olu Moloye's thoughts interrupted my reverie. Olu had been a good friend and collaborator. We shared a love for jazz and as fellow anthropologists, we had collaborated on some work.

"Yes, he is." I had forgotten my own first impressions. "He rarely shows his fierce side, Olu. Usually, I only see the friend. I'd hate to cross him."

"In the old days, Prof, there were Northerners like Joseph who attached themselves to one or another of you whites. Good God, no one dared offend that white or else!" Here he made a gesture accompanied by the sound of a throat being cut.

I laughed, "I don't think Joseph would cut anyone's throat. He's really quite gentle and a Christian."

It was Olu's turn to emit his deep and satisfying laugh. "And I thought you were a *good* anthropologist!" he said.

After they left, Joseph and I said our own good-byes. We relived our experiences.

"Dr. Frank, when you were a young man, what did you want in life? Did you want to come to Nigeria? Did you always want to be a professor of anthropology? What did you really want?"

What indeed, I wondered. How could I answer that question? But if I could discuss it, really discuss it with anyone, it would be with Joseph that night.

"Well, Joseph, like most American kids when I was growing up, I went through a lot of *quando mi facia grande* (when I grow up) dreams." I had slipped into a bit of Italian and translated for Joseph. The words of that old Italian song came easily to me and, on his insistence, I taught the song to Joseph.

For a time, he sang to me again, once again the dutiful son. Then I continued, "I had once planned to be a priest; I even went to the seminary but that didn't pan out. Finally, when I went to college, my English prof encouraged me to teach college. He told me to go on to get my Ph.D. right away after my bachelor's degree. I didn't go right on, unfortunately, but after paying my dues to life, I did."

Of course, I had to explain my errors in life on my way to my Ph.D. Joseph was, remember, a persistent interviewer. Finally, I turned to him.

"What about you, Joseph? What are *your* dreams, *abokina* (my friend)?"

"I have dreams of learning," he began rather poetically. "I wish to attend the university and then begin a singing career. You know about my training in the East. I learned from my Filipino and American friends that *everything* is possible if you just work hard enough. You know the song, 'When You Wish Upon a Star'? Well, I've wished upon a star."

"Joseph, you have mentioned your fiancée. What are your plans there?"

"I expect, Dr. Frank, that I'll marry soon after you leave. I wish you could be here. This lady is as beautiful as Ladi. Our children will be as beautiful as yours. One day we will meet again. We'll work in the North among my people. I pray God, Dr. Frank, that our families will meet."

Tears filled our eyes as we said what we thought would be our final good-byes. Neither of us embraced the other. To do so might appear too effeminate. Friends though we were, we were not sure of how our open display of affection might be taken. But we shook hands and clung to each other's hand for some time. We spoke through tears.

"Sai anjuma, Dr. Frank. I am going to catch a midnight ride back to Gusau. There is a taxi I can get at the market."

"Is it safe, Joseph? There are armed robbers on the road."

"Don't worry, my friend, God is with me."

"Joseph, wait. I have saved these pots and pans for you and

some clothes. It's not much. Here are some music tapes and books. Can you carry them?"

"I can."

"Well, Godspeed and safe journey."

The next morning I went to wait for my ride to Lagos at the mission station. The USIS run to Lagos was revving up when I saw Joseph.

"Dr. Frank, wait. I decided to wait one more morning before I left. The good sisters have waited this long for me. They will wait one more day."

We laughed with tears in our eyes.

"I am glad, my friend. I thought about our friendship last night. You will not be forgotten. I'll tell my students about you and write about you."

I knew Joseph would like that. He had read all my reprints and often asked me about the people in them. Once he hinted that he would like to be in a book. At the time, I hadn't responded. We said our farewells again, to the amusement of the Dominican community and scattered others who had come to wish me a safe journey. They found it amusing to see me openly sentimental instead of masking my feelings behind an ironic pose. But Joseph and I told each other verbally and nonverbally how much we cared for one another. We knew that we were indeed "soul mates," that color, race, ethnicity, and culture became meaningless categories, weak attempts at classifying the unclassifiable.

I thought of Joseph on my ride to Lagos. I did not look forward to spending three or four days in Lagos with USIS personnel. But my plane was not leaving until Sunday, and it was only Thursday. I had to check on final plans and arrange for an "expeditor," someone who helps a traveler negotiate the intricacies of Lagos's Murtallah Muhammad Airport. It was a useless task, since he never showed up in any case. Eventually, I wended my own way through the Kafkaesque horror of Murtallah Muhammad Airport and left Lagos.

Arriving in London, I began to piece my life together, reflecting on my good fortune in encountering Joseph, and wondering whether I would ever hear from him again since contacts and friends fade from our lives, leaving us to wonder "Whatever happened to . . . ?"

I found the answer when I went to my mailbox one day some months after reaching home from London. There it was—an air letter from Joseph! The colorful Nigerian stamps signaled to me before I even picked the letter out from my mailbox. My pulse quickened as I tore open the envelope with eager anticipation. The letter read,

Dear Dr. Frank,

How are you? It has been a while since we last saw each other. I hope all is well with you and your wonderful family.

Thank God, we are fine here. Father Peter sends his love. I see him when I visit my junior brother who is in the seminary with him in Ibadan.

Dr. Frank, do you remember the beautiful lady Ladi whom I sung to you about? You have that song on video, I recall. Anyway, I have married my fiancée who looks like the famous Ladi. We now have a fine young boy. I have enclosed pictures of our wedding and our child at his baptism. You know us Dakakari people! The honeymoon comes before the wedding! Maybe someday we'll be fully civilized like you Americans.

I am going to change jobs soon, Dr. Frank. The good sisters in Gusau are nice, but they can't pay me enough for me to save money to go to the university, raise my family, support my brother, and help my Father in Zuru. Remember that wishing star, my friend.

I have also enclosed the answers to the questions you sent me in your letter. I have drawn pictures of our Zuru huts and diagrams of those games we discussed after the Bond movies. Thank you for the tape recorder. I am afraid to send tapes in the mail but when you get here, I'll give you them. Thank you for the money you sent.

Good-bye, my friend. Write soon. Please, God, we'll work together again in *my* part of Nigeria.

Your very good friend—and adoptive son,

Joseph Nathaniel Manga

The letter compelled me to reflect on what my experience with Joseph meant to me. For one thing, it reinforced my conviction that for those of us who relish referring to ourselves as humanists, much of our work takes the direction it does because of the contacts we make in the field. We crave human companionship. As I noted earlier, human companionship makes more of an impact on my spirit than theoretical conclusions.

Cross-cultural friendships are possible and even common in the field. In this day of blatant pandering to the politics of difference, it is necessary to note the satisfaction and joy of discovering our common humanity in diverse settings. That discovery is what anthropology should be all about.

Joseph has his dreams, but what will happen to them? His singing career will be taken up with singing in choirs, at best, and lulling his children to sleep. He deserves so much and will get so little. Knowledge has only increased his possibility of pain and disappointment. And yet—he seems so content. Each day appears to bring him a new delight. He remains confident that there is no challenge he cannot meet. He has shown me through his quiet self-assurance how to prepare for life. I often listen to the tapes of his singing when I am blue, and Joseph still sings away my blues.

ALAN R. SANDSTROM

THE WAVE

FIELDWORK AND FRIENDSHIP IN NORTHERN VERACRUZ, MEXICO

Critics of anthropology sometimes forget that field research is impossible without the active cooperation of the people who are the object of the study. Friendship is more than a psychological nicety for the anthropologist — it is essential if the work is to succeed. Friendship cannot be faked, nor can trust, and a phony is easy to spot. Nonetheless a certain wariness often characterizes two people trying to understand each other across a cultural divide. The successes of earlier anthropologists in forging friendships and making allies among the peoples with whom they have lived has greatly increased our sympathetic understanding of other cultures and has opened the possibility of authentic communication among different peoples. Critics of the anthropological enterprise can only base their objections upon the knowledge about culture established by previous anthropological research.

In this chapter, Sandstrom recounts some of the struggles in making friends in a Nahua village in northern Veracruz, Mexico. The Nahuas are heirs of the ancient Aztecs, and well over one million of them continue to speak the Nahuatl language and share a culture rooted in the rich traditions of their pre-Hispanic past. The story tells how miscommunication can abort friendship and how judging the actions of others is always a risky business. It is about trust and the ways that crisis sometimes reveals someone's true character. Finally, it is an account of the emotional toll that friendship can exact regardless of circumstances.

Bartolo Hernández and I were both in our mid-twenties at the time we first met. As a novice ethnographer, I had just arrived in the community of Amatlán, a Nahua village in the tropical forests of northern Veracruz, Mexico. Bartolo, along with several of his agemates, had come to visit me under the corrugated iron roof of the two-room schoolhouse. Each man was dressed in loose-fitting pants and shirt of gleaming white cotton, and each carried a machete in a brown leather sheath slung over one shoulder. They stood respectfully, feet together, glancing at me discreetly from time to time and murmuring to each other in their native Nahuatl. The men had come to satisfy their curiosity about this stranger and what he wanted, as well as to introduce themselves.

"What's your name?" a voice in the dark asked in halting Spanish.

"Alan," I replied.

Following a brief silence, another voice tentatively attempted the unfamiliar sounding name by asking, "Adán?"—Spanish for Adam. After repeating Alan several times without influencing the way they pronounced it, I accepted my new name and for the first time began to realize how difficult it was going to be to establish an identity across a linguistic and cultural barrier. Clearly, whatever I told people would necessarily be interpreted according to their own understandings.

I asked their names in turn, and I remember that the last to speak was Bartolo. He countered with his question, "How long will you stay here?" I told him that I hoped to stay for two months but would return for a longer visit in about a year. In fact, I was working under a summer grant from my university and would return to their village only after finishing qualifying examinations in anthropology and securing funding to support a longer field study. At that moment, however, I was not really sure whether I intended to return at all. I was finding the first hours and days in the village to be lonely, difficult, and even threatening. Although trained to expect adjustment problems and fatigue, I found the experience to be more trying than I had anticipated.

I had arrived in the village the evening before, after an exhausting two-day journey aboard dilapidated buses and a hike of several hours under the tropical sun. The destination of my journey, a place I call Amatlán, was home to 600 people, all of whom identified as *masehualmej*, or Nahuatl-speaking Native Americans. Anthropologists at the University of Veracruz directed me to this remote region after I told them that I wanted to conduct ethnographic research among traditional Nahuas. The Nahuas are the largest Native American group in Mexico, and some of them are descendants of the Toltecs and Aztecs. Despite their importance as an ethnic group, no anthropological study of their village life had ever been published. I had come to Amatlán to fill in this gap in the ethnographic record.

After an awkward arrival and some confusion as I explained who I was, village authorities agreed to let me live in an unused corner of the schoolhouse. It was July, and the children were on summer break. I can barely recall Bartolo that first evening. We had very little time to become acquainted visually as the brief tropical twilight gave way to total darkness under the canopy of trees. His face and personality have long since fused in my memory with those of his companions. Yet his friendship was to prove decisive in my work and even my life.

As that first conversation continued, I became lucky when I asked my visitors, "Will you help me to learn Nahuatl?" This question seemed to solve the problem of my ambiguous status as well as allay the fears the men may have had regarding my motives. I was now a student of their language and thus had some reason to be there. They laughed, exchanged comments with each other in rapid-fire Nahuatl, and appeared to relax. They took to the teaching task immediately and began to list all the words they could think of as I rapidly wrote them down.

The solution to culture shock is to make friends, but given the intrusive nature of fieldwork and the marginal position of the ethnographer, that is easier said than done. Added to these problems, I was to discover that the very definition of friendship and the symbols used to express it vary cross-culturally. My own struggles to overcome these barriers centered ultimately on Bartolo, but it was to take the passage of years before I succeeded. He came to the schoolhouse to visit on several occasions, always accompanied by other men. I counted him among perhaps a dozen people with whom I became acquainted that summer. But my initial stay was too short for us to surmount our differences in life experience. Try as I might, I did not feel that I knew who he was.

When I returned to Amatlán the following year, I once again had to deal with that feeling of apprehension and loneliness mixed with despair that can occasionally overcome the fieldworker who is far from a familiar world. The excitement tinged with fear created an edgy sense of mistrust that sometimes made it hard to reach out to people. With no electricity, running water, bathrooms, or means of external communication, and faced with a damp, tropical climate in the summer and a dry, cold climate in the winter, I was often physically uncomfortable. As I became used to conditions in the village, the people must have undergone their own adjustment to having a stranger in their midst. They had remembered my previous visit, but upon my return I was once again a spectacle and an object of curiosity. The visitors laughed a great deal and came to loiter around my quarters in large numbers. Yet, just as before, the novelty of my presence began to wear off within a week or two and fewer people came by to spend the day.

As life in Amatlán settled into a routine, my circle of acquaintances grew. I made contact with Bartolo again, but he was preoccupied with village politics and rarely had time to visit me. He was friendly but distant and either thought that I would not be interested in local affairs or felt that he could not yet confide in me. There were dangerous developments surrounding Amatlán that involved the invasion of private land, but at that time I was not able to learn all of the details. It was a topic that people did not wish to discuss with me. I pieced together that a number of younger villagers had cleared the land on a cattle ranch about half a day's walk away. The struggle split Amatlán into factions, but although feelings occasionally ran high, no crisis erupted while I was in residence that year.

During this period, an incident occurred that illustrated some of the complexities and perils of forging friendships across a significant cultural divide. While Bartolo remained in the background, seven or eight men in their early twenties continued to come around daily and even accompanied me to the arroyo to bathe. The group of young men narrowed itself to about three or four as peripheral members drifted off and, in retrospect, seemed to stay away from me. The remaining men were the first to reach out, and some of them became my earliest friends in the village. They visited often, answered questions about community life, and offered to help in my work. I was grateful for their company and for relief from the boredom and loneliness of my initial several weeks in residence. More than that, for the first time I was beginning to feel optimistic about my prospects in Amatlán. It was not until later that I began to notice that something was amiss. Hardly anyone came to visit me except these new-found friends. Furthermore, it seemed strange that while all other males in the village were busily engaged in horticultural activities, my friends seemed to enjoy days of leisure. As I attempted to expand my social horizons, I realized that I had made the classic mistake of a novice fieldworker—I allied myself with the first people to approach before I found out who they were. As it turned out, they were village malcontents who, having been rejected by much of the community for failure to reciprocate in one or more exchange relationships, seized the opportunity to escape their low status by associating with a foreigner. Other people were avoiding me because I kept bad company.

Personally, I liked these misfits, and they were of great help to me in overcoming initial problems adjusting to village life. One in particular, Juvencio, spent time showing me important sites, such as the best places to bathe and get drinking water, and he even served as my guide to the distant market town. He was also very patient as I elicited word lists in Nahuatl and asked him the proper way to say things. Our interaction was awkward at first, but we had gotten used to each other. He was respectful, it seemed to me, but no more so than most of the other villagers I met.

One day as I was recording words, Juvencio said, "Adán, I need to buy something. Lend me fifteen pesos." He was not demanding or aggressive in his request, but nonetheless I was mildly alarmed. Lending money was a practice I wished to avoid, not only because I felt that it could lead to trouble if too many people became indebted to me, but also because as a graduate student I did not have a great deal of money to lend. On the other hand, the amount he requested was minor, and I trusted that he would not take advantage of me.

"Sure," I said, and reaching into my pack, I took out some bills and handed them to him. He immediately got up, mumbled something and left.

I had no idea for what purpose Juvencio borrowed the money; nor did I really care. Juvencio seemed unchanged by the loan and continued to come around and apparently enjoyed keeping me company. After several weeks had passed and he made no effort to pay me back, I grew concerned. Had he forgotten about his debt? I knew that he had sold corn at the market and must have earned some money, yet no offer to repay the loan was forthcoming. I did not care about the money itself, but I was worried about the reputation I would develop if it became known that I was such an easy mark. Again I was faced with negotiating my identity in the absence of cultural guideposts. At this time, I was still puzzled at the difficulty I was having in getting to know a wider circle of people in the community. But I felt that it was important to establish a clear precedent with regard to money lending. The message I wanted to convey was that while I was prepared to be generous, I expected fair treatment in return.

Juvencio arrived one afternoon, and I tried to bring up the debt in a gentle, nonaccusative manner. I said as delicately as I could, "Juvencio, did I lend you some money?"

There was a long silence, and he finally replied, "What? What do you mean? What are you saying?"

"You know," I said, "the fifteen pesos I lent to you. Well, I need it so that I can go to the market tomorrow."

"You what? What are you talking about? I don't know what you are talking about. Do you need problems? Why do you say these things? We'll see about this. We'll see about where this is going." He left me abruptly.

Juvencio's response surprised me. He offered no excuse and acted as if I had insulted him by asking for the money. Later, he brought along his two brothers, and they instigated a heated conversation.

First one, then the other brother assaulted me in rising tones. "Hey, gringo, what are you saying, why do you talk like that to my brother? Is it trouble you want? What can you do? You didn't lend anybody anything. Hey, *pendejo* [stupid wimp], why are you causing all of this trouble? What can you do against us? Do you really want more trouble, do you want us to do something?"

I replied calmly, "Look, I lent fifteen pesos to Juvencio, and I need my money back. I am not asking for a favor, nor for trouble, just for my pesos."

"Is my younger brother a thief? Is that what you are trying to say in front of everybody? What goes here? Hey, gringo, are you accusing my brother of stealing money from you? Are you stupid? Don't you see everyone here? What do you want? What are you doing here?"

The situation had obviously grown far out of proportion, and it was clear that Juvencio and his brothers were prepared to make a public scene. This was just what I wanted to avoid, and I could not believe that they would want such a thing. The scandal had become the talk of the village, and only the Mexican schoolmaster assigned to Amatlán, who was himself an outsider, seemed to share my interpretation of the situation. He told me, "Yeah, that's what a lot of these people are like. They've done that to me on a number of occasions." That only the schoolmaster appeared to agree with me should have been the tip-off that there was a profound cultural misunderstanding behind this controversy.

I had no one to consult but myself, and so the internal dialogue began.

"Do these people view me as a rich gringo who does not need to be repaid? What have I done to give that impression? They are obviously treating me like an alien who does not merit common courtesy. Are they simply greedy and have found me a convenient target to exploit? Maybe it is time to get out of here."

"No wait, this doesn't make sense. Of all the indigenous groups in Mexico, Nahuas have a reputation for being generous to a fault. Didn't people warn me never to admire possessions in a Nahua house because family members will immediately offer them as gifts? I have never had anything stolen and borrowed items, except money, have always been returned. People have been bringing me gifts of food with little thought of repayment, and villagers have often mentioned how important it is to be generous."

"Yes, but other people I know have since asked to borrow money from me, and I suspect that they would not pay it back either. This seems to be a pattern. All right, it was never very much money they requested, even by village standards, but clearly a problem is developing here."

This one-sided conversation continued for weeks without helping to resolve the puzzle. Meanwhile, I gradually entered into the routine of village life. I witnessed ritual kinsmen exchanging gifts of food or clothing on important occasions such as Day of the Dead celebrations. A person who wished to deactivate the relationship simply stopped the flow of gifts by neglecting to reciprocate. I documented godparents showering godchildren with a steady supply of small presents, and I noted that children are expected in return to treat these ritual kinsmen with respect. Gift giving was clearly the currency of much village social interaction, and I came to realize that reciprocity lies at the heart of many Nahua practices.

Even Nahua religious rituals are forms of symbolic exchanges between human beings and spirit entities. Villagers sometimes refer to a ritual as *tlamanilistli* [offering] in Nahuatl, and the core of each ritual occasion is an elaborate gift of food, cornmeal, tobacco, copal incense, and other valued items. Before people consume a soft drink, they spill a few drops on the ground for the earth. Women leave eggs by the springs in exchange for taking water, and a man makes a small offering when cutting down a tree. I came to understand that formal exchange suffuses the Nahua social and cultural world, providing it with structure and a mechanism of expression.

As my knowledge of Nahua culture increased, I began to reflect on the problem I had with Juvencio. Clearly, as a North American outsider, and thus in the eyes of many Nahuas an obviously wealthy person, I was defined as someone of relatively high status. By borrowing money from me, Juvencio was formally initiating friendship, but a friendship between two people of unequal status. He was willing to accept the position of being indebted to me (albeit for only a small sum) in order to allow us to interact as exchange partners. What I took to be an inexplicable act of irresponsibility and a threat to my status was in fact a humble and elegant expression of his desire to establish closer ties with me. In responding to his gesture in the way that I did, I affirmed that it was I who lacked generosity, not to mention common politeness. Here was a clear case of cross-cultural miscommunication. But I only figured this out after I had left Mexico, and it was too late to make amends. Meanwhile, the shortage of arable land in Amatlán forced Juvencio and his family to leave the community. When I returned, they had moved on and joined others in the risky game of invading the land of a wealthy cattle rancher. I never saw him again.

Over the next decade I returned to Amatlán for short periods of time. I tried to keep up with my many contacts but was never there long enough to develop deep and permanent ties with any single person. One problem was that the village fissioned twice in the interim as extended families left to form new communities in areas where land was more abundant. Relations between these daughter villages and Amatlán were sometimes hostile, and it was difficult for me to visit people I knew in them without offending some community members.

Making friends with Bartolo took a very different course. During my brief visits to the village, I would sometimes see Bartolo in the distance, but for some reason he never came to talk to me. He smiled and waved when passing by but acted like a stranger, neither hostile nor particularly friendly. I became convinced that he was avoiding me, but I could not imagine why. But in 1985, when I arrived for a second year-long stay in Amatlán, accompanied by my wife and three-year-old son, Bartolo seemed a different person and approached me as if I were a long-lost companion. The day after we arrived he came to our quarters with a broad smile on his face. He looked older but had grown more handsome as he entered middle age. He greeted me with, "So you have come again, Adán," as he reached out his hand so that we could touch fingertips in the traditional Nahua greeting.

Not knowing how to respond to this overture, I said, "Yes, it's good to see you again, Bartolo, how are you? What has happened? Everything has changed around here."

"Yes," he responded. "We have moved the houses into rows to make room for the electric lines." And he recounted how villagers had petitioned the federal government to have electricity brought into the community. Everyone appeared to be excited about this development, and Bartolo shared the prevailing view that electric power represented progress.

We reminisced about the past, and he explained what had happened in the village since my last visit. I learned who had died and who had moved out. I was puzzled at this turnabout in his behavior but did not know how to ask him why he seemed changed. Then, in one of those remarkable denouements that fieldworkers often experience, I finally learned the reason. One evening, as he sat on the same porch with the corrugated iron roof where I had first met him, he spoke to me about some of the events in his life.

"Do you remember when you first came here, Adán?"

"Sure, that was almost 15 years ago," I replied.

"That was a long time ago now. After you left that first time, the *comisariado* [a village leader] petitioned for more land. Well, the land we were granted by the government was claimed by Villa Hermosa even though they do not have official recognition. My *milpa* [field] was one grabbed by those bastards from Villa Hermosa, and I had to fight back. My brothers and I stood watch over the milpa day and night, and our friends from here said they would help us. Things became very tense, and one day we found Juan Martnez dead, murdered with a machete. Juan was my cousin, and his milpa was next to mine."

I interrupted, "But I thought that your father-in-law, Aurelio, also from Amatlán, was accused of the murder. Why would Aurelio kill someone from his own community?"

"Well he didn't, but things get confused in these situations. Then the militia was called in from Ixhuatlán [the county seat]. I was blamed for helping with the murder because it was my milpa that they took, but it wasn't true. Anyway, my family and I fled to Papantla [a Totonac town 100 miles south of Amatlán], where I have an uncle. I stayed there for ten years, fearing to return even once to see my friends and relatives."

"But surely you came back on occasion? Why, I saw you when I was visiting. You waved at me, don't you remember?"

He looked puzzled and replied, "No, I was gone. They would have killed me if I had come back, like they almost did Aurelio. But wait, you probably saw my brother Raúl. We weren't speaking to each other—still don't. We haven't talked since I was married."

"But I swear it was you. Look, you have three brothers, and I know each of them."

"No, Adán. I have four brothers; Raúl is my twin. But he wouldn't have come to tell you about me because he is against me."

No wonder I felt ignored during those intervening visits. People in this region often go by a number of different names, and so I was unable to draw a connection between the two men. Bartolo and Raúl had become estranged over an obscure dispute in the distant past and always avoided each other's company. This explained why Raúl kept his distance from me during the years while Bartolo lived in exile. The person I thought I knew really *was* someone else.

Bartolo was a person of respect who had served the village in various leadership positions. He walked with a proud bearing and exhibited the polite formality that characterizes the ideal of Nahua social interaction. Like me, he was entering middle age (I turned forty that year) and he, too, had a small son. His stature was slight by Anglo standards, but he was of average height compared to other village men. His hair was jet black, and he sported just the shadow of a moustache. When I first met him in the early 1970s, Bartolo wore the men's traditional white outfit, but by 1985 he was dressed in Western clothing purchased in a regional market. This change in dress signaled shifts in ethnic identity that were sweeping Amatlán, as well as most other Native American communities in the region. The old division between Indian and Hispanic was being replaced with new identities that had not yet solidified. Although he exhibited the quick wit and readiness to laugh I found in many Nahua villagers, I detected an unusual sadness about him that I did not observe in other men.

He seemed to enjoy visiting us every evening, and we eventually began discussing in depth the kinds of cultural information that I was seeking. I introduced him to Mexican red wine, which he preferred over the powerful clear rum that was available locally. Because of its color, he jokingly called the wine medicine, and he talked about his visits as "coming for his medicine." He reciprocated by inviting my family for dinner on many occasions. Over the months, Bartolo showed that he was willing to work with me, and we spent long hours reviewing kinship data, village history and maps, word lists, and other sources of information about Amatlán.

As our friendship grew, Bartolo became invaluable to my research. He willingly answered questions when I posed them, but his real contribution owed to his knowledge of the people in Amatlán. Once I formulated a question or expressed an interest in some area, he would direct me to the person best able to provide me with reliable information. He often accompanied me as I went to visit these key people to introduce me formally and allay fears that they may have had regarding my motives. Bartolo rarely offered himself as an authority, and only on occasion did he innovate by suggesting topics that might be of interest to me. He acted as my entré and guide into the heart of Amatlán's social world.

Bartolo never asked to borrow money, but if he had, I would have understood the signal better following my experience with Juvencio. I believe he saw his position as equal to mine and thus avoided establishing our relationship on the unequal basis that a debt would signify. Following Nahua practice, however, he actively engaged in exchange. Every so often, one of his children would arrive with a gift of food for us. In return, I would give Bartolo a cigar or a kitchen utensil for his wife. When we left Amatlán for several days to go to the city, I would always bring back some small gift, for example, a carpenter's tool or, on one occasion, a quartz watch. After a while it became apparent that our exchanges were escalating and that we were ready for a more formal acknowledgment of friendship. The invitation came one afternoon when Bartolo and his wife arrived for a visit. They both sat for hours making small talk as we consumed rounds of soft drinks. This waiting period is customary in Nahua culture when people are about to make a request. Finally, Bartolo spoke to the point: "We would like to ask you to become godparents to Israel, our son."

After the brief pause that is considered polite, I responded, "We would be honored. When can the ritual be arranged?"

Bartolo consulted with his wife inaudibly, but it was clear that they had thought out their plans ahead of time. "Following the *tlacatelilis* [winter solstice] offering next month, the shaman will hold the rituals for people who want to become compadres."

Compadrazgo, or ritual kinship, is one of the most important formalized relationships between two people in Nahua culture, and we were deeply flattered. Technically, the relationship is between the godparents and the designated child, but important ties are also formed among the four adults. At three in the morning, at the close of the four-day winter solstice observance, we four parents waited in a line before the main altar in the village shrine. The shaman cleansed each of us by taking up sacred palm brooms and brushing us, all the while intoning a deep chant. Next he brushed us with beeswax candles and then handed them to us so that we might burn them on our home altars. He instructed us to shake hands and address each other by our newly acquired kinship terms.

After this brief ritual, we entered into a new relationship with Bartolo and his family. We never again called each other by name, but instead used our ritual terms of address, compadre and comadre. Bartolo's child technically became our ward should anything happen to his parents, and we assumed responsibility to supply the boy with clothes and gifts during certain rituals. In essence, we became co-parents, and the interests of our two families were merged.

After becoming ritual kinsmen, an interesting shift occurred in Bartolo's pattern of reciprocity. Gifts were of a more traditional sort and had deeper symbolic meaning. For example, when the new corn had ripened, Bartolo invited us to his house for dinner. As we were about to take our leave, his wife lowered her voice so that she could barely be heard. This usually signaled a show of great respect.

"Compadre, comadre, here is something I made for you." She then presented us with a large bundle tied up in new red bandannas.

"Thank you, comadre," I responded, having no idea what she had just handed me. We immediately opened the bundle, and the gift turned out to be a very large *xamitl,* a tamalelike cornmeal cake steamed in banana leaves, freshly made from sweet young corn. She explained that this special dish was prepared only at this time of year, and it symbolized the corn spirit in its aspect as a child (*pilsintsij*). Called a *xamconetl* or *xamitl* child, the cake was approximately the size and shape of a newborn infant bound in swaddling clothes. The gift allowed me and my family to join villagers in the symbolic recognition of the ripening corn and in celebration of the corn spirit. This was a significant time of the year for all villagers, and the gesture by Bartolo and his wife was meant to include us in the community.

Something changed, too, in the nature of the topics that Bartolo was willing to discuss with me. In general, villagers were reluctant to speak of highly personal matters. I was surprised and gratified, therefore, when Bartolo revealed to me a great tragedy in his life. We were sitting on our porch together, as usual, when he suddenly fell silent.

"Compadre, did you know that we had a baby last year?"

"No, I hadn't heard," I responded, waiting for him to continue.

"He was a beautiful baby, big and healthy, always smiling. I don't know what happened, he stopped eating. He was fine, and then he just stopped eating. He looked good, healthy, but we couldn't give him food. I brought in a shaman, and I walked to Ixhuatlán to take him to the clinic. Nothing we did made a difference. One day we woke up and he was dead. What could have killed him?"

I had no reply. Bartolo was clearly still grieving over the loss of the baby, and with tears in his eyes he told me what an extraordinary child it had been. He quickly turned his head to regain his composure. This is a gesture that I had witnessed on several occasions in Amatlán. Overt expression of emotion by men or women causes disharmony and leaves the person, and others nearby, susceptible to disease. This is one reason people rarely reveal how upset they are. Bartolo was protecting my family and me from unanticipated consequences of his emotional state. To make matters worse, Bartolo's wife miscarried in the months before we arrived. I will never forget the anguish in his face as he revealed these misfortunes.

The year spanning 1985–86 was a period of momentous change for the people of Amatlán. The houses had been consolidated from scattered groupings, based on relations of kinship, into a grid pattern, to accommodate the introduction of electricity into the village. People seemed excited about the prospect of electrification, and many had purchased light bulbs that would represent their link with urban Mexico. Others were talking about buying the inexpensive television sets that had flooded the country from Japan and Korea. Since my previous stay, Amatlán had become almost a parody of the modernization process. Already the traditional thatch-roofed houses had anomalous electric meters attached to bamboo walls. A lone wire led to the interior of each house, powering one bare light bulb. Equally momentous was the arrival of Protestant missionaries from Texas and

Louisiana. These Anglo evangelists had entered Mexico illegally and were taking advantage of economic instability in the region to make converts. Amatlán was not exempt, and several families had rejected their traditional beliefs to convert to the new religion. This situation threatened to divide the village and undermine social solidarity as well as people's identification with their Nahua heritage.

Bartolo aligned himself with the traditionalists and continued to sponsor and to attend village rituals dedicated to the pre-Hispanic deities. Interestingly, his twin brother, Raúl, joined the Protestants, further widening the gulf between them. I, too, was eventually forced to take sides and, while trying not to alienate the converts, chose to continue my relations with members of the traditionalist camp. It was in this context that I was invited by the leading shaman of Amatlán to attend a major meeting of shamans in a neighboring village. They were gathering to make preparations for a pilgrimage to a distant sacred mountain to petition thunder spirits for rain. Several people from Amatlán wanted to attend, and I offered to take as many as would fit in our four-wheel-drive vehicle. This was a rare event, and I wanted to witness and photograph as much as the shamans would allow. Bartolo and his son also expressed a wish to attend, and I made sure that there was room for both of them. The trip took several hours over very rough and often hazardous trails that meandered through deep arroyos and along narrow ridges. Everyone was relieved when we finally arrived, and we found that indeed there was a veritable summit conference of shamans who had gathered for the pilgrimage.

I was very busy over the next several hours taking photographs of the preparations and interviewing participants. There was an offering to the water spirit, dancing before an altar dedicated to the seed spirits, singing by a specialist in visions, countless blessings using the sacred walking sticks of the thunder spirits, and many other fascinating episodes. This event was of great interest to me, and I was very much occupied during it. I noticed that the other visitors from Amatlán were also actively participating in the event. I was surprised, therefore, when Bartolo approached me and spoke.

"Compadre, I am tired and wish you would take me back to Amatlán. I have things to do and want to leave. I thought that we were only going to stay for a few minutes."

"But, compadre," I answered, "I want to see this offering. Can't you wait for a little while longer?"

"No, because Israel wants to leave now."

What remained unsaid was that I was the child's godfather and so should abide by the boy's wishes. This rush to depart was highly unusual behavior for people of the region, and it was certainly uncharacteristic of Bartolo. Although I put him off, we did end up leaving earlier than I would have wanted. I never learned Bartolo's motives for leaving, but I remember thinking that ritual kinship is a double-edged sword. As a ritual kinsman, he could ask me to do things that normally would be out of bounds.

I was reminded of the incident at the meeting of shamans from time to time as Bartolo began making demands of me that I was unsure about. By this time he had more than demonstrated his friendship, but there were disquieting aspects about our relationship that I did not know how to interpret. Even after we had become compadres, I was confronted with situations that caused me to question Bartolo's motives and trustworthiness. For example, one day while I was visiting him he fell quiet, as if he were about to say something significant.

"Compadre, my family would like a television set."

"You want a gift?" I said, taken aback.

"They all want to watch television here in the house," he replied.

I was undecided what to do about this request. In the first place, I was uneasy about the effect television would have on village life. What changes would it bring? Would it raise unrealistic expectations? Unsure about television's impact on my own culture, I wondered if the programs, many of which are dubbed versions of series originating in the United States, would give a warped view of life in other parts of Mexico and the world.

Stalling for time, I answered, "Compadre, I don't have to tell you that watching television is a waste of time. You have seen it before. People just sit for hours and watch, and they don't get any work done. Are you sure this is a good idea?"

He paused a moment and said, "Yes, compadre, they want it."

Despite his answer, the prospect of actively promoting television in the village initially struck me as almost irresponsible. Previous to this time, the only television set had been that of the schoolmaster, powered by a car battery that had to be carried by mule for miles to be recharged. Another concern was that a television was quite a costly item to request. I had more than kept up my end of the reciprocal exchanges over the months, and this added expense seemed to suggest that I was being taken for granted.

I told Bartolo, "Let me think about it."

My solution was to put off the request for as long as possible so that I could gain time to decide what to do. I slowly came to see that, from Bartolo's perspective, his demand was not unreasonable. As ritual kinsman and friend I should be willing to share resources and help out his family, just as he had helped us out. Our family should certainly want his family to be on the cutting edge of technology in Amatlán. After all, in the intervening weeks other families were acquiring televisions. It was not as if his would be the first.

The day finally arrived when we had to leave Amatlán to take care of business in the regional town of Tuxpan. A number of villagers had purchased television sets by this time, and the community was officially electrified. Although the power was constantly interrupted, and brown-outs lasted for weeks on end, the small bulbs did cast a dim, cold light in people's houses. I had decided to fulfill Bartolo's desire and purchase a portable television for his family. The dam had been broken—others were already exposed to reruns of "Dallas," along with commercials exhorting viewers to buy the latest in dishwashers or bathroom-cleaning products. As we left, Bartolo told me that he would cut a long bamboo pole for the antenna and await our return. Several days later I delivered the equipment and helped him hook it up. Just at the telling moment, the electricity went out for three days, and when it came on again, it was at half power for a week. Eventually we managed to get the apparatus working well enough to receive two channels. For the next several evenings, Bartolo did not come for his usual visit. He was at home watching television.

A few days later when I went to visit him, I found the television on and the entire family in the house. It was the middle of the day, and they were tuned in to a soap opera that was interrupted every few minutes by commercials. The program was similar in format to a U.S. soap opera, with the love triangles, melodramatic music, and endless plot lines. There on the screen were urban Mexican actors and actresses dressed in the latest fashions, wearing cosmopolitan hairstyles, driving sports cars, and living in palatial houses. These figures in their bizarre surroundings must have been fascinating to Bartolo and his family. The program was obviously aimed at urban housewives and seemed remarkably out of place in this thatch-roofed house in the tropical forests, miles from the nearest small town. Here was Bartolo's wife grinding corn meal with a stone *mano* and *metate*, making tortillas over her cooking fire while listening to the character on the screen agonize over whether to stay with her rich doctor-husband or run off to Europe with the Austrian ski instructor. And here was Bartolo listening to mouthwash commercials as he squatted down to sharpen his machete on a well-worn block of sandstone.

I was glad in the end that I had purchased the television for Bartolo's family. In the first place, it was what they wanted. But more importantly, it provided them with a window on the rest of the world that they otherwise would not have had. Admittedly, it was a strange and biased view presented, but the villagers were capable of evaluating the information that came to them over the screen, perhaps even more so than people raised on television from childhood. My fear that this electronic link to urban culture would waste their time was apparently unfounded. Bartolo resumed his evening visits and did not talk much about the television. Some days later he casually remarked to me, "Compadre, the television is boring." After this, when I visited his house I noticed that the set was often on when I arrived. Family members would be in the house, but nobody was actually watching the screen. As in many U.S. households, television was being used to provide background noise while people directed their attention and activities elsewhere.

Bartolo made a second problematic request a few weeks later. He asked that I take him and his family to the city the next time that I left the village. This seemed on the surface a fair request, but there were difficulties associated with it. Bartolo wanted to take along three of his children and his wife, as well as a ritual kinswoman of hers. Even with the improved roads, it is a full day of travel from Amatlán to Xalapa, the capital of the state of Veracruz. Most of these people had never ridden in a vehicle before. Neither Bartolo nor his family had ever stayed in a hotel, eaten in a restaurant, used plumbing of any kind, slept in a bed, or crossed a busy street. They had introduced me to their world, and I was willing to introduce them to mine, but the logistics involved were boggling.

I realized that from Bartolo's perspective the trip would be a minor inconvenience for us. We went to the city anyway, and what possible bother could it be to have a few more people along? He, like most villagers, simply assumed that we were wealthy and the expenditure would not matter much. In fact, we *were* wealthy compared to many villagers—I estimated that an average family could get by on less than $300 U.S. per year in cash.

Eventually the need to take action on my ritual kinsman's second demand arose, when my family and I had to return to the capital in order to consult with anthropologists at the University of Veracruz. I prepared for the worst as I informed Bartolo of our plans. He seemed eager to go and left immediately to make arrangements. As the day of our departure drew closer, he informed me that his children did not want to go with us and would remain in the village. Later, his wife's ritual kinswoman decided that she had better not go because her family feared something harmful would happen to her. The day we left, Bartolo's wife backed out too because she was concerned that she would get sick in the truck. That left just Bartolo and a much simpler situation to handle. In the end, however, even Bartolo seemed to be having second thoughts. Many people I talked to in Amatlán spoke of travel to the city as an excursion into an unknown world. When villagers recounted a trip to a major city, their narration would take on a mythic quality, like an odyssey in which they were lucky to escape alive. On the other hand, people stated that the urban world is full of excitement and new things as well. Bartolo weighed the costs and benefits and with trepidation committed himself to accompanying us. I was gratified that he trusted me enough to come.

As he climbed into his seat, Bartolo grew quiet. Our progress was very slow as I maneuvered around large rocks and holes and skirted deep gorges along the trail. After four or five hours we arrived at a crossroads where several small stands were set up to sell soft drinks and food. I suggested that we rest a while, and Bartolo slowly climbed out. I bought soft drinks for everybody but could not find Bartolo anywhere. Finally I spotted him off by himself, away from the crowd of people gathered at the stands. He took the soft drink and quickly drank it and handed the bottle back to me. I was slightly puzzled at his behavior but thought no more of it at the time. He followed this pattern of keeping a distance from us while we remained within the region of Amatlán. Once we had gotten far enough away, he did not seem to mind as much being seen in our company.

I had experienced a similar situation in which villagers did not want to be seen with me. Several months previously, I had walked to the market with a group of village men. We talked and laughed all along the trails, but as we approached the market town, my companions fell silent. When we entered the market, they drifted away in the crowd, and I was left alone. I was puzzled by their behavior and thought hard whether I had said something to offend. After a few hours, I headed back for the village and found my travel mates waiting for me on the trail. They said nothing about the incident, but I learned later that Indians sometimes get into trouble with the townspeople for being seen with foreigners. For Bartolo, to be associated with obvious outsiders could only mean problems. If we were missionaries, he would be perceived by traditionalists as betraying his Indian identity. If we were anything else, he still risked trouble from local ranchers, cowboys, and other upholders of the Hispanically dominated social order.

Throughout that day we traveled south toward Xalapa, making much better time once we connected with the Panamerican Highway. Bartolo was very still next to me in the front seat of the vehicle. He stared intently out the window at the scenes passing by, but he spoke only when spoken to. In mid-afternoon we stopped at a small isolated restaurant perched on the side of a hill overlooking the Gulf of Mexico. Bartolo told me that he had never actually seen the Gulf before, although the body of water plays an important role in Nahua mythology. I knew that in Nahua belief, the Gulf is home to a drunken water deity who threatens the world with inundation. He is now said to be chained at the bottom of the sea, and his occasional movements and growls of rage cause storms to roll inland from the water. The sea is literally the edge of the world in Nahua mythology, the source of life-giving rain but at the same time a dangerous place inhabited by bizarre creatures. It is not considered to be a setting where human beings should venture, and even approaching the sea warrants great caution.

Bartolo was obviously fascinated with the water, much as a person can be mesmerized by a great chasm or a ferocious animal. The sheer horror of it transfixed him. As my wife and son entered the restaurant, I took Bartolo to get a closer look. The land gave way to gigantic volcanic boulders that formed the beach at the water's edge. About fifteen feet below, the water was turbulent and roiling as waves crashed onto the black, jagged rocks. A storm far out at sea must have been agitating the water, although the weather was clear and calm where we stood. Bartolo continued to stare at the water and became fascinated with the large black crabs that scurried over the rocks below.

I walked out as far as I could on the rocks to get a better view. I was about ten feet over the water, and well above the wave action. Bartolo stayed back, obviously wary of the violence of the waves and their continuous din. Then it happened. Out of nowhere, and completely unexpectedly, a huge tongue of water shot six feet over my head with a deafening roar. I had never seen anything like it before. The water poured over me as I staggered under the shock and weight of the cascade. As I was about to pitch over the edge to sure injury on the jagged rocks below, I felt Bartolo grab me and yank me back toward the shore. We both stumbled over the uneven rocks, completely soaked, and rapidly beat our retreat back to land. Bartolo had a wild look in his eyes, and my heart was pounding at the thought of how close I had come to tumbling down. The Gulf appeared to reach up and grab me, and only the quick thinking and courage of Bartolo had prevented tragedy. I had seriously underestimated the danger of the rough water and nearly became its victim. Bartolo's apprehension about going too near the violent waves turned out to have been well founded. In reacting as he did, he overcame a tremendous antipathy to the sea that originated in Nahua conceptions about the angry and irrational water spirit. Despite his inexperience around the open water, he exhibited remarkable courage in his successful effort to keep me from falling. It is no exaggeration to state that Bartolo risked his own well-being in order to save me.

I gasped, still out of breath, "Thank you, compadre, I almost went over." He was clearly shaken and merely nodded his head in acknowledgment.

Nothing more was said about the incident for the rest of the trip. I tried to bring up the misadventure several times, but my companion seemed preoccupied. Bartolo returned to his silent vigil in the front seat, and he stirred only as we approached the city several hours later. Here we were entering another danger zone, one as precarious as the seaside. He did not act outwardly nervous or afraid, but he was clearly on guard. He asked how people found their way around the maze of streets, and I pointed out street signs and the numbers on buildings. He wondered where people lived and what they did to earn enough money to survive there. Mostly, he expressed amazement at the noise, the noxious exhaust from buses, trucks, and cars, and the seeming frantic activity of the hordes of pedestrians.

We stayed in Xalapa for several days. Bartolo appeared to adjust rapidly to urban living, but I could tell he felt out of place. In restaurants he always ordered chicken *mole* (enchiladas in a spicy sauce made from chile peppers and chocolate), even for breakfast. This was familiar food, and he showed no interest in experimenting with other dishes. He slept on the floor because he could not get used to a bed, and he spent long periods of time in the bathroom experimenting with the hot and cold running water. We toured the city a bit and spent many hours working on village kinship charts and genealogy. He appeared to enjoy the ambience of the city, but in the end I think he found it overwhelming. He purchased presents for his family and carefully packed them away in his carrying bag. This I took as a signal that he was ready to depart. When we announced our decision to return to Amatlán, he was clearly very pleased.

After a very tiring day, we arrived back in the village. People came out to observe our return, and Bartolo retired to his house along with about a dozen kinsfolk and friends to recount his adventures. They all sat around in a circle, and Bartolo told about the journey in remarkable detail. I was surprised at how he was able to remember the most insignificant minutiae and to put incidents in the proper context. During his silent ride he had been concentrating and memorizing all that he was seeing, so that he could recount his story when he returned. He told of trucks, towns, huge fields of corn and sugar cane, vast markets, the foods we ate, the beer we drank, and the people we met. He told about the sea and showed everyone some seashells that he had picked up. His narration recounting the incident of the wave was particularly detailed. He told how the water reached up and almost took me over the edge, and everyone was riveted by the scene he depicted with his words. In proper Nahua style he downplayed his own role in saving me, stating simply that he pulled me back at the right moment. After he had finished, people asked questions, made comments, or contributed their own stories and then slowly drifted off.

In the remaining months of our stay in Amatlán, life returned to the normal routine. Bartolo continued to come for medicine in the evenings and helped direct me to informed villagers. We kept up our small exchanges, but we both knew that the time was drawing near when my family and I would be leaving. I would like to say that after Bartolo saved me that day we somehow became closer friends, but I cannot. Things stayed about the same between us, and I think that we did the best we could considering how different our lives were. He never talked about the trip we took except on one occasion. We were sitting in silence one evening as it was getting dark, and he said, quite out of context, "Compadre, you looked after me very well in Xalapa."

I think this was his way of thanking us, and I replied, "Compadre, you looked after me very well that day by the water." He and I had nothing more to say about the incident.

The day before we were to leave, Bartolo called me to his house. This invitation was out of the ordinary because he asked me to come alone, and no mention was made about a meal. He offered me a seat indoors, and without the usual prolonged waiting period reached up into the rafters and brought out two newly made *bateas*. These are multipurpose, oval wooden basins, hand-carved from tropical cedar, and an essential item in every Nahua house. People use them to carry things, for washing clothes or food, for bread baking, and any number of other uses. He asked me to select one as a going-away present. As I looked each one over, I realized that they were masterpieces of the woodworker's art. I had known that Bartolo enjoyed working with wood, but I never realized that he had a reputation as the best wood craftsman in the village. I chose one, and he nodded his head in agreement. I asked him when he had made the batea, and he said that he started working on it after I had mentioned that I would like to take one home with me. That comment must have been made many months previously, because I did not remember saying anything like it to anyone. As I left, he asked me to leave the batea with him and said that he would deliver it before we left.

The morning of our departure, Bartolo did not show up with the batea. I wanted to say good-bye to him, and so I walked to his house after we had finished packing the vehicle. Nahuas often weep when people part, as an expression of friendship and solidarity. The show of emotion in this circumstance is an exception to their general avoidance of such behavior. Even so I was unprepared to see Bartolo in tears at the prospect of our leaving. He had stayed in his house so that people would not witness his state. I was profoundly touched by this display and felt a sense of sadness that is difficult to describe.

I said awkwardly, "Good-bye, compadre, thank you for everything you have done."

"Good-bye, compadre. When will you come back to Amatlán?" And as we parted company, he added, "It is important that we remember this day."

I carried the batea to our vehicle, loaded it in back, and drove off. After traveling all day, we stopped for the night, and I took out the batea to admire the beautiful job that Bartolo had done. I was having a hard time shaking the morbid sadness that I experienced in his house that morning. I noticed for the first time that he had written something in Spanish on the rim, undoubtedly after I left his house the previous night. The message simply read, "TRABAJO HECHO POR EL SR. BARTOLO HERNANDEZ MIERCOLES 2 DE ABRIL DE 1986" (WORK DONE BY MR. BARTOLO HERNANDEZ, WEDNESDAY, APRIL 2, 1986).

But the most significant work of Bartolo was to have the empathy and patience to reach out his hand to a visitor who might well have come from another planet. The two of us managed to overcome

JEANNE SIMONELLI

THE REFLECTING POOL

FIELDWORK, LEARNING AND THE NAVAJO WAY

In the past twenty years, "doing" anthropology has become more and more complex. In the days when we traveled long distances to far-off places, our fieldwork stayed in the field. Now, the distances have been narrowed. Informants have become consultants. Consultants are our friends. As such, they can board a plane in their land and come to visit, spending long nights in earnest conversation about truth and meaning and enlightenment and expectations. In the days when we wrote only inscrutable manuscripts circulated among colleagues, there was no one to dispute the validity of our work except another "expert" in the area. Now, our consultant-friends are critics, editors of our written words, commentators of their lives, and ours.

"The Reflecting Pool" is a result of this new era of fieldwork. It is ethnography in a broad sense — a product of the interaction between an anthropologist and a Navajo woman and her family, in a world in which ceremonies, alcohol, peyote, and Christianity are just a few of the ways of dealing with rapid change. It takes the reader not just into the physical and spiritual fabric of Navajo life but also asks questions about the mainstream American world that the Navajo people are expected to enter. The piece chronicles the friendship and spiritual journeys of two women while also addressing concrete issues that arise when the federal government tries to operate a popular national monument on lands belonging to native peoples.

Lend me your dreams, shepherd
That I may walk with you within the red walled canyons.
Land of your mother's mother's mother;
The long flow of memory, passing.
In charcoal is your history, visions of the conqueror—
Mounted, wide black cloaks, swirling
Under flat hats, the cross and the sword
Searing your tentative cornfields.
Walking on, I see blue, and golden buttons.
They came again, the "steam eaters"
Burning peach and apricot orchards
Leaving hogans death filled with the ghosts of children.

And I, daughter of Columbus,
Come to you in your dying pastures
Seeking the wisdom of centuries,
The gateway to the sacred winds.
I know somewhere a grandma stands, facing east
Blessing sunbearer as he prepares to take another trip
Across the dazzling blueness of the canyon sky.
Lend me your dreams, shepherd sun
That I may fly with you, and be healed.

An extended version of this essay will be published as *Canyon de Chelly: Crossing Between Worlds* (Santa Fe, NM: School of American Research Press, 1996).

195

Finding the Trail

It began with my daughter, who loves horses as only a young girl can, and with my own passion for mesas. She and I live together in a small community in rural New York, a place of sweet, gentle green hills, where brief summer is followed by endless November. In the winter of 1990, the gray was particularly damp and dense, the snow forgot to fall, and the deep turquoise skies of Arizona and New Mexico drifted in and out of my waking dreams. An anthropologist by trade, I'd been teaching for five years, including a biannual summer program "on the road" in the Southwest. During our five-week rambles we stopped at national parks and monuments, following rangers through ruins and canyons, up and down the hand-and-toehold trails. I'd always admired these well-versed tour guides, and as the winter wore on, I decided to realize a childhood dream—applying for a job as a seasonal park ranger.

It was December when I filled out the lengthy National Park Service application, choosing two sites for potential employment. My choice of park was based on dual considerations. I'm happiest in the dry heat and juniper piñon woodlands of the Southwest, so it had to be in that part of the country. Even more important, it had to be a place where Rachel, my eleven-year-old, could spend the entire workday in the company of horses. I picked Mesa Verde, Colorado, because it was close to a large tourist town that I assumed would have horses; and Canyon de Chelly, Arizona, because of the riding stable located at the mouth of the canyon.

Endless November was moving into its fifth month and the spring semester drawing to a close when someone from the interpretive branch at Mesa Verde called, offering me a seasonal position.

"I have a pre-teen daughter," I told the woman.

"We're sorry," she answered. "We can't have children here. Housing, you know." I was disappointed and wondered if my career as a ranger was doomed before starting.

Three days later, a wet April snow was falling when the phone rang. This time it was the chief of interpretation at Canyon de Chelly National Monument. Visions of sunlight and warmth filled me as he described the open position. I was needed as a seasonal ranger by May 10; the position lasted through Labor Day; they wanted to pay me to hike and talk and do the things I normally did for recreation. Once again, I described my young liability.

"I have a child," I told him, waiting for rejection.

"Great," he answered. "We'll put another bed in the duplex. This is a Navajo park. One of the other seasonals has a baby. We're family." Compared to Mesa Verde, Canyon de Chelly seemed special.

As a single parent and homeowner, I was plagued by logistical dilemmas in the days that followed. What about the house? Who would care for our loving, neurotic dog? What should we tell Rachel's elementary school, where the term dragged on till the end of June? In spite of these problems, we were ready in time, our summer lives packed into two large suitcases and a cardboard box. Less than twenty-four hours after I turned in my final grades, we flew out of New York's hesitant spring to a waiting ride in Albuquerque.

The approach to Canyon de Chelly is not encouraging. The town of Chinle sprawls in often-swirling sand at the main inter-section—a cluster of convenience stores, fast-food franchises, coin laundries, and video-rental establishments. The low complex of Chinle schools is surrounded by a chain-link fence cluttered with hand-lettered signs announcing community activities. Further down the road, a red-striped chicken bucket offsets the hexagonal shape of the local Catholic Church. To either side, the pale, fragile-looking layers of Chinle sandstone look like unkempt remains of strip mining rather than a natural formation.

As we approached monument headquarters, I was apprehensive. I'd been to the canyon as a visitor and knew it was nearby and spectacular, but in the past I had ignored Chinle and the daily life of the Navajo people. Now, I was looking through a new lens—at the open-range cattle rummaging through sparse vegetation at the side of the road, at the government-built housing falling into disrepair in the dry dust of fenced enclaves. As we drove, I talked with the two soft-spoken Navajo rangers who picked us up at the airport. They were in Albuquerque to shop for the three-day training hike and orientation for new staff that would take place in the canyon. We were to be joined by Navajo and non-Navajo naturalists, healers, archaeologists, and others with special knowledge of the region. I was assured that Rachel was welcome. In fact, other kids would meet us as we hiked a twenty-mile stretch of the north side of the canyon. It seemed like a great way to learn, and I looked forward to it as we were taken to our three-room duplex to unpack and begin the summer.

The training hike was an introduction to both Canyon de Chelly and the people with whom I would work for the next four months. Together, we staffed the Visitor Center, hiked the trails, and presented programs. The workday was ten hours long, but I seldom looked at a clock. Some days I was up and out by 7:30 A.M., dressed in ball cap, shirt, and hiking shorts, ready to lead the morning hike. On others, I was in the amphitheater at 9:00 P.M. in full dress uniform, welcoming people to Canyon de Chelly through a multimedia evening program. Within a week after arrival, Rachel apprenticed herself to the local riding stable. She was given her own mount and accompanied her Navajo co-workers guiding visitors through the wash, while I held forth to a trailing group of morning hikers. I was learning. I was looking.

Like the tourists who come to visit, the Park Service is at the canyon as a guest of the Navajo people. Home to the Navajo since the early 1700s, Canyon de Chelly continues to be both a place of residence and a location of great sacred significance. At the same time, visitation to the area is increasing, as the canyon gains a growing reputation among tourists. The legislation establishing Canyon de Chelly as a national monument in 1931 gave the National Park Service primary responsibility for the management of prehistoric resources and visitation, in order to "preserve its prehistoric ruins and features of scientific or historical interest." As I worked, it became clear that today's goals are broader and more complex. Visitors are encouraged to experience the canyon's scenic and archaeological beauty. At the same time, they are reminded that they are on Navajo land and must respect the privacy of the residents. Moreover, tourism must take place in a way that does not cause further deterioration of the archaeological resources.

The Navajo Nation retains ownership of the land, creating a relationship between the park service and the Navajo that requires constant communication. Though the monument provides employment for a number of residents, many Navajos continue to suspect the federal government's intentions. The fear that the government will eventually force residents to leave their homes, fields, and flocks is one that constantly resurfaces. When the decision was made to designate the canyon as a protected area in 1931, few Navajo were involved. Today, tribal members are closer to policy decisions than they were then, but after renewed discussion in the 1990s, responsibility for management still belongs to the National Park Service.

I came to Canyon de Chelly to be a ranger, not an anthropologist. More than half of my co-workers were Navajos from the canyon who were skilled in translating their culture for the benefit of first-time visitors to the area. The remainder of the staff were non-Navajos. Many had training in some branch of anthropology or natural history or were volunteers with education and interests that coincided with the Monument's needs. As we worked, we engaged in a continuous exchange of values and perception—Navajos testing the white point of view, non-Navajos slowly opening the cloak of our own beliefs.

As I walked through the deep corridors of the canyon, pondering the remains left by prehistoric dwellers or exchanging shy greetings with time-worn grandmothers, something was happening. As an anthropologist, I was enthralled by the struggle to create a balance between cultures taking place among my Navajo friends and their families. Academic questions formed in my mind. Could the volume of tourism be increased without altering the cultural terrain? Would it be possible for the Navajo to continue to use the canyon's resources to meet their physical and spiritual needs without altering the natural and archaeological landscape? Could the Park Service preserve and conserve the archaeological resources while also encouraging visitation? How did the Navajo view the process of change? To what extent did they want to share in the values and goods being brought into the area?

At the same time, as a human being, I watched as the flickering tongues of a bonfire sent dancing shadows against the canyon wall during the training hike. Later, I listened to the stories of creation and continuity, learning of the Navajo Way. As the weeks passed, I found myself asking questions long silenced by the need for security and material comfort, by work and school and parenting, by VCRs and automobiles. Now, hiking side canyons and scrambling up the talus slopes, perennial issues surfaced. How did my beliefs and values contribute to a world on the verge of ecological crisis? How had I ignored the interconnectedness between living things that was so basic to the worldview of my Navajo co-workers? What was the shape of god, and could I discern it?

In spite of this, as the summer progressed, I was sometimes disappointed by how long it was taking to develop friendships with the other rangers. In fact, Rachel was learning more about Navajo culture than I was. Taken into the family of her "employers," she picked up some of the language and spent much of her time in their home. But as the summer drew to a close, I found myself invited to spend some days in the canyon with one of my Navajo co-workers and her family. Though I'd worked with Margarita Dawson for almost four months, listening to her sweet and musical voice describe Navajo traditions to fascinated visitors, we'd just begun to talk to each other. In a sense, we were thrown together, the only two seasonals left as Labor Day approached.

One evening, as the long hours of work drew to a close, Margarita suggested that we hike down to the canyon floor along White House Trail. Her sister had a hogan there, a traditional Navajo dwelling, near the junction of the two canyons. As rangers, we took that trail at least three times a week, and I swore that it was so familiar I could hike it in my sleep.

The night was August chill and new-moon black as we made our way into the canyon. We started down, and I stepped cautiously, following instinct and my companion, convinced that she must know the way. After ten minutes we paused, measuring the shadows against the slope of the path. Margarita's voice floated across to me through the darkness.

"Where's the tra-il??" she called, incredulously. We stumbled into each other, laughing and shuddering as we remembered the sheer drop to where the wash bubbled through, six hundred feet below. We picked our way carefully in search of the dried mud switchbacks. Margarita's words continued, lilting and comforting, in the place of flashlights.

From down below a horse whinnied, startling us as the sound echoed against the sandstone.

"It's that white horse," Margarita said. "That horse's been down there close to fifteen years. He's wild. Nobody can catch him."

My pack and sleeping bag bounced off my back as I bent to find a line of marking stone amid the low grass and gravel. I pictured the horse easily, a constant observer during my morning hikes. Suddenly Margarita turned. The trail was where it should have been, a little to the left and just beyond a line of swaying greasewood. We stood in the night, relieved and reassured, talking of our lives and dreams. As with the trail, the way was there before us. We began walking it together in that quiet evening of acquaintance, cautiously at first, the beginning of a journey of question and discovery for each of us and our families and friends.

One of the friends who would come to know Margarita and her family was photographer Charles Winters, a friend and co-worker of mine in New York. Charlie and I were both admirers of Lewis Hines and the photographic social documentaries of the 1930s. We had worked together to produce a book in that tradition, which focused on the decline of the family farm in upstate New York.

Before leaving Canyon de Chelly, I asked Margarita how she felt about a similar project that would focus on her family and the families of the other Navajo rangers. I believed that Charlie's photography would allow us to give something back to the Navajo people, who would have to tolerate the intrusive lens of the camera and the awkward presence of the anthropologist, if we were to produce a lasting document of a changing way of life.

Margarita passed the farm book around, then invited Charlie and me to come back during the winter. After much discussion, we worked out an arrangement with the Park Service wherein both Charlie and I would provide volunteer services in exchange for canyon access. He and I returned several times during the next four years. Sometimes we were together, sometimes alone. At times the visits were wondrous; at others, they were painful reminders that understanding and friendship come slowly, and only after much time, conversation, and contemplation.

July 1991

It was July and hot. Charlie had arrived the previous week, and he, Margarita, and I walked down to her land at the Junction at 9:30 A.M., under a burning sun. Reluctant to hike with heavy packs, we had hailed a Thunderbird Lodge tour truck and put Carla, her daughter, on it with the gear and water.

Margarita had begun to expand her homestead, inching toward her dream of reestablishing a farm at the old location. The newly enlarged shade house sheltered a double bed, which sat on a frame of gray plastic milk crates. With their openings facing out, the crates could also be used for storage. A few cabinets had been built by an uncle, and a small dome tent was pitched so that its door opened into the arbor. In front of the kitchen area, faced stone blocks from a dismantled hogan waited to be made into a cooking hearth later in the day.

We walked back toward the canyon wall to the apricot trees laden with ripe fruit. Margarita climbed a tree, shaking a limb so that the fruit could drop to where Carla and I stood with buckets. We ate greedily of the sweet and juicy apricots before taking the remainder back to the shade house to be split and placed on plastic dish drainers to dry.

Margarita was nostalgic. "When I was little, there was an orchard of apricots and peaches, and the family would fill the wagon, taking the fruit out of the canyon to dry or sell. It was a happy time. I remember driving the horses past the irrigation system." She paused. "We still had irrigation then—it came from pools and springs where the canyon walls come together back there. We had so many apples, growing behind fields of corn and squash." Of the apple orchard, only two gnarled trees remained, and these were sorely in need of pruning. One solitary peach tree struggled to survive in the dry soil.

We had come into the canyon to work, to fit into Margarita's days off as many of the tasks of building a home and farm as we could accomplish. We began to dig out the old fire circle, shoveling rich ash into boxes that we hauled out to the deep furrows of a plowed field. The ash removed, we enlarged the pit, circling it with the heavy stone, facing the opening to the east. A red tailgate from an old Ford pick-up, reflector still in place, became a shelf and grate across the pit for cooking. Once the grate was positioned, Margarita built a fire, and we began to prepare supper by dropping a bundle of fresh-picked Navajo tea into boiling water.

The smell of the paint burning off the tailgate mixed with the rich odor of bread frying as we cooked this first meal in the new kitchen. It was a strange menu, canned foods and noodles and finally, the thick pads of a prickly pear roasted over the coals in the fire. Margarita was experimenting, reaching back into the apricot-summers to remember exactly how it was that her grandmother had made this food.

We pulled a charred pad out of the fire and turned it over carefully. The center was soft, and I tried to peel off the burned skin as you would do with a roasted pepper. Margarita looked at me skeptically.

"I think my grandmother did it different," she said with a laugh.

After dinner, Carla took Charlie and me over to a small cave at the back of the property. It had handprints and pictographs and a star ceiling. The falling night was exquisite. A clear coral wrapper of light illuminated Carla and the irregular rectangle of the cave's entrance. The air was filled with swirling cottonwood tufts, like the sideways blizzard of a winter snow. We sat quietly for a while, and Charlie photographed. Finally, the light faded and the sun went down. We climbed back out, tired and ready for bed. A pregnant canyon kitty mewed in the darkness, her cries echoing off the dark mass of Dog Rock, looming solid against the blue-black horizon.

We'd vowed to greet the dawn as any grandma would, rising before the sun to try and reach the peninsula rim before the light, Up Yei trail we went, groping for sand-filled hand-and-toeholds, legs screaming. I heard a cock crow but could not tell from where. We walked silently, Margarita ahead. She was dressed in blue warm-up pants, with a red-and-white-checked shirt, her thick black hair pulled back. At the top of the trail, she stood watching her piece of land drowsing in the dawn below. There was the persistent cry of a rooster and the tinkling of a goat bell from over on the south rim.

"When I was little, we went up this trail in the mornings to the goats who were corralled here, then climbed back down, all before breakfast. It seemed so natural," Margarita remembered.

A criss-cross of old twisted wood made up the goat corral, while a series of tossed boulders formed a natural pen close to the edge of the rim. A storage area of flat piled sandstone and upright slabs stood at the perimeter. There were grey pottery shards scattered everywhere—Navajo-made—near an old hogan that stood silently. Its door was perfectly placed, to look toward morning's arrival. Beyond it, a datura bloomed in the shaded light. Some of Margarita's family had been born in that hogan, when its now-skeletal roof beams were covered with mud mortar and the wind was louder than the sound of the autos heard making their way along the canyon's South Rim.

The sun peeked through, its orb poking through a slit in the hogan. A few rays hit the aqua berries of a juniper, as blue as Margarita's warm-up pants. We walked down to a point above the farm, to the place where gathered firewood had been thrown down to the canyon floor. A great deal of wood filled the cut now, all juniper splintered by the fall. One piece stood upright, embedded in the soil.

We came down from Yei separately. The day before, Charlie and I had climbed to a ledge in a side canyon near the farm. In a back crevice, a baby's burial had eroded out and was now visible. I told Margarita about it.

"I checked on that burial," she said when she returned. "I don't like going near it, but I wanted to be sure everything was okay. I added some cover, and it made me think. I walked through some places I haven't been in a long time—remembered my family and what we used to do each day."

Somewhere near noon, with no sign of the needed July rain, Margarita and I headed into the field to water and prune the fruit trees. We gave some water to the young peach tree that struggled to stay alive in the brittle, cracked soil. We tried to remember the correct season to trim back dangling branches.

"When do you prune?" I yelled to Charlie, who had remained in the shade house.

"Any time you got the shears with you," he replied, sharing rural New York farm wisdom.

Since we had the shears and the saw with us, it seemed like a good time to cut down a few ambitious Russian olives growing on a high ledge above. It was a short but steep climb, using eroded handholds, and it left us below ochre, red, and white-painted panels of antelope and Hopi figures. A round stone-and-mortar storage cyst in the narrow alcove, which once held dried corn and fruit throughout the winter, now was empty and crowded by the trees. We walked to the end of the ledge and talked, close and warm, sharing bits of our lives and memories. We talked about Margarita's marriage, now heading for divorce, and about the young man with whom I was involved. We talked about our daughters growing up without fathers and about our own philosophies of life. Finally, we took the saw and began to cut. In the crack at the back of the ledge a line of blue yucca grew, and in the damp moss of the sandstone seep, a tiny piñon. We cut the olives, ruthless water eaters, and took great joy in throwing them over the edge. We talked about reestablishing the irrigation and about bringing in Navajo and non-Navajo student groups to work.

"What do you think it would take for me to run the farm again, the way it used to be?" Margarita wondered.

I thought briefly about my own land in New York and its idle acres.

"A hell of a lot of courage, and a good deal of help."

October 1992

"I don't know what we're gonna do with the sheep," said Margarita, matter-of-fact.

Margarita, Charlie, and I were standing near a small juniper fire, warming ourselves from the midnight chill. We had just driven forty miles in the darkness through the Chuskas to attend a Ye'ii'bechai healing ceremony. Though it was only mid-October, the nighttime temperatures were in the twenties, and frost kissed the piñon and ponderosa of the high country. The thundering storms of summer were fast asleep.

I looked at Marlene curiously. "What sheep?"

We'd come over from Tsaile in a Geo Metro with Aunt Noreen, who had been asked to join one of the groups of dancers participating in the ceremony. A series of small fires edged a grassy runway leading up to a large hogan. I could hear the faint sounds of singing from within the hogan as we waited for the first dancers to appear.

Margarita leaned closer to the fire, warming her hands as she spoke. "I just talked to Noreen. They asked her to be lead dancer for her group. That means that she's got to dance at least three times, probably stay until 4:30 A.M. It also means that the patient's family is gonna give her a sheep."

I nodded, thinking about the luggage space behind the back seat of the Metro. It was just about the right size. "Is it dead or alive?" I asked calmly.

"It's a live one," Margarita told me, surprised that I needed to ask. "It's a big one." She looked at me, and we laughed and decided to worry about it later. The night was just beginning.

We had arrived at about 11:30 P.M., parking the Metro amidst a sea of pickups. Looking around the groups of people huddled near the many fires, I saw that there were only two other white people—*biligána*—present. As on other occasions, I felt uncomfortable, as though I'd come to be a spectator at someone's personal consultation with his doctor. Even after three years, I wasn't sure if Charlie and I were welcome.

The fires burned brightly, but there was no central bonfire as there had been at the summertime Squaw Dance. At the far end of the corridor stood a circular brush arbor, the Yei house. In the glow of the firelight shining from within, I could just discern figures moving about, but their features and their identities were hidden to us.

This was the last night of a nine-day healing ceremony, the night that the Yeis and Talking God danced. As we waited, speaking in quiet tones, four dancers approached. All male, dressed in white clay and elaborate kilts, masked and feathered, they wore broad collars of fresh spruce. In one hand, each dancer carried a gourd rattle; in the other a spruce bough. Deerskin medicine pouches hung across one shoulder, a foxtail dangled almost to the feet. They stood silent and unmoving in their high moccasins, waiting before the hogan. Clad in buckskins, masked like the others, Haashch'ééltí'í—Talking God—was with them.

Moon was a lazy half, lying on her side. Her long beams mixed with firelight as the patient and medicine man joined the dancers. The patient was a young boy, and he sat swaddled in a blanket, before the line of dancers. The healer was tall, gray-haired and robed. Slowly, the Ye'ii'bechai began to dance, singing, shaking rattles, repeating purposeful steps four times before returning to the Yei house.

The patient entered the hogan, and the guests began to talk and move about. Across from us, a small trailer served as a concession stand, selling coffee and snacks for the long night's vigil. A loudspeaker system gave a running commentary in Navajo on what was happening. Suddenly, the voice switched to English.

"I realize that there are some Anglos present," said the booming voice. My heart dropped. How embarrassing it would be to be asked to leave, to be told we were unwelcome. "Please don't take any pictures," the voice continued.

Charlie and I looked at each other. They were talking about *us*! We nodded in the darkness, agreeing that we wouldn't have considered it. Ceremonies, we had learned, were not an appropriate place to take pictures. Photographs were accurate records—they showed exactly how people were dressed and what they were doing. You couldn't alter a small detail as you did in the telling of a story to outsiders.

The speaker continued. "I want to thank you for taking the time out of your busy schedules to come and support my grandson for this time of healing. Thank you for coming. You are welcome."

I looked toward the voice in amazement. It was as if he had sensed my awkwardness and had gone out of his way to dispel it. I realized then that healing was a community endeavor, one in which all your friends joined to give support. When you were ill, out of harmony, you were not left to suffer alone. It was a subtle touch. Standing in the firelight and darkness, the mystery of the night was multiplied, and the healing reached from the patient to encircle all those waiting. I thought about inviting my entire extended family to my next doctor's appointment.

Thirty minutes later, the sound of the gourd rattles began again. This time there were more than twenty dancers, paired men and women. The men were dressed like the first group, the women in skirts and full blouses. We spotted a masked dancer in mossy green, with the body and features of Aunt Noreen. She was at the head of a long line, dancing with her partner, as the patient again waited in his seat near the door of the hogan. The dance was slow, solemn, and methodical, comprised of paired Ye'ii'bechai, who were blessed by the patient between repetitions.

As we watched with fascinated concentration, we noticed a solitary dancer who wore a costume that was the reverse of all the others. As he pranced by, his foxtail waved from his mouth instead of his bottom.

"What's he all about?" Charlie asked curiously.

The dancer was going from spectator to spectator, performing elaborate pantomimes that left the crowd laughing. When he danced, he was one step behind. When he sang, he was one beat off.

"It's the clown, the trickster," I said to Charlie. "He bawdily mocks the entire ceremony and lets you know that the sacred ways are not inflexible." In his dance, the clown reminded us that what was up was also down, what was here was also there, what was life-threatening could become life-giving. I was glad to see him; he made me feel good, but I fervently hoped he wouldn't single us out for ridicule in front of the entire community.

Noreen danced all night, a masked figure moving through the moonlit hours. In the dawn, the sheep went home to Black Rock, becoming mutton for the new day's dinner. Watching the Yeis dance, I sent my prayers to the young patient and shared the night's blessings in return. I saw no human dancers that night—not Noreen, nor the Trickster nor Talking God. The players in that frosty clearing were the Yeis, alive and earthbound, endowed with the unmeasured power of timeless ceremony.

Although the October days were still long and golden in the cottonwood sunshine, winter was approaching. The sheep would soon be at their winter camps, the fall piñons dried and stored near the apricots of summer.

"You know, there was a biligana who came out here last summer and wanted a ceremony," Margarita told me, as she swept aside the layers of russet dust that had settled on the battered table in her canyon kitchen. We were down at the Junction, a final visit for me before I returned east to finish the fall semester.

"I went to this medicine man and asked him if he'd do it, and he said yes. But he told me it would cost the man three hundred dollars for one night's sing. I didn't know what to think about that. It was so much money. I asked the singer why it was higher than for a Navajo. You know what he answered?"

I shook my head, surprised that he would consider doing the ceremony in the first place.

"He said that when he does a sing for one of us, he knows that we have at one time been in balance, that something has interfered with our knowledge of this land and our relationship with the Holy People. There is *hozho*, it has been disturbed, it must be reestablished. For white people, though, it is different. You are so far away from harmony that he must first work to bring you to a base, to a starting point. You were not raised with our traditions and our beliefs, and so, to help you in our fashion, he must first clear away the residue of your own way of life, the chaos, the uncertainty, the disturbance. Then, and only then, can he begin to heal you."

To me, the explanation seemed logical and the price reasonable. We pay eighty dollars an hour to a psychologist; in that light, three hundred dollars for an all-night sing was a bargain, a down payment on understanding in a rapidly changing world.

Margarita opened a cabinet and took out a can containing dried Navajo tea. "How's your family?" she asked. "Are you going to bring

Rachel out for her *Kinaaldá* when she begins to menstruate?"

I shook my head. "No chance. She won't leave that horse," I answered. My daughter had gotten a horse of her own and now never left home.

"And your man?" Margarita continued.

"Not perfect," I said sadly.

We made some tea and a light dinner, deciding to take a short walk. The evening was chasing us, and we walked partway up Yei trail to meet it. In the low light, the canyon walls were a thick dusky rose, dotted with muted blue-green. The sun fell slowly through a raggedy bank of gray-purple clouds, layers of mesa becoming three-dimensional steps as the white glowing rays reached them. There was a steady hum from the road opposite on the South Rim, as persistent as the dusk wind across the rock. In the distance, a few lights began to glow from Chinle, autumn night beginning for the shift on duty at the Health Service hospital.

We started down; down again, against oncoming darkness. Our feet picked carefully along deep steps and ancient ledges filled with sand and lengthening shadow. Once on level ground, we walked silently to Margarita's waiting Suzuki Samurai. Turning once to watch the encasing night hug silhouetted stone, we locked in the hubs and gunned the engine. Plowing through the chill and mounded mud of the wash, we drove out of the canyon, silent—our separate lives mingling into oncoming winter.

Side Trips

In the summer of 1991, twenty of my students from the State University of New York joined members of Margarita's family and clan at her place near the Junction. Though the New Yorkers looked forward to the opportunity to learn about Navajo culture from the Navajo people, they soon realized that they were to play a similar role for Margarita's young nieces and nephews. Sharing work, meals, music, games, and dance, the groups spent three days in an exchange of ideas and customs. Residents from around the canyon dropped by, on hearing that there was a bunch of biligana visiting; turning us into the curiosity that the endless tour trucks made of the canyon residents.

The experience was wonderful and difficult. Grandmas marveled at the sight of men cooking, watching them add innumerable spices and vegetables to a typically bland mutton stew. Many of the students were vegetarians who—as good anthropologists—broke with their own traditions to eat meat. Several tried their hand at shaping bread, spinning the dough in the air with typical East Coast pizza-making skill.

"We don't play with our food!" scolded Margarita's mother, Karen. She had just corrected another cook who used a knife to stir the stew. "You don't stir with a knife. You cut with a knife," she told him, as Margarita translated.

There were times when we visitors fumbled, inadvertently hurting or offending those who had opened their lives. But at other moments, there was understanding and shared peace. One student, sensing the relatedness of all living beings, later wrote:

"This morning we listened to grandma Karen pray for all of us. I realized that . . . we are all brothers and sisters. Faces are different, but people are not. We are all one. There is no real difference. I did not need a translation."

Among our group that summer was a Japanese exchange student, a loud and exuberant young man who hailed the People as long-lost cousins. While the Navajo were not as quick to embrace him as a relative, they spent hours talking about what it was like to be a stranger, an outsider in another culture.

"Say something in Japanese! Sing a song," Noreen prodded him.

The student complied happily, offering a moving Japanese rendition of "Rudolph, the Red-nosed Reindeer" to his laughing audience.

In all, the visit was a success, a formative experience for all. Over the next year, the two groups corresponded, and in the spring of 1992 one of Margarita's nephews was chosen to represent the Navajo Nation on a visit to Japan. It was a startling proposition: to leave the reservation, to go beyond Phoenix, to cross the ocean, to visit a completely alien land. The family met and talked long and hard, considering the possibility as one examines a faceted stone. In the end, they drew on the experience of the summer before, their meeting with the American students and with one from Japan in particular. They agreed to let him go.

Returning, the youngster slowly described his journey.

"Auntie," he told Margarita wide-eyed. "Everywhere I went I was so famous!" It was the first of the exchanges that took place that year.

In the warm, wet northeastern August of 1992, I met a plane in Syracuse, New York, bringing Carla Dawson and her cousin Dezbah for a two-week visit to my rural home. Driving across the miles of rolling, verdant hills, the girls were astonished. What were all these tiny towns with ramshackle white buildings leaning lazily toward evening?

"Jeanne," Carla asked in her soft, teasing voice. "Where's *New York*?"

We picked up my daughter Rachel at the horse farm where she'd been working for the summer and stopped for two cheese and pepperoni pizzas on the way home. The pizzas spilled over the sides of the cardboard boxes holding them, filling the car with an East Coast aroma. At our house, in the mother-of-pearl dusk, the sign in front dubbed it the Evening Inn Farm and bade the travelers welcome.

In rained the first night, warm and inviting. Carla coaxed the other girls into a midnight roll in the thick green grass. I was awakened by the sound of their laughter mixing with the steady patter of rain-drops, the gentle downpour on soft lawn that would be a desert luxury. In the next days, the three girls were joined by a teenaged friend of Rachel's. The girls wandered the streets together, going to malls and movies, or dancing in the living room when the adults weren't looking.

Early one morning, we piled into the car and drove "downstate" to catch a commuter bus into New York City. On the way we stopped briefly at a sprawling suburban home, with an in-ground pool, twenty-five-year mortgage, and two-earner family. The girls were impressed, even my own daughter. But as we bumped along the New Jersey Turnpike in the bus, we counted the hours of commuting it took to support that kind of life, and some of the glamour vanished.

Approaching the City, the bus moved into the tiled, looming gullet of the Lincoln Tunnel.

"We're driving under the river?" Dezbah, asked fascinated. "How?"

A twenty-six-year veteran of life in New York, I was still con-founded by roads that drove under rivers, so my explanation to the girls was decidedly vague. They remained in awe when we arrived moments later at the Port Authority Bus Terminal on Forty-eighth Street.

The smell of browning pretzels mixed with the acrid fumes of too many buses as we hit the streets of Manhattan. Taxi horns blared as cars skimmed the curbs, drivers yelling obscenities in five languages. It was hot and steamy, a haze obscuring the tops of endless buildings as we navigated down packed streets to the Empire State Building.

Hot, palpable smog lay as a mantle above the city, reaching far across New Jersey. We looked down to where the mouth of the tunnel disgorged an endless stream of vehicles, marveling that we had just been below the river. Returning to the teeming pavement of Manhattan, we stopped at a souvenir shop. The proprietor looked at our group, the four of us dark-haired, wide-eyed, and ill at ease.

"Come inside and look at the cameras," he invited in flawless Italian, sizing us up and deciding it was the only possible nationality.

We returned exhausted to our mountain haven. The girls went to spend the second week with Charlie at his house a few miles down the road. They visited dairy farms and helped milk the cows. They went to a dinner with local poets, and Carla read some of her own poetry. Like most teens, they got bored hanging out with adults, but they had a good time.

At the end of the visit Carla and Dezbah flew back to Arizona. In a long family conference, they told of experiences, of stopping to pray as they had been taught, even in the alien terrain of New York State. Grandma Karen was proud that they had turned to what they knew and remembered.

The winter of 1993 was a hard one for both Margarita and me. Our personal lives were in disarray; her marriage finished in divorce, and my two-year relationship ended. We spoke on the phone, mingling our individual sadness. Margarita went to her mother for advice and in the spring she wrote:

> Jeanne, if you don't mind, as a friend, if I give you some support in the Navajo Way. I'd like to share several tips during troubled times that my mom gave me and it helped me a lot: You are the child of Mother Earth and Father Sky. They made *you*, only *you*, at a particular (sacred) time and place and nobody else or with nobody else, not your mom, father, grandfather, son, daughter, or husband (boyfriend). Because you are so special, child of Mother Earth and Father Sky, you are given only a few years of your lifetime to enjoy and treasure your loved ones on Mother Earth. You will never end your life with your loved ones, you will depart each other one after another. . . . When your time comes, you alone will be chosen to go back to Mother Earth and Father Sky for eternity. . . . No one departs or dies in a finished task, you die or depart preparing, not complete. . . . Your husband (boyfriend) comes into your life as a stranger, he will always be a stranger and will leave you as a stranger. You never deeply will be in love with him, you are put together only to try and make a peaceful, beautiful life—to produce. Besides, this stranger is not part of your clan, his flesh blood is totally different from yours. Your flesh blood is who you should care for . . ."

At the end of May 1993, Margarita Dawson left the park service after seven years of work. Her programs had reached thousands each year. Her words touched some visitors in a way that changed their lives. School groups began to come into the canyon and spend time on her land. She began to work toward her dream of establishing the Canyon de Chelly Diné Institute, a nonprofit cultural and educational center to teach Navajo youth and others to live in beauty with themselves, society, and others.

In the fall of 1993 I visited Margarita alone, as friend, leaving all anthropological intent at home. Carla was away at a Tuba City boarding school, a trial stay that ended in December. Margarita and

I hiked deep into the canyon, to a wonderful spot I'd never been shown. Then, we stopped at Black Rock to visit her mother, Karen, and two of her mother's sisters, who were just finishing a special ceremony. I walked into the house and greeted the older women.

"*Yaa' at' ah*," I said.

Karen, nodded. "*Out*," she said, meaning yes.

I looked at her, a little puzzled. She always greeted me with a big hug.

Karen turned to Margarita and said in Navajo, "Tell my daughter I'm sorry I can't hug her. We can't touch anyone until the ceremony is over."

Margarita translated, and I nodded in understanding. "Out," I said.

We had come to make sure that the older women had everything they needed. We'd seen Karen's husband, Leonard, out gathering plants, but he kept his distance during the ceremony. The three sisters seemed to be doing OK, and for a few moments I was envious of their warm, easy interactions with each other.

In the winter of 1994, Margarita joined her newly founded Diné Institute with an organization called Trees for Mother Earth (TFME), which was in its eighth year of bringing non-Navajo high school groups into the canyon area to plant fruit trees. Margarita became canyon coordinator for TFME, traveling all over the country during the late winter to raise funds and interest school groups in the project. We talked on the phone, setting up a canyon stay for my students during the upcoming summer.

I had come to Canyon de Chelly in 1990 as an anthropologist, a professional outsider, realizing that I was a person who thrashed about in the realities of other cultures because the one I was born into made no sense to me. In the intervening years Margarita and her relatives had shared much knowledge with my family and me, as we all attempted to create a balance between the logic of tradition and the relentless demands of the twentieth century. In exchange, I showed them the life I knew and tried to portray their lives in writing, with beauty and dignity. I watched Margarita grow and mature even as I sensed similar changes occurring in myself.

As the writing of this work progressed, I sent copies of the text back to Margarita. She read it to her family, and they made comments. They had asked not to be identified by their real names but were concerned about the names I'd given them.

"This is the twentieth century," said Noreen. "We want twentieth-century biligana names like Sue, or Joe." I'd used many Spanish-sounding names. Later, they decided to stick with these original choices.

Margarita commented on my writing and corrected places where I'd gotten something wrong. In the end, the fieldwork and the writing was a partnership, part of the exchange that this whole experience became—something Margarita talked about when she visited my classes in New York in March 1994!

This cycle of visits to the Navajo began in 1991, at the time of the Gulf War. That conflict was short-lived and is now just a memory. Almost four years later, daily wars continued to rage at Canyon de Chelly and across the reservation. Snow, floods, mud, and drought are cyclically occurring trials. Alcoholism, poverty, frustration, and uncertainty remain battles fought from day to day. Tradition, ceremony, pride, and ingenuity are the weapons used to fight them.

In the coming years, Charlie and his family and Rachel and I will return to the Canyon and its families. Relieved of the burden of documentation, we can just visit.

As anthropologists and as travelers, we go to the field of human experience to learn about relationships, to live in the physical and spiritual fabric of someone else's life, and then we leave. Returning home, the months are held in small spiral notebooks filled with scribbled thoughts and observations or seen in colored blankets displayed upon our walls. Within the familiar trappings of our own lives, we are somehow different. Like the image in a hall of mirrors, we are ourselves, reflected in their lives, reflected in ours. The legacy of the experience called fieldwork is change, subtle and blatant. Its challenge is not just to see and know other people, but to see ourselves in the reflecting pool of their realities; in the company of men and women, to learn what it is to be human.

JOHN O. STEWART

CARNIVAL MOURNING

Stewart was born in Trinidad and spent his childhood there. Consequently, his fieldwork on the island was as much an exercise in the excavation of self as anything else. Stewart recognizes the relationship between self-discovery and friendship in the wake of shockingly painful moments he recently had at the loss of certain friends in the field through death on the one hand and a less easily explained alienation on the other. As he reflects on these friendships that no longer exist, he reconnects with an earlier version of himself.

"Carnival Mourning" explores one set of possibilities in which the intersection linking friendship and identity is considered, with carnival and the "mopping up" of revolutionary guerrillas that occurred following the 1970 rebellion in Trinidad as significant backdrop influences. The symbolic relationship between carnival and revolution needs no elaboration. In this explanation individual identity stands at the third corner of a triangle, and friendship is the force that energizes and elucidates the relationship among all three.

I

They are dancing down below. They are jam-packed on the open patio and all around the narrow green pool. All in between the chairs and tables. Dancing. The music is sweet. Even from where he is up on the fourth floor the music is sweet, coming through as he cracks the window. Tenor pans on the melody, bass pans rumbling the beat of what must be a new calypso. He wanted to open the window wide and let the music come flush into his face, but this window is spring-locked and can open no further. To save the air-conditioning, they say. Which they put in for people who can't stand heat. People who don't know how to take heat. "People from America don't know how to take heat. . . . So give him a room with conditioner." That's what Phyllis Coudray said last year. Those were her words, her instruction to the middle-aged clerk beside her who was handling the keys. He had smiled and said, "I born in Trinidad, you know," and she had with a sweet smile of her own returned, "But you're away long time, not so?"

That was Phyllis Coudray . . . whom the new clerk on the desk tonight claimed she did not know. "I only working here since the hotel went on strike last week. Let me ask the doorman. He might know her . . . Carl! Carl! . . . This gentleman here is asking after one Phyllis Coudray. You know what to tell him?"

215

Carl, almost as tall as the door itself, is dressed in a green uniform. He has no holster clipped to the broad belt around his waist but carries a heavy nightstick swinging at his side. Beneath the dark visored cap his face is solid in the jaw; he has the mended nose of an experienced fighter. He does not know Phyllis Coudray either. "I on this door nights, going three months now. I never see nobody working here by that name . . ."

"Do you know Rodney?"

"Who he?"

"He was the doorman here carnival time last year. You know him?"

"No. I never hear 'bout no Rodney neither . . ."

No Phyllis Coudray, no one who knew her, and suddenly it seemed he had come a long way to face emptiness and disappointment. It never came up last year, where she lived, what her private life entailed, or where else he might find her. And all through spring, summer, and the fall he'd felt no need to write or call either. Carnival was a memory carried in the gut, and he was pleased to leave it there encysted in its own mystery. Then winter came, and in one of those enclosed moments when he was safely indoors from the Chicago cold, warming himself in front of a fire, the drum vibrations rose. Echoes of a melody rose spontaneously. Slowly, leisurely at first, lazy slivers of sound arching through his consciousness. The sound of voices, drums, a chanting from the sky, coming from somewhere inside him too, echoing, taking shape in the form of Phyllis Coudray. This Creole woman who stepped out of the pages of history for him last year, from the boudoirs and marketplaces of the eighteenth century, a cocktail of the races intoxicating wherever she passed through salon, street, or yard, or the lobby of an old hotel, Phyllis Coudray. Cocktail of the islands, dancing to the drums of jouvay, Phyllis Coudray, her arms raised dancing through the heat of the day, into the dark night, through the unbroken hours of sweat and hot handling, and he had to see her again. And here he was. Only she is not here, and no one could tell him where to find her.

"How long you're staying?" The new clerk wanted to know. She would not have been a courtesan in Europe, or a concubine in New Orleans. She is New World Asian. One of those whom a certain writer calls "the beautiful Asiatics"—or something like that. She did not carry the flavor of lilac and caramel. She is slender. her dusky skin is smooth, her narrow face as flawless as a newborn. There is the aroma of the garden rising from her hair as she bends to make the entry. Her fingers are slightly bigger than the pen with which she writes. She's new. She does not know Phyllis Coudray. But she gives him the same room—fourth floor, two doors west of the elevator. If he had the calypsonian's talent, he could make a song out of this.

He should go down to the dance below. Pan music always drives his pulse to a pitch bordering on loss of self-control. It demanded surrender to the instincts for union. Reunion. With what, didn't matter. With whom? That didn't matter much either. Reunion with what one of the people's poets called "the force." Phyllis could be in the crowd down there, dancing the way she did last year. Then again she might not be. For now, he'll wait. No need to rush down there and possibly come up empty. For now he'll wait, and trust to destiny. He would, as a matter of fact, sit down and make the first entry in his field log the way he is supposed to do. There is a certain satisfaction in that. It is, after all, what the Research Committee expects him to be doing. It is what as a professional ethnographer he promises to be remembered for—a scientific observation of the carnival—and this was the textbook way to get started. On reentry to the field catch all immediate details at the first opportunity. Repetition dulls. Tomorrow this room will not feel the same.

i

When we landed at dusk, I had the strongest feeling that this was an inappropriate time to arrive. I don't know why. It was just a feeling. I say "dusk," but really what I mean are those few moments between sunset and full darkness that comes so quickly in the tropics. The hills above Piarco still showed a tint of red from the sun already out of sight, but shadows down below were swiftly making the coconut palms around the airport indistinct from the general background of green—the first color to lose its outline to the night.

The airport was not as busy as expected. No 707s disgorging streams of passengers jostling to be first inside the terminal. Instead, I see three C-5s on the tarmac. They look quite out of place and menacing. Their bomb-shaped noses tower above the clutter of local craft, and nothing in view matches the powerful angle of their slanted gray wings. Gray is not a popular color at carnival. It is the color of death and mourning. Is this part of the world to be shaken by that thunder from the clouds that shattered so recently over Vietnam?

Off our plane disembarking was quite orderly. Even among those coming home from New York for the festival there was none of the usual spontaneous shouts, the salutations, the bragging about how much fete true aficionados would put down, the hurried exchange of addresses and telephone numbers, and promises to "catch up" with travel partners for some highlight or the other. Too quiet. There was no steel band at the gate. Many uniformed police, though, and others who were clearly officers, though they wore casual clothes. There were lots of guns in evidence. The uniformed men all wore holsters, and those in casual dress carried bulges in their hip pockets.

Through immigration, then customs, and out into the lobby, people seemed subdued. The volatile gestures and rapid talk I remember from last year, very little of it was there. There were Canadians in the lobby—lots of them. Some South Americans. The bunch ahead of me through the lines were West Germans. They laughed and talked. Their excessively pink faces were sweaty, and their eyes glittered as they talked, switching from their own language into English, then back and forth. The whole world comes to Trinidad for carnival. Yes. But where were the Trinidadians? The dusky faces here to pick up relatives and friends were almost somber. They hung back. A few, fashionably dressed, carried their bags with straight faces, children dutifully at their sides.

In the back of the taxi that carried some Germans and myself through the canes of Caroni, then past the roadside vendors installed on both sides of the highway, on into the city and the old hotel, my uneasiness remained. The Germans and the Indian driver chatted all the way. Trinidad is a safe country, he kept telling them. Nobody to bother you when you're making your spree for carnival. What about tickets to the Dimanche Gras show?, they wanted to know. No problem: he knew where to get those. And what else could he do for them, a trip to Maracas? To the bird sanctuary? Did they want to see the Moruga volcano? "You have to have something to do after carnival, you know, and you can't trust everybody," he kept saying to them. Perhaps they will visit Tobago.

All through the lighted streets of Port-of-Spain, past the waterfront and on through Independence Square, where I could see the small black and white police cruisers, my uneasiness remained. All up to the empty space behind the reception desk where there was no Phyllis Coudray, but a delicate clerk who kept her flinty eyes on business, and Carl, the new doorman who had never heard of Phyllis, and up to this familiar room the uneasiness remains. The steel band is playing down below. Around the pool they are singing and dancing. From the window four floors above, the shimmering leaf-shaped pool casts its green light back onto the dancers, the tables with their nests of upright bottles, the empty chairs, the band squeezed into an angle where the stem would be if this were in fact a real leaf.

ii

Beyond the outdoor lighting of the hotel, the night is dark and silent. Within that large silence the music of the steel band rings out clear and sweet. It is a brave music. I listen and I call on it to displace my uneasiness as I sit here in this room of a gone era. Shuttered doors on the closet caked in stiff white paint, polished mahogany floor worn pale between the bed and bathroom. The single bed has its tight top sheet folded back; a small cedar desk with chair off to the right, and at the foot of the bed a carved mahogany washstand with nothing on it except one glass and a thermos jug of ice water. A room built for gentlemen on field duty—down to the brass call button in the wall above the pillow.

Stalwarts of the old regime would have passed through here. New clerks to the colonial secretaries and colonial attorney generals waiting for their official residences to be freshened and readied. Auditors, investigators, commissioners from the Home Office on their way to some further outpost, or here on his/her majesty's service. A room for such as these. Despite the air conditioner fastened into the window it carries still the humid mustiness that must have marked for them the difference between civilized home and the domain known as "the colonies." This is one of the oldest hotels in the city, and the owners must have a great nostalgia for colonial times. They have tried to keep this place just as it was in the days when the Union Jack flew over Government House. The concessions in modern plumbing and a pedestal television set make little difference. Darkness coils at the corners of the ceiling, and I smell more than a suggestion of sweat and decay coming from the old wood.

iii

Down below, the green-lit pool reflects its rippling shadows among the dancers. The steel band music is very sweet. They go round and round. I should be there among them. In Chicago I never think of myself as missing the steel band. But I do hear something special in it.

Once, almost thirty years ago, I wanted to play pan. At daybreak that year, when the bands came out for jouvay, when the "Free French," then "Bataan" drummers chipped on by, I heard myself in the music. In the company of other young boys whom I didn't even know we followed the band. For miles around town my heart marched in great strides to the boom right up ahead, and what of me remained quivered on the refrain repeated over and over again on the ping pong. But the true center of harmony and force bared itself in the many voices of the tenor pan. A person could ground there. And even though one may never know where the journey of this force will end, when daylight came up, the serious faces on the drummers, men who in the everyday world would have been closed strangers, this was exactly the same hard face I wished to borrow. And I borrowed it too. And marched. Even when the battles broke out, and with all the other boys my age I ran for cover from the flying bottles and stones, fighting myself for a safe place from which to see the main knife fights, even then I didn't change that face, and it would only be a matter of time before I came into my own daring. Those around me had better know that. I sent signals too. I turned my school cap *backward, turned my shirt wrong side out, and hovered near the boom again when the bands got past each other. I would be a warrior when my day came.*

But I was a child; and those who make decisions for children had other plans for me.

That music down below reminds how deep a tearing had occurred when I first left Trinidad. I didn't know it then. Leaving was the path to glory, fame. The promise of a brilliant, professional future could swathe over the jagged edges of family and friends left behind, the sounds and smells of Christmas, the metamorphosis of carnival, that time of year when men became truly what they were—kings or warriors, thieves or robbers, clowns, or the dreaded devil. But the warrior king I would have become, with stick or knife in hand, the blood-catching band around my forehead, dancing in the heat of the people's voice, he never quite died. Surreptitiously nurtured upon unsung lavway he survived beneath the gauze, and perhaps if I had been more attentive time would have turned out differently. Perhaps if I had been more attentive I would not have gone so many years without acknowledging his voice inside. But that's nonsense. Because even now I go for months in Chicago without feeling the difference. It is the music down below that makes me take in shallow breaths, and tells me how we acquiesce in loss, and warns I won't ever be satisfied because it is the only satisfaction. It can't be bought: it can't be stolen: it can't be borrowed. It comes, and I can fly exalted wherever it crests, or toss in its nether rumble as it goes. There will be no sorrow should I fail to find Phyllis Coudray. I don't go to the glitter of that pool down there. I stay in this room, and turn to my "work" to fight this trembling.

He turns off the air-conditioner, and now the steel band music comes in more clearly. He returns to the chair at the little cedar desk and gets out a second loose-bound notebook. These pages are already covered with double-spaced typescript, between commentaries in his small handwriting along the wide margins. He searches through the pages, then stops to read. He searches again, then stops to read again. This is his manuscript. This is the text in which he explains the symbolic structure of Trinidadian culture . . . based on what he had learned of formal theory, his experience as a son of the soil then anthropologist, plus what had to be taken from history, and scrupulous observation in the field. In this delineation of a symbolic structure at the heart of Trinidadian culture the textual strategy is orthodox. Four sections to historical background—"Pre-Columbian origins," "Spanish Colonialism," "British Colonialism," "Post-colonial Independence," then chapters on the economic system, political system, organization of domestic life, the religious and educational systems, urbanization.

He has more than three hundred pages, and yet not much of it comes close to saying anything real about a symbolic structure. What is a symbolic structure? So clearly stated as a theory—even if he didn't fully understand all that he should about lateralization—a symbolic element linking clusters of performances in everyday life was still not an easy thing to specify. A concern at the heart of much of his brooding. He turns the pages rapidly and comes to the last section. The regular typescript gives way to yellow note paper covered in his cramped handwriting. He leans forward and props his brow on the heel of his hand now. He pulls the notebook closer. And with the concentration of a surgeon going over a procedure for tomorrow he slows down, and goes over the pages carefully, one at a time.

This is why he's here. This is why, he had told the Committee, he had to come again to the island. One more time he had to come, since here somewhere there must be the key to fully unlock essentials that he knew inside, but that nevertheless resisted when he assumed to express them in a formal fashion. He hopes there is such a key. And this time he would very carefully pay attention to the small details. Write them down. Put them in place. So that they would bring life to the understanding on these pages. Bring substance to the abstract analysis already on these pages . . . *beliefs, the great majority of them, do not normally find an outlet in practice . . . When patterns become obsolete, practice will generally disappear while belief lingers . . . on the other hand, in certain cases, practice survives while belief is forgotten, and new reasons for practice are invented . . .* he writes on the last page. *Nowhere has the divergence between practice and belief been more ardently cultivated than in these Western territories, the former colonies, where thought evolves slower than a snail's pace.* This time he knew exactly where he would look.

And this time he would treat the ideas one by one, and settle for a partial structure if he had to, one which could later be expanded. The process, after all, could be unending. But the ritual confrontation, that was it. A system of echoes—that was it—where an unnamed, perhaps unacknowledgeable third party figured in the trials between men, and in the linkage between layers of social thought and performance. A third party that belong to no one, that masked itself at will, that multiplied its voice at will, imposing the test of farce on every duel.

Under the weak table lamp that leaves all corners of the hotel room in darkness he writes—*One of the crises in Trinidadian society has to do with the relocation of central power from strong men and lineage heroes to more widely integrative and growing structures. This crisis is more often addressed as a political problem, but it pervades other social arenas as well, since the shift involves the whole conceptual order of society . . . The gayal and the stickman continue to be power predicates, but on a vastly reduced scale, and for an almost negligible number of people. (The gayal has been supplanted by the marketplace in which one side always wins, the other always loses.) But it is not difficult to find people with powerful stickfight stories. The image of the "bois-man"—lone warrior carayed against the sky—is imprinted on the national imagination. He is survivor of an archetypal order—that may well be regenerated should the conceptual network of power relationships shift to make individual heroism central to social structure once again. (Do the young guerillas in the bush think this way?) Symbolically, the traditional gayal was gateway and arena. It was the gateway to community, the arena where communal expression of the ancient combat myth was acted out (and life in Trinidad is nothing if not combat) . . . The true stickman is a fierce character: the fighter who is both hero and fool/sacrifice . . . The grace with which he receives or delivers the telling blow protects all from chaos and dispossession . . . When a stickman dies no special attention is given to his burial. Other stickmen attend the funeral if they regard him as a friend or kin, but not out of allegiance to any stickfighting brotherhood. . . .*

. . . In attempting to account for the decline in stickfighting it has to be taken into consideration that the stickman traditionally needed a good measure of hero-worship, and the present society is much less disposed to grant such to any individual or class of individuals at this time. . . . Yet, the political violence which threatens now promises to be of such irrational proportions as to make the ritual stickfight appear quite humane . . . and on he writes. In time, he's consulting the books on theory that he's brought along with him, making revisions around his fresh paragraphs, and additional notes either on the manuscript page or on individual index cards that he stacks neatly from right to left as he goes along.

At fifteen after midnight the steel band is still playing. He straightens up and stretches. It would have been nice if he had remembered to bring a bottle of rum with him up to the room. A drink would go well now. But this hotel has no room service at this hour.

If the music was mixed with other sounds before, they are all dropped away by now. The drummed melody clean and sweet through the cracked window reigns as though it were the only sound in the world. And when he looks down on the patio, the dancers are still there, yet something about them has changed. Not many jumping and marching about in between the tables. Clustered on the cleared space before the band they dance in a single mass, bobbing and grinding in unison, and when they raise their voices in the chorus of the calypso it is cleanly airborne. No stragglers. And as they repeat again, and again, he submits to the tempo. His knees flex up and down in unison. And finally giving way to the now earned desire, he leaves the room for downstairs. He is mildly awakened again to his desire to see Phyllis Coudray and wonders what might he say if he really sees her.

The small courtyard is fenced right up to the outer wall of the hotel. There is a bougainvillea arbor along the long side of the fence; the pool sits in the middle. Lush decorative plants around the deep and far sides form an inky tangle, which nevertheless takes on a festive shape, with small red and green lights dangling in between the foliage. Giant ferns, fine leaf palms, and poinsettias, he could recognize these. Ixora, lilies, and blooming hibiscus. Beyond the blazing spotlights hung on tall poles around the bandstand empty space goes up to the sky, murky dark at this hour, and sprayed with stars. The steel band sound fills everywhere. On the wooden bandstand decorated as though it were an overgrown sea shell the players are deeply concentrated on their drums. Some are dancing as they play. Some, the front line players, and their drums are actually down on the wide concrete patio. The sound is powerful. It buffets inside his open shirt, and he feels the rhythm thudding into his viscera. He is elated but stays calm as he walks toward the music.

The round patio tables are littered with empty beer, rum, and whisky bottles. Paper cups, plates, and glasses. The hotel workers in their uniforms, some of them are dancing. A smaller group of three or four stand quietly reserved near the pool, tired, perhaps, but clearly disassociated. The dancers are drunk. Everybody is drunk. He will soon be drunk himself, whether he drinks or not, because it is the music. The dancers are in a tight knot, there's hardly any space between them and the band. They are drawn up to the band, tighter and tighter as they chant the refrain. Some are coupled, holding tight, others independently give their bodies to the night. There is no other like the odor of rum and sweat, flavored with perfume gone stale; none other like the mixed sound of drums and voices in unison chanting, chanting, chanting. Everybody is dancing, bouncing in the rhythm. The West Germans are there. The Canadians are there. The dusky brown faces of local Trinidadians. Some in their swimsuits.

There is a waist-high rope that separates the dancers from the musicians. He could see the musicians' faces now. And if there was a sentimental desire to see Phyllis Coudray, it doesn't matter now. Time spins. He's really hearing now, and he wants to see the music. The rows of black men, their faces quietly stern over their instruments. Some play with their backs to the dancers. The soprano players in the front line never look up. Their heads bob in a rhythm that comes behind the flashing of their hands. At its center the music is so deep and sweet, he willingly takes it in. It will make something out of him that he's striving for. That's what it says. And he stands there, feet rooted to the concrete patio, but from his knees up flexing now in imitation of what he might have been had he become a steel band player. He wants to play. All inside him he wants to play. He cannot play. Then he steps nearer, near enough to touch their hands, let them know he is vibrating too, and if it were somehow managed that they could hear his drum, he would give back a sound as deep and mellow as they were making on the metal instruments.

They run through the chorus one more time, with all the drums in unison on the last four bars. They bring that song to a close. "Which band is this?" he says to the player nearest.

"What band . . . ?" The player is a lean man with tight, strong face. The veins bulge in his forearms, and sweat runs in a steady stream down his open chest. He wipes his forehead with a blue handkerchief, wipes the handles of his mallets and puts them in his hip pocket. "What band is this . . . ?" He has broken teeth, and his breath smells of heavy rum. Then he turns to an older player next to him and says, "This fella want to know what band this . . ."

The older player is short and spare. "What band . . . ?" He is still caressing his drums with his rubber mallets. His round eyes stand out bare, boldly, in his bony face. "What happen, he some sorta tourist or something?"

"No," he says. "Not exactly. I'm no tourist, I come from here, Trinidad. But I'm living in the States now . . ."

"Oh . . ." the older drummer says. He turns to tightening the screws that hold his drums on their metal stands. The young one is wiping his forearms with his handkerchief, and looking at the dancers who are drinking now, and opening into tense, ragged talk, waiting for the band to start up again.

In that moment, one of the Canadian visitors comes shuffling up, waving an open bottle of Scotch. "You fellows sound go-od," he says. "Really go-od. I'm jumping the whole carnival with your band . . . " and still shuffling to some echo in his head he passes the bottle to the drummer with the blue handkerchief.

The drummer takes it, hesitates briefly, as if waiting for a glass to materialize, and when it doesn't he puts the bottle to his head and takes a drink. He passes the bottle to the player next to him and says, "We're not on the road, you know. Not this year. We are in the ban on bands playing in the carnival this year."

"No road march this year," the second one who had finished taking his drink says, without looking at the Canadian.

"No road march . . . ? Then where will you be playing?"

"Right here," the young one with the blue kerchief says. The bottle comes back to him and he takes another drink. "We're playing here 'til Sunday night. Then Monday, Tuesday we're in we yard."

"That's where?" the Canadian takes the bottle handed back to him.

"We're right near the fly-over. You ask anybody where the fly-over is and they'll show you. We're feting whole day Monday and Tuesday . . ."

He walks away from them. What is there about him that makes people react this way? As though he were unreal: unbelievable. Evidently, what he feels inside does not make its way to the surface, and this has happened before. How many times had he seen the change, even in friendly strangers? A greeting, open, warm, friendly, until he speaks or in some other way signs whatever it is he feels that makes them close, and they withdraw as though annoyed with themselves for having made some mistake. He had seen it many times before, and in spite of the adjustments he'd willed himself to make in what his eyes did, how his voice sounded, there was something yet about him that cut off others, or perhaps not let them in even as he tried to, or maybe just put them on their guard. He feels no choice but to turn away from the band, drift off.

If he could find Phyllis Coudray, she'd know there is no boundary around him not to be crossed. Last year it was instantaneous. She'd come out to the poolside dance after the desk was closed and found him sitting at a table. "Carnival's no time to sit down alone," she'd said. They danced. When they embraced her short, curly hair fit just beneath his chin, and there had been no barriers between them.

Drifting back through the dancers now, hardly looking at their faces he knows she is not at this dance. If she were, his feelings would have directed him to her already. He sees other women to whom he could probably talk, but none gives him a sign of specific attention and he passes them by.

He hears snatches of humorous talk coming from among the men, but none of it is for him and he passes on through. He hears laughter and anticipation in the merry voices waiting for the band to start up again on the patio, a certain crackling bravado against loss or weariness. The promise of a deep thrill is strong in the smell of sweat and rum, as he makes his way back through the dancers, while off above up in the night the sky and stars are going about their business. He leaves the dancers around the glittering pool behind, walks out of the courtyard through a side door, and enters the narrow alley which borders the western side of the hotel. As he goes up to the corner the surrounding buildings are all dark and quiet. The high overhead globes send a dim light that barely reaches down to the empty street. If he turns left once he gets to the boulevard, he would soon come to The Savannah with its open fields, spreading trees and benches, and the coconut vendors with their mounds of nuts.

From the patio dance behind him, the steel band rhythm rises to the sky once more. The dim night where he walks pulses, and he wishes that he were not alone. Last year there was Phyllis Coudray walking softly beside him, leaning on his arm. The perfume in her hair kept the live pulse between them cantering, and later, after the monstrous heartbeats came, it wasn't just the case that they had gone no further than the colonial room upstairs. With Phyllis Coudray he had soared into a traveler through time, one from whom the world could keep no secrets. There were no secrets between them. Together they were elevated into a revealed world where heat and cold, fear and elation, cry and laugh, adoration and disdain were all the measure of each other. He misses her. It is Phyllis whom he misses. He does not want to think about her, or feel the absence of her flashing smile too fully in the dark.

He will think, why is it that men should feel this need? Why must we drug ourselves on companionship in order to encounter who we are? Didn't the species have another option somewhere in the past? What was it that led us to prefer this alienation-hunger-reunion as our formula for confronting time, a future? He wills himself to come forward with thoughts that transcend Phyllis, to not dwell on her, but he doesn't quite succeed.

She's in the mellow rumble of the drums that he still hears, she comes down from the warm starlit sky, she takes shape in the shadows of the night and he cannot keep her enlarged presence from reaching deep into his viscera with memories of the way they danced, and walked these same streets in the dawn of last year's carnival. They had danced around and around The Savannah drinking, laughing, touching, immodestly insane in the vast jouvay crowd. They had marched and shuffled together in the oneness of the crowd, drummed on by the melodic pans and voices raised in a chant to the mysterious power that held them where time stalled, and the suspense before daybreak seemingly would last forever. That space between night and day lasting forever. A dream. Discovery of a new self. Dreaming that makes and remakes itself on the memory of her face, her hands, the traipsing rhythm of their legs in unison.

So that he walks not toward The Savannah at all, but instead winds his way down to Independence Square, where the old women vendors in their tight headties sat along the sidewalk with their backs against the closed shops, their trays of fruit, candy, cigarettes, newspapers, lighted by flickering flambeaus—just as in his childhood days when this was Marine Square, heartbeat of the carnival, calypsonians in their makeshift tent, stickfighters in their gayal, and all the verandas gay with parties dancing to the brass band syncopators. Now Independence Square, it is no longer fashionable. The old Spanish-style colonial buildings are rotted and rusty. Ghosts are about their business here. Beneath the stunted, dust-laden trees in the median what should have been temporary vendors' shacks look permanent. Some are still open for trade in food and crafted goods, but most are shuttered and deeply withdrawn from the night.

Other changes too. Flickering neon signs in red, gold, and green. The Tuesday before carnival, and already policemen on horses. Policemen in pairs on every corner, aloof in the stiff black uniforms with pistols at their waists. Beggars turned in on their patch of pavement for the night. A few taxis still cruising, some stragglers calling after them "Arima!" "San Fernando?" "I goin Couva, boy!" "Ai, Petit Valley!" Behind one of the ghostly hotel verandas a small brass band plays the same calypso tune he'd heard at the hotel, but the music is desultory. Tired. Before the street doors to the hotel, several night women cluster. They are, most of them, young Indian girls dressed in tight skirts, no earrings. One says, "Pssst . . . !" in a half-hearted way as he walks by. Another in a sailor's hat does a lonesome body grind and sings far behind the music.

He turns and walks past them again. Walks with the smell of the waterfront on his left, until he comes to where he could glimpse the open water itself. There are crafts out there, he could tell from the slow-heaving lights; but mostly nothing else beside the dark water. Ahead, people mill slowly out of the Young Brigade Calypso Tent. The show is over. They come out steadily, some talking and laughing about what went on inside, but heading directly for their cars parked along the road and in the nearby lot. There is no lingering. Tuesday the week before carnival, and there are no rowdy after-hours sidewalk parties. The police stand in twos and threes on nearly every other corner with nothing to do, their backs straight, their faces hidden in the shadow of their caps.

On past the calypso tent the whole neighborhood is still. He hears no wild Indians practicing their cries. No robber speeches being committed to memory. But he does hear drums coming from a distance. He listens closely, and from somewhere in the hills that surround the town he does hear a tenor pan ringing plainly on the slight breeze. Somewhere up there the soloist is practicing without accompaniment and for the whole town, what of it that's awake, to hear. The mellow riff comes over and over, fading at times, then strong again. He will never know the player. Yet as it comes and fades, he feels the music as a personal gift of peace and warning. Would Phyllis have felt the same? Would she have been able to show him what to do with such a feeling?

Back at the hotel he makes the entry in his diary. Then he sits at the half-opened window looking down on the pale green pool, now totally deserted.

II

It is too early for most of the guests to be at table. He is there only because he had been unable to sleep in the clatter of the window air-conditioner and had to turn it off. Without it, the air in the room grew close and heavy, and even though he had finally dropped off, he'd slept fitfully; and before six o'clock it was clear that lying in the bed damp from constant sweating would do nothing for the headache tapping at his temples. He'd got up, showered, and come down for an early breakfast. At the entrance to the dining patio the middle-aged Chinese cashier sat reading the daily paper. Her green and white flowered dress flowed copiously over the stool behind the cash register, and she'd never raised her eyes to greet him as he came in. A Trinidadian family of four who, by their conversation that he could not help but overhear, had recently become Canadian citizens, were already at their table, and at the far end of the patio two waiters in their black and white uniforms with towels draped over their forearms stood like silent sentinels. One of the German couples he'd noticed on the plane came in behind him, both looking haggard and gray, as though the coming carnival had already sucked too much energy out of them.

The patio is the uncovered end of an open floor between the lobby and the first, looking out on a row of tall yellow crotons glistening with beads from an early watering. Behind the crotons is a taller hibiscus hedge clustered with dark red flowers in between the green leaves. Here the air is not as thick as it was in his room. The swatch of sky that he could see is still cool gray, not yet shimmering with the day's heat that's to come, but as he waits for one of the waiters to reach the table, his throbbing head promises to get worse before it passes. Perhaps breakfast will help. He sits with his eyes closed, congratulating himself mildly between the reddening throbs on having handled the disappointment of not seeing Phyllis Coudray with fair success. After breakfast, when he feels better, he will make some telephone calls, or talk to the maids who knew everything, spend the rest of the morning if he had to, locating her. He hears the waiter from a distance at first, not realizing the spare middle-aged man is standing at his elbow.

"Good morning. Coffee, sir?" He feels the presence hovering at his shoulder, and an anger he did nothing to summon swells up in his throat. He rubs the back of his neck to let it pass, then answers, "Yes. Please."

"Sweetened?"

"Yes."

"And would you want anything else for breakfast, sir?"

The anger he feels could have something to do with Phyllis Coudray not being there, or with the hard-boned gardener in raggedy clothes who had come out to trim the hedge, or with the sky that would in time be so hot as to make this passing hour a dim memory, or with the steady throbbing in his head, or with something else about which he knew nothing.

"And would you want anything else for breakfast, then, sir?" the waiter repeats, while over at the hedge the gardener lights a cigarette and begins clipping at the already neat hibiscus branches. Must he wear such ragged clothes? With his knobby old man's knees exposed? Why was he so solemn? While the waiter in a voice as mild and solicitous as the gardener's bowed attention to the bush repeats, "Sir?"

There is the Chinese cashier buried in her daily news, the German couple behind him talking in their rough accents, the Trinidadian-Canadian family instructing the children on proper table manners, and he feels that something ought to be done although he doesn't know what, and he hears the words drop out of his mouth "Do you have to wear such clothes?" in a voice at once strange and familiar. He is not himself.

"Pardon?" The waiter in his baggy black pants, frayed long-sleeved shirt topped with a black waistcoat, seems bemused. He stands there in his broken shoes, spare, his staunch shoulders subtly square, and with delicate fingers flourishes his pencil and repeats with his pad waiting, "Pardon. . . ?"

"Why must you wear such clothes? Why don't you dress in something . . ."

"We are always well-dressed at this hotel, sir . . . This morning we have bacon and eggs, sausage and eggs, ham and eggs, toast, juice . . ."

As unexpectedly as it had erupted in him his anger dissipates. The gardener is stooping now. He's taking a rest. The cigarette dangles from between his lips, and he faces the bush steadily, almost as though he were in a silent conversation with it. "What kind of juice?"

"Orange, grapefruit . . ."

"Fresh?"

"Tinned, sir. Our juice is always tinned. Locally here in Trinidad. But there is fresh grapefruit if you prefer, sir."

"Yes. Grapefruit and toast."

"That's all?"

"Yes, that's all."

"Most of our American visitors like our scrambled eggs with their toast . . . sir . . . ?"

A rush of pity wells in him—for the waiter in his spotted uniform, the gardener in his ragged clothes, himself too, and he looks away. Silent. With a smile the waiter leaves his table, walks stiffly to the far end of the patio and disappears through the door to the kitchen.

There is no music. He misses the music. Last year with Phyllis Coudray at his side there had been no time for angry thoughts or pity. Music. There was the constant flow of music, and after breakfast they went back to sleep again, until late in the afternoon when she shook him awake and said they must go down to the sea. The steep cove some distance beyond Chaguaramas Bay was green, and parrots screamed in the bois-canot trees as they stepped hand in hand into the water. Music. They could hear it coming through the trees. They splashed, and rolled, and floated lazily in the water, until restored, refreshed, they'd returned to the dance again, until the next day, and the next, until it was time to say "See you next year?" and she'd replied, "No promises."

The grapefruit half sits on a thick plate, but it is neatly diced within the rind, and the coffee has a creamy aroma. The toast is dark brown, crisp, marmalade the color of champagne. Music will come again, for sure. Tonight, tomorrow night, there will be fetes to be explored, and he goes to the lobby to find a daily newspaper. At his table once again, he sits and sips his coffee. The aroma is creamy, and he will have room for a second cup. He scans the news. As he knew it would, the front page story features the preliminary rounds in the carnival competitions. The toast is crisp, and the marmalade carries a touch of cinnamon. Photographs of the kings and queens who will appear on Dimanche Gras are there in their grand though unfinished costumes. He scans the paper through to the back page, and is brought up abruptly. Across the top banner line he reads—GUERILLA SHOT IN MORUGA FOREST (NO. 27). Beneath the headline there is a picture of a young black man dressed in a plain white T-shirt and dark pants, pleasant looking, with his hair in tight, long braids hanging down over his ears and shoulders. The body is sprawled in a grassy drain beside a dirt road in the bush.

He folds the newspaper along the original creases and puts it aside. The face in the photograph seems to resemble Rodney's but he is not sure. He finishes his toast. The remainder of his coffee has gone cold, and he sets it aside. He uses the old linen napkin with its starched holes, then rises from the table. In a stroll charged with drawing no attention to itself, he sets off to his room to find his notebook.

I REFUSE TO DOUBT

AN INUIT HEALER FINDS A LISTENER

Friendship in the field is an unlooked-for but valued result of the anthropologist's work. The stories that are burned into the mind of the visiting stranger are those rich with a resonance that affects both the friends. Furthermore it is the events recorded in such stories that show the most direct path into the deep levels of the culture. This is due simply to friendship.

In a north Alaska Inuit village, Turner was looking for such a friend, a healer, because she felt in herself an old, unused urge to help the sick. Claire's and her own aim turned out to be close, though Claire's was one aided by rarely experienced abilities. She healed by a kind of extraction of the ills of the body, always powered by prayer while her hands worked with great intelligence. Closely recorded examples help to make this clear.

In a small village in the north of Alaska lives a healer whom I will call Claire. Her people may generically be classed as Inuit, tribes possessing a long history of survival in climatic regions that would scare most of us. Their religion, now largely defunct, once recognized various classes of spirits and the power of shamanistic contact with spirit helpers.

Why did I go to the Inuit? Research leads one where it must. I had been studying from a very close-up view the work of ritual doctors in Africa (1986, 1992) and chose to publish my material in a more humanistic style than was the norm in academia, at the same time including much context and analysis. Now came a chance to study a non-Western woman healer in a different culture, a personality who was one of her culture's most richly complex members.

I lived for a year in this Alaskan village, which I am naming Ivakuk, "Hunting," because that is how the inhabitants always lived. I myself was hunting down some of the peculiar details that might possibly be associated with the people's traditional healing and which

My thanks are due to my sponsors, the Wenner-Gren Foundation for Anthropological Research and the University of Virginia. The help given by James and Mary McConnell is warmly acknowledged. I am particularly grateful to Claire and the healers for their patient instruction of a rather obdurate pupil. I also thank many other individuals in "Ivakuk" and the north who must be nameless, people who have instructed me or made my way easier.

233

might be making the healing work. However, in doing the research I found I caught neither subsistence food nor mere fieldnotes, but a living and dear and fascinating friend.

In Ivakuk there were nine healers, seven of whom were women, and there were at least five child apprentices learning the craft. Claire was the principal practitioner in the village, with a clientele on one side who supported her, and on the other, detractors who preferred another curer. Like the various healers whose work I studied and whose stories I heard, Claire possessed gifts of clairvoyance and direct healing that went beyond the provenance of the medical profession.

Claire told me this story: "A young man came to me about his back. I passed my hand along his back and I prayed. Then I *saw* the original accident. I saw that kid fall off his snowmobile and become twisted by his gun because he couldn't get it off his back." She said to me, "You know what it's like—it's like fantasy. I might write a book."

Claire told me that the young man with the bad back answered her, "Yes, that's exactly what happened, ten years ago." His back was already healed.

This kind of gift appears to resemble the Inuit ability to make spirit journeys, as recounted in former times. Claire had moved back in time and to a different place, and had *seen* what happened.

I remember my first meeting with Claire. This is the story. I was thinking the time had come to visit her—though wouldn't she be secretive and reserved, as Native Americans are said to be? I found my way to her prefabricated house. Now it stood before me, painted dark red, with wooden steps going up from the tundra gravel toward a door on the left. I ascended and knocked. Would she be at home?

A distant voice hollered, "Come in!" I opened the door. It was pitch dark inside. Ah, there was another door beyond: this was just the storm porch. Shutting the first door against the bitter September wind, I opened the further one and found myself in a large living room.

A small woman was busying about and turned to me. She had a fine oval face and straight look, somewhat like an unthreatening version of the dark-haired sybil in Michelangelo's Sistine frescoes, only carrying in her eyes the more delicate epicanthic structure of the Native American. I introduced myself to this healer person, thinking, "Come on, Edie, your own dad was a doctor. And you're not just an anthropologist. You're fascinated by healing for what it is. You've seen a thing or two." This woman had some gift I did not rightly understand. I was ready and open to hear.

She knew that I was ready as we sat down.

I started out, "I've heard of your work. I've a great respect for Inuit healing."

"What made you interested in it?" she asked.

"I once saw my husband, Vic, heal somebody. This man had a heart attack in our living room, and his heart stopped. Vic put his hand on the man's heart, and it started again. I wondered what was going on—if I might learn what's behind it. I've respect for what you do."

"*I'm very glad.* I've been getting discouraged, frustrated."

"Are the medical doctors getting you down?"

"Yes."

"Don't let 'em," I said. "It's a good work you're doing."

She explained that she had just come in from the distant village of Bristol. "They flew me there to work on some of the sick."

She and I liked each other. Her adopted children crowded around, Jeanie, seven, and Ann, ten. She also had older adopted children and two grandchildren. We began to talk about our families and grandchildren.

Then she was silent, pondering a minute. "Inuit healing is *different*." She lingered over the word. "Come into the kitchen and talk while I work."

In a few minutes she was due to attend a teleconference education class in anthropology at 5:00 P.M. and needed to hurry. "Anthropology?" I thought. "She could *teach* them that, couldn't she?"

Did she have to go out right now? She'd just come back from a trip, and now she had to go out again. The kitchen was high with dirty dishes—the family hadn't washed them for days. But she told me how proud she was of her family, proud of her grown-up son of thirty: he had recently obtained his first job and bought a TV and stereo. "I'm *proud*," she told me.

She suddenly turned to her daughter of nine, Ann, and spat a command. "What math homework do you have?" Ann showed her the book.

"You can do that quickly. Do the dishwashing, then the homework."

"I'll do the dishwashing," I said, and got to work. It was easy because there was plenty of hot running water.

A message came over Claire's CB radio. She cocked an ear. "Claire. Claire. Come on in," the voice said. "Go at once to Atiq, she's sick, she's throwing up."

The anthropology class would have to be missed because Atiq, an elderly lady, came first. I had learned to respect Atiq too, a healer and a bold personality. Before leaving, Claire opened the refrigerator where she kept three bags of a herb called stinkweed. This was *Artemisia tilesii*, wormwood, the best of the Inuit medicines. Claire took out some of the boiled infusion, a dark fluid, and she drank a cupful; she handed me a little to drink. It was bitter. She said it would give her strength to heal. Quickly she grabbed her coat and left for Atiq's house. After finishing the dishes, I thought for a moment and decided to go to Atiq's too.

As I approached Atiq's door, a woman came out. She passed me and jumped on her Honda ATV.

"How is she?"

"Atiq plays too much Bingo," she said sharply. "So of course she doesn't eat properly. That's why she's sick." This was the head of the clinic health aides.

I went into the house. There were many people in old Atiq's living room. I made my way along the passage to the bedroom and found my friend Clem, who was Atiq's adult grandson, at the entrance of the bedroom. His flat features were loosened into solemnity, unseeing. I peeped into the room. The old lady with her familiar face—though now her little pinched eyes were weary—was lying on a mattress on the floor, not on her bed. She was still clothed in her skirt and a fine blouse. Claire was at her side with seven-year-old Jeanie sitting between her knees, acting as her healing apprentice.

Atiq's senile old husband was sitting on the unoccupied bed. He arose and stood near, then went wandering off down the passage. After a time back he came again, and this went on all the while—the old man shuffling to and fro, to and fro. Ardell, another health aide, was sitting on the unoccupied bed, backstage as it were to Claire. Claire told me Atiq's stomach was in the wrong position: it was hard and tight. Claire could feel air pockets that were stopping the stomach from working. There was something wrong that was causing Atiq to vomit blood. Atiq had not been able to eat for three days.

The house was occupied by many people. I went back to the living room and greeted the elders, Kaglik, who was Atiq's brother, and Atiq's son, Clem's father. Both of them were old men. They sat like statues on straight chairs. There was silence. I felt a little frightened. Then I went back to Atiq and tried to massage her feet to relax her. But she vomited, groaning, and lay back; then she vomited again and muttered something in Inuit. Claire was working on Atiq's stomach with both hands, working deep into the folds of the old stomach flesh. Claire had "good hands," as the Inuit often said: those hands could soothe the body and take away pain. At one point Claire spread both arms out with her fingers wide in a gesture of relief. She was tired. In Inuit parlance Atiq's stomach had risen and was jammed against the heart and lungs, stopping the organs from functioning properly.

I went to Ardell, the health aide. "What's wrong, d'you think?"

"We don't know. I'm going to have to phone the hospital and get them to send the medevac plane. The senior health aide gave Atiq some Mylanta. That's all we are allowed to do."

Meanwhile Claire was softening Atiq's stomach to bring it down into the right position. But the air pocket gave trouble. As I stood in the doorway, I saw the old woman's face become contorted; then I saw it blank out to nothing. Claire held Atiq's head hard and held on, drawing Atiq to her. I started to pray. Clem looked fearful, as if death penned; perhaps it did. The old lady reared up again in agony to vomit, then fell back. Her body blanked out, and her head sank back. Her whole personality seemed emptied. I went on massaging her feet while Claire massaged her stomach, bending her head very near to Atiq's. At one time Claire put her hands on Atiq's stomach and lay her head upon her hands, right on Atiq's stomach.

Ardell, the health aide, watched, then took herself off to the clinic to make the phone call to the hospital at Bristol. I left the house to fetch some snacks and brought them back to feed Claire and the others. When I returned, I looked at the scene through the door and thought of the Pietà. There it was, the lax figure and the supporting forms: "Oh, Atiq, I'm sad for your pain, sad." I kept praying that Claire would heal her. Everyone involved has to do what she knows how. Atiq lay there exhausted; was she failing or was she resting? Claire stayed right close to her, head to head, with her hand always on Atiq's stomach, warmly there with the "different" knowledge in it, as Claire put it, an intimate contact. I thought, if only they'd done that for me when I was in hospital in 1983 for agonizing stomach cramps.

Atiq stayed as she was, still vomiting occasionally. Each time she vomited we looked anxiously at the clock, wondering when the plane would come. But she did rest. Claire began to talk cheerfully. I loved Claire's ordinary conversation, again about her grown-up son and his new TV. We laughed, subduing our voices. The others all talked in Inuit. Netta was now drinking 7-Up, talking herself, vividly complaining in Inuit about her stomach. She stretched out her feet, which had been reincased in her tube socks. The old man entered the room in his tortoise crawl and stopped at her outstretched legs. After a pause he just managed to walk across her legs and go to sit on the bed.

Atiq asked for some tea. There was a quiet rush to fetch her a cup. Clem began to smile. Gradually we became aware that the immediate crisis was past. We waited.

The plane was flying over. Everyone heard it. The people in the living room, dressed in grand printed velveteen-and-ruff parkas, passed to and fro to look through the windows, telling each other, "There it is." Clem, being the adult grandson, started worrying about intravenous feeding, IVs—"She must have fluids. The doctor will have to do the IV in the house; the ambulance is too small." Clem's wife fussed over what clothes to send with her. Even so, they forgot her dentures.

As we stood waiting, Clem said to me in his slow voice: "Her spirit went out of her body three times. Three times it went out of her, and Claire brought it back and pulled it down into her stomach. When it leaves for good, it goes up through the hole in the top of the head." I touched my long-closed fontanel (the site of some of my headaches—a place that was aching a little that day).

Clem smiled. "That's right, there."

I surmised that Claire's healing acts of drawing back the fleeing spirit were basically the same ones that used to be carried out by the ancient Inuit shamans. But this occasion had been *now*.

I stood with Clem, still frightened for Atiq's safety, finding I was already dominated by love for the old lady, for Claire, and for this crowd which had become my crowd of "forever" acquaintances. "Forever?" After three weeks? I realized that a leaping tie of love had come from them to me and back again; I was involved.

There was a stir. The ambulance was here in the shape of a new, yellow, low-slung vehicle outside the door. The white pilot came in; then a tall, dark-haired white man, distant of manner, who turned out to be the doctor; another very beardy little fellow, quite fun; then a huge white ambulance man, easy to talk to. The place was full of people milling around in a confused way. I peered into Atiq's room. A blond nurse was already inside the room, putting a blood pressure sleeve on Atiq's arm. The team became occupied in following the stereotypes of "medical practice." They took the blood pressure, pulse, and temperature, asked questions, and then the stretchermen gathered in the bedroom.

Clem told the doctor, "She's been spitting out very dark stuff, black, like blood." The doctor came into the bedroom and looked into the old lady's vomiting can. "A little blood," he said disparagingly. I returned to the living room, and the doctor came and stood by the wall. We grew silent. After a moment the ambulance men emerged from the passageway with their stretcher—Atiq was inside. They carried her out of the door and into the ambulance. We saw her wrinkled face lifted to look out of the ambulance; then the tailgate was shut, and they were off to the airstrip.

The following day Claire had to send in her assignment for the teleconference course in anthropology. She wrote well and knew the facts and traditions for the subject of her essay, which was on subsistence. After all, her husband was a hunter and she was his absolutely indispensable hunter's wife. Who would process the hunting meat but her?

The next time I visited Claire, I found her living room crammed with five large plastic laundry baskets full of dirty laundry, and the sofa was piled high with clean clothes. She was cooking bacon and eggs for her husband, who was back from his construction job. People kept coming in and out to consult Claire about their food stamp forms, for she was also the volunteer food stamp official in town. She said to me, "Have some coffee," then dashed into the utility room where an old-style washer-agitator was working, in the process of rinsing a full load of men's jeans. An electric mangle was attached above it. I helped her mangle and turn the clothes inside out; then she made me put them through the mangle again. I helped with much of the laundry, hung up the jeans on the overhead pipes, swept the floor of the living room, and folded the clothes piled on the sofa while she talked and worked alongside me. She was speaking of healing and how healers could feel the pain of the sufferer. (It struck me that this "feeling" would well be covered by a possible concrete glossing of the word "sym-pathy"— "feeling" "with.") Given the power to heal, it would not help much if Claire herself developed the sickness in some mystical way. However, she was able to block the harm of the disease halfway up her arms while she worked on the sufferer's body. She was still able to "feel the pain, feel where it is." This was different from feeling swelling, lumps, heat, and throbbing in the body. It existed as some sense of the misery of the tissues.

She told me how a woman 250 miles away called her on the phone and said, "I'm having a miscarriage." The woman was four months pregnant. When the woman spoke, Claire's second sight told her what was wrong, and then Claire knew what to do, also by virtue of her second sight. She gave the woman the corresponding instructions and the fetus was saved, and later the baby was born full-term.

Claire said yet again in her soft voice, "My healing is *different*." She went on: "The doctors say to me, 'You're wrong, Claire.' They think I'm trying to predict—I don't predict, I *know* when someone is pregnant and for how long. Then it turns out I'm right. The health aides say, 'You must go by what the doctors say'—but I *know*. They finished my contract at the clinic; I don't know why. One woman came to me. She put out her hand and said, 'Don't touch me.' She was scared. I didn't touch her. I told her she was two weeks pregnant. I *knew*. Later she had the test, and she was pregnant."

"Why should people be scared of what is so good and useful?" I remarked.

Claire turned back to her cooking. There she was, slaving for her family, waiting on them with food and services.

"I'm glad you came," she went on. "For thirty years no one's helped me in the house." She picked up a glittering peacock blue velvet bathrobe, wet from the washtub. "I made this myself, for my husband," she said proudly. Her husband was in the back room watching TV. She went in there later to hang up the nicer things, knitteds and so on. I was thinking how her gifts needed backing up, and how mundane was her husband's construction work in comparison—except when he was hunting.

Claire talked a blue streak. She said to me, "You are different." I told her that I knew other countries where I had witnessed unusual healings—Africa, Brazil. I had even seen a spirit. Then I talked about Atiq.

"If you hadn't been there when Atiq was so sick, she might have died," I told her.

"I saw the spirit leaving her several times," Claire said, just as Clem had told me earlier. "I had to be there. The health aides just up and leave when it's five oclock. What would Atiq have done? You can't just leave."

She caught me washing the half-moon Inuit knives. "You have to wipe them dry at once," she warned me, drying her own on a towel.

"—Or they'll get rusty," I said. She had ten half-moon knives inserted in the groove behind the sink.

Her living room bore photographs of relatives crowding the walls, just as my own mother used to crowd her own walls. Claire had a large color photograph of her mother-in-law. The face was thrawn and severe, yet with a kind of cheerful beauty that burned in the high-cheeked Inuit face, well framed by a fur ruff. There were trophy pictures of animals the family had caught. There was a picture of Jesus praying at Gethsemane, beautiful and sad. There was the usual large clock and a sewing machine in its table with an Eddie Bauer down jacket waiting to be repaired, the zipper already tacked into place—her husband's favorite jacket. A milk crate stood against the wall with neat files for the food stamp job, with easily available forms. Claire ran things well.

There were no photos of Claire herself, so I give a pen portrait of her. Claire looked out from herself, all alive, from that oval face with the high brow, with a considering look in her eyes: she was an immediate character, with strength and energy. She moved with an easy walk and big fluid motions. When I came to know her well, she used to take off her jacket in my house and sit down, ready for anything, her eyes a little hooded as became an Inuit (it was rude to look straight into a person's eyes). She was capable; she asked for what was not on the table, such as honey for her tea. We'd talk. Her voice wandered into great variations of tone, from rasping when in a state of uncertainty—still with self-assertion; sometimes slumping in falling tones—in complaint, still with that rasp. Then, when she was musing or reminiscing, her voice became wandering and soft, musically keyed, her eyes inward, her mind seeing pictures that leapt into existence one on top of the other—her voice leapt as the pictures came. And when teaching me language pronunciation, her voice went like this: it carried tones of sorrowful rasping, searching, and persistence, coming near to despair with a frog in the throat and much doubt—then a little hope. She tried again, "*qa-aggaq!*" and I repeated, "kargak," wrongly, and her hands flopped uselessly by her side. She laughed, cackling like the grandmother she was—a young grandmother.

I knew a certain thing about her from long ago, and I could not bear to think about it. It was when she stood before her burning house in which lay her first three children, her own children trapped and dead. Her spirit must have been dead and tortured inside her. A screaming impossibility, Claire.

Already with six more children—adopted this time—and two grandchildren, with an easy job she liked, sitting in City Hall, typing on a computer, running the teleconferences as well as taking the courses—this was the life (only they had begun to cut down her hours). And a telephone, and a CB radio.

The radio crackled and said, "Claire, are you on? Come and see little Lee, he's hurt." She went, unhooking her jacket and donning it as she strode down the office stairs out to her Honda ATV and whirled off—with little Jeanie and myself on the back. . . . She entered the house, all gentle, already *knowing* the trouble, for there existed a preliminary time of clairvoyance for Claire. Inside the house the child was screaming (shades of the burning house). He'd taken a jump off a high shelf and gone crash on both knees. Now he couldn't stand and couldn't walk and was on his mother's lap crying. Claire brought up a chair and sat opposite Lee with Jeanie kneeling close by to watch. Like me, Jeanie was very much interested. Claire took the child's foot gently and turned up the pants leg. Lee's crying got worse. Claire turned her hand over the throbbing knee, almost not touching it.

"I can't hurt you, *I can't hurt you*," she told him as an obvious truth, in her musical voice. "See, I'm making it better." She was so used to seeing inside. Claire's hand was like an X-ray, so she used to tell me. All inside was as clear as daylight. The mother held Lee, and Claire felt both lower legs, not the knees. Lee's crying began to give way. She felt down the muscles of each lower leg, drawing down the legs neatly and together. She worked each ankle, the flat of the foot, and the toes, bending them gently until they were flexible, showing Lee how good they were. Her hands went back to the knees. The right one bore a bruise and a big swelling below the kneecap. She placed the kneecaps one after the other centrally and pressed them gently into position as if they were jigsaw pieces, completing the action by pressing carefully with her palm. She went to the better knee and worked the dimpled areas while swiveling the leg back and forth. Then she returned to the swelling on the right knee. I noted that she left the trickiest side until last. She pressed the swelling slightly here and there, and I saw it diminish a little. She left that work alone for a time and turned down Lee's pants legs. He slid off his mother's lap and tried a few steps, using his legs like little sticks.

Claire chatted to the mother about financial matters. She turned to Lee. "Auntie Claire's going to make you some mukluk boots. How about that, eh?" Lee was busy making eyes at Jeanie.

"Come on my lap," Claire told him. "Auntie's going to work on you a bit more." She caressed the swelling on the right knee again, showing me how it was going down.

"See? It's simple." Before my eyes the swelling went away altogether, leaving the normal muscle curves visible around the kneecap. I was attending carefully, remembering now the occasions when Claire had managed to teach me to heal. Once, under her careful tutelage, she had made me heal an injured rib on her own back. This is what happened. She said, "There." I put my hands on the place. OK, I felt a nasty lump on the rib; but not only this. It was as if it were sending off rays or something; there was a kind of sizzling. What I experienced was an odd message of misery, a call—"I hurt!"—coming out of that bit of sick human tissue. I felt a rush of sympathy for that pain. "Poor Claire." The lump and its mushiness was not just a sign of its physical disruption. My hand knew that and knew it was there to help. I began to work it tenderly in Claire's fashion. To my surprise, the swelling began to go down until it was just a sliver and went away. How? Rationally speaking, I don't know.

And I also experienced being healed myself and noted how the pain seemed to leak away from my body and just not be there anymore.

Now Claire drew down Lee's pants legs and let him go. He walked easily. She went to the sink and washed, getting rid of whatever it was. "The pain goes into my own arm," she would say. "My hand gets hot. *Hot!*"

She went on talking. Lee's mother was hard up, awaiting a welfare check. The place lacked a carpet, with torn vinyl chair seats and only a garish rainbow window shade to cheer the room. Lee was now jumping from the empty stereo shelf to the sofa.

"That's how he did it in the first place," said Claire. "Jumping and falling on his knees. Stop that." We left before more treatment might become necessary.

Claire's healing tantalized me. As the process was indeed deeply physical and focused and particularized, the healing itself was very hard to explain verbally. Claire would say— having seen TV— "It's the power of mind over matter." Was it that? She was working intimately with matter, with her actual hands on actual bodies, searching and taking out pain. "Cancer you can feel—little things—" She drew on paper:

and also drew 1 1/2-inch lumps. "These little things are in the skin or muscle itself, not moving, in it."

"Can you get them out?"

"You can work on some of them and get them to go. Not all, not all at once. You can cure it."

I thought to myself, "Does the mind enter the hands and cure the body?'' Other healers said, ''My old hands are gone, these are God's hands.'' I saw in this a theory of healing corresponding to the old Inuit shamans' theory of healing by spirit possession.

Claire told me how she knew when she herself was pregnant, against the opinion of three out of five doctors. She had twice been operated on for cancer; now she was healthy. Once she told me she was very tired; she kept on yawning. She said it was because she had been working on a pneumonia patient—''I took the trouble into myself.'' The grateful pneumonia patient, now cured, gave her a huge ornate clock decorated with a silver swan, which she put up on her wall.

On another occasion Claire was on a plane trip with her relatives. The weather was tricky. As they started across tundra and ocean for the distant village, she saw a bright, sharp line right across the sky—golden, not cloud-colored. As they rose, higher conditions became bad, with 60-mph winds and cross gusts. This was extremely dangerous flying weather. ''But we flew in the golden line all the way and the plane was perfectly steady. We landed fine.'' She spoke in a tone of outrightness and wonder, a proposition for my belief, a marvel that does happen. There were old accounts of shamans creating a similar tube of quiet weather in which their dogsleds traveled safely in stormy weather. It was quite obvious to the Inuit that there was such a power.

As for Claire, she constantly ascribed that power to a source outside her: ''The good Lord gave me the gift of healing.''

We can follow how that gift developed from the way the Claire described her life history. At first I did not know how to go about obtaining her life story, from a cold start as it were; but eventually there occurred a small special event that stimulated us both. One day I was awkwardly trying to ask Claire about her memories of childhood, but the awkwardness only increased, and conversation became impossible. Then in came old Auntie Nora, who had no thumb—it had been eaten off by bees when she was adopted as a baby. Auntie Nora was tiny, well under five feet tall. She started talking to Claire about an illness of hers, epilepsy, which only bothered her when she was nervous. She said she was conscious during her seizures, feeling bad all the time. And she went on to complain that her nephew used to take her welfare check away from her for food purchases, so that she had no spending money. She was full of complaints.

When she eventually tried to put on her parka to leave, I saw her try to close the zipper. Having no right thumb, it was a difficult matter.

''She needs a tag on that zipper,'' said Claire.

I happened to have a large tag on the side zipper of my purse—it was a brass triangle with JR on it. Claire and I managed to get it off and put it on Nora's zipper. Nora was very pleased and hugged me, and from then on my awkwardness vanished. Suddenly Claire began to pour out the story of her childhood. She told it as if it were happening now, in a voice that gathered richness as it went along. I listened spellbound. At last all the honey and tea, the language sessions, her awareness that I did in part actually feel with her in what she was doing, her actual seeing of me as a person, came together and formed into her spontaneous tale.

"I was born at the time they had that epidemic, measles. I never did get sick. There were a few of us who didn't. The epidemic was more powerful before I was born, and it was subsiding. I was born in August or September when it was at its worst. So many people got it that they had to use tractors to bury them when they died. They couldn't figure out *how* it was I lived. I remember my grandfather when I wasn't yet a month old; he died when I was about two months old. I described what he looked like, what he was wearing, how his hair was, and his complexion; and upstairs that little hole in the window—it wasn't really a window—and the bed rolled up, and the floor, I gave descriptions of how they pulled the bed up, the cupboard on this side, the table and on it the white cup with a red rim around it. To the right there was a stove, and it had a little door where they put in the firewood, and there was some driftwood on the floor. And on this side there was an oven, and they were making biscuits that summer, and there was something on top. On this side there was a nurse who had helped me be born, and I described her. I was one of the last ones to be born before she left, which means when you get right down to it that I must have been about a month old at that time. And they were giving shots, and there was a thing on the window—an emblem of the Red Cross, and there was a big sign. I couldn't see the word QUARANTINE, I saw it backwards. They said they took those off that summer when I was a month or two old. They had to have those signs on there if somebody was sick in the house.

"And what happened was this. I remember getting up, trying to stand up. I knew my feet were for standing up, I knew what my hands were for, I knew my eyes were to see, but I couldn't stand up, my legs wouldn't hold. They did hold if I went like *that*"—Claire shoved her legs—"and I kept going like that, and then I would roll over and use my hands like this"—Claire shoved with her hands—"and I was going on like this, until I got to that place where there were people talking. My mom said I was about a month old when this happened. I almost fell down from that place, and they could *never* figure out how I rolled from that bed. You know? And I explained it to her later, and she said, 'Claire, it can't be true, you were only about a month old, just a little baby.'

"I could go all the way back to about a month and a half. All those years I could flash back"—she snapped her fingers, her warm-olive face amazed, telling me. "I could go way back and remember *every* word they said to me. If I just think about it, it comes back to me, picture that house, I could just *feel* it, I'd *be* there—as I described visiting and listening to another old lady. I used to rub her back. I didn't realize she had back trouble and that the only time she felt good was when I was there and had been massaging her. 'Yeah,' she'd say. 'Go like that.' And then I'd get my hands and press. I remembered her house and can describe it. Not long ago an old lady told me, 'That was my mother.' She said, 'What I want to know is what you did when you used to rub her back for her. Describe the house. No, you can't!'

"But I did. I was only two years old.

"I remember that I had long hair and an old lady used to braid it. I was a year or so old when that woman died. I was one year old, and I remember her. I told my mom about the little tiny braids. But when I do that I picture everything. For some reason when I was growing up I could understand everybody; but I couldn't speak, maybe because I was small. When I was growing up, the most I could do was when they let me work on their fingers or their muscles or back muscles or arms. The old people taught me. They said, never use your fingernails, keep your fingers flat and massage the people. You could *press* them, but not use your fingernails at all. But they used to get me all the time for broken bones, fingers, hands, arms, and back, and I didn't do anybody's stomach. Those old people wouldn't let me touch those until later on. My mother, grandmother, and great-grandmother were all healers, and I learned from them. I remember healing someone when I was four, just like my daughter healed my stomach when she was four.

"When I was a teenager I used to work on myself. There was never anything wrong with my body. I was new. I can't really say I learned it. I *feel* it. I get the symptoms from those people. I—they get sick. That's the most important part, the feelings, and I know it, I always felt it. I could *sense* it. The old people would hardly ever let anybody watch them work on a person. I had the authority to do it, authority to watch; I was *given* the authority by the old people. I could, my grandfather did, my grandmother did, my great-grandmother did. It went down from generation to generation. I'm one of the very few people that could work on myself. It's very rare. I have to pray about it a lot of times, though. I don't do the healing myself; I know the good Lord gave it to me, so I'm not going to take all the credit for it. I just never *doubt* it too. I *don't doubt* and I *refuse* to doubt. It's one of the main things.

"Like the other day I was getting bad symptoms in my side, in my stomach. I lay down but I *couldn't* get it away. And the next day a woman came to me with all the symptoms that I had the night before I saw her. I couldn't eat and didn't want to eat; I wasn't really nauseated, but I was uncomfortable. And here she was thinking about me all the time. Every time I work on her, I get her symptoms beforehand. It's more powerful when they think about me. I was affected really easily by that, badly affected. Sometimes I just feel for them to come, and I know they will. You talk about somebody and they'll walk right in. It's happened like that so many times; I always know it. But I could block it off. Another good thing about it—it goes on until they come, and then it'll go away. So any time they come in, after I work on them it goes away. If they don't give me anything I just constantly have it, and I don't like that. Most of the time I ask to work at their house so that I can get a bite to eat or something to drink. They're giving me something.

"When I was growing up I benefited from talking to people. I always had that, with old people. I was never scared to talk to them, although I was supposed not to. Me, I always wanted to find out.

"At one time—I must have been about seven, I was never scared—there was this old lady, she probably had epileptic fits, and everybody used to be scared of her. We were out walking. My cousin told me, 'I bet you can't go in there and talk to her.'

"And I said, 'I bet you there's nothing wrong with that person. All she needs is somebody to talk to, it's just that nobody visits her. How would you feel if nobody visited you? What she needs is somebody to love her or talk to her, and so. . . . .'

"I was not allowed to go there. But I could! I went in there. When I closed that door, I didn't have the nerve to go on. We knew that her daughter was out; the daughter used to say, 'Don't go in when I'm out.'

"I went in. You had to go through a door. When I looked over in this area outside—it wasn't too far away—there was a dog on a chain. I was more scared of the dog than anything else. The chain couldn't reach me. In order to get away from the dog I'd have to go inside. It wasn't growling at me. That feeling. It wasn't mean. A low growl.

"When I knocked I heard somebody in there. I braced myself and went in. The first thing I noticed was a skin curtain. Usually doors went up like a curtain. There was a small kitchen, with one bed that had a curtain. This old lady walked out. She was *old*! If her hair had been combed she'd have looked pretty. She was clean. Her clothes were not really dirty, it was as if she had slept in them for two days or so. She had a chain on her hand or her leg, I can't remember, her leg. I remember her hands: her nails were really long. She tried talking to me, and I told her the only reason I went in there was because of my cousin; and I asked her, 'Don't tell my mom.'

"She couldn't talk because her tongue was like that, she was tongue-tied. But she *could* have. Anyway I told her she could have, and went back.

"I asked my mom about her. I forgot I wasn't supposed to talk to her. I kept thinking about it—why didn't they comb her hair? 'Mom, how come you don't comb Kinnaun's hair? How come they keep her on a chain?'

"She said, 'You were there!'

"I said, 'Where?'"—Claire smiled.

"Mom said, 'You were over there, weren't you?'" I never did lie to my mom.

"'Yes. But I pitied her.'

"'What did she say to you?'

"'I was trying to talk to her, I was being nice to her. But I didn't *touch* her.'

"When that old lady was young—about twenty—she got lost. It must have been after her daughter was born—she had twins, you see. After her twins were born she went out—and her mind was boggled, she couldn't think. Instead of going home she got lost. It was a long walk. There was all kinds of water all over the place, she must have forgotten which way she went. At that time it was just a small village anyway. She got lost. I don't know if this is true or not but her track turned from the leg of a human—she had no foot—to a brown bear's legs. Maybe a brown bear was around, I like to think that way. I may say that she later died. She ended up in the insane asylum. They sent her back home and she eventually died. But all she needed at that time was affection."

All this time I was making assenting noises and pouring out more tea and honey. Claire's voice and her speaking style were inseparable from the subject matter, and the story came in a series of vivid pictures. The style itself spoke of great self-confidence such as one encounters in the personal histories of exceptional people. For instance, "*I* dared to visit the old lady"—no one else did. She understood speech practically from birth. The subject matter and style were all one with the flow of knowledge, "I just knew." It was a life that unfolded by its own dynamic: the unitary principle was very strong in her.

She had at least four episodes of what is labeled by psychologists in our culture "fugue" or "psychosis"—but we do not have the right to label them psychosis. They appeared to be the classic irruptions of shamanic experience just as the ancient Inuit knew them, typically lasting for four days, during which something fearful, a spirit of the dead or of an animal, first afflicts the incipient shaman, then changes its nature into a helper.

The first episode was related by a friend of Claire's. About twenty years previously Claire was in Anchorage alone, for reasons unknown, staying in an expensive hotel for four days. There she had some kind of transformation. (The friend looked disturbed on recounting this.) The friend continued, "Claire told me on the phone—I was at the airport—that she had had some kind of revelation about me. There were certain things that would happen. A person who didn't know Claire's powers would think she'd gone crazy. What she was doing was glossolalia. This was a bad time for Claire. I've no idea what she went through in that hotel for four days all by herself."

Some years later Claire again had a very bad time. At her peripheral vision she would continually see a devil figure. According to an close affine of hers, an educated woman, Claire kept uttering a whole lot of blah-blah-blah nonsense words. It was glossolalia again. This greatly upset the affine. Claire told her, "Don't be like that, you don't think I am anything, do you? I can't help it, it comes to me." But at the end of it Claire could pray to Jesus, and afterward her healing was stronger. The affine, who later also signed up as a student in the anthropology teleconference course, told me that she came to realize that the personality of a shaman or healer could not be expected to be like that of other people.

A further episode occurred during my own fieldwork. One Thursday when I went to see Claire, I found her smoking all alone on her couch, very depressed. She wouldn't say a word. Then she said in a dull voice, "My husband has gone north, he doesn't tell me where, maybe he's drinking. He hasn't come back. Here I am with all the kids and the bills and everything." She shut her eyes, turned to the wall, and wouldn't speak anymore. As for me, I sat there crying and furious with men in that dim place, and frightened because she was angry. Was she angry with me? Claire finished her cigarette and went to sleep. I left, having kissed her. I loved her and it hurt me too. On Sunday when I visited her again she was not around. Her husband was back and told me she was in her bedroom, still feeling bad. I left her some pears and went home. Later still Claire was herself again. She thanked me for the pears, laughing. "I hid them in my room in case the kids got them, and I ate them all myself." What I saw had all the hallmarks of the shaman's episode.

During a later visit yet another episode seems to have occurred. I had just arrived and heard that Claire had returned from hospital, where she had been a patient for four days. I went to her house.

"Where's Claire?"

"Washing dishes," said young Ann.

I entered the kitchen. A small dark figure was at the sink, and she didn't turn around.

"Claire, Claire, look here. I've brought you something." She still didn't turn. Her gray hair was scrawny, her figure thin. I immediately thought, "An episode again? Isn't this fieldwork pitiful! My dear friend caught up in . . . something so mysterious! OK, I have to try to understand."

Claire peeped into the shopping bag I brought and saw peacock blue velveteen for a new parka, and a peacock blue zipper. She turned convulsively and flung herself into my arms. We were crying. I stroked her wild gray hair and haggard face.

"Dear Claire. You've given me everything, my sweet friend." When we recovered she told me the doctor at the hospital had given her the wrong medicine. She was really mad at him. "I'll get an attorney," she said. Now she was off all medicines and was feeling better by the minute. I wondered what the doctor thought he had prescribed the medicine for.

The four-day period puzzled me. An old account has survived about an ancestor of Clem's, the shaman Kehuq. When Kehuq was a young man, he was out on the tundra when he heard the sound of paddles up in the air. He looked up and saw a boat floating in the sky. It landed, and Kehuq saw within it a shaman with one big eye, who danced and gave him pleasure. The vision disappeared, and by the time Kehuq reached home, he had forgotten about it. Late that night Kehuq started up naked and left the tent for no reason. They brought him back, but for four days he was crazy and could not eat.

But when he recovered, Kehuq could dance. When he did so, his spirit left him and he was possessed by the tutelary shaman's spirit. Kehuq taught the people the shaman's songs and also taught them how to carve the shaman's face in wood. He was now gifted with supernatural powers.

This is just one of many accounts featuring a four-day crazy period, typically followed by a supernaturally successful hunting period, also by healing gifts and other benefits.

One of Clem's brothers also had four-day episodes in which he would not talk to anyone. Furthermore Jean Briggs (1970:254–255) mentions that during her fieldwork among the Inuit of Canada, the father of the family with whom she lived appeared to become withdrawn at periods, with the same moodiness and dislike of disturbance as Claire. The so-called "arctic hysteria" (Foulks 1972) may not have been a matter of light deprivation so much as the four-day crazy phenomenon. My own late husband, Vic Turner, suffered black periods from time to time. We both noted that they lasted for four days.

I do not know exactly what happened to Claire during those four-day episodes. I think she was only learning about herself gradually—including what she learned from her readings in the anthropology of her own culture. But she mainly learned because of a shadowy return of faith in her own traditions, battered as those traditions had been, when she was young, by a determined Christianity. And her life's focus was on using her gift. No systematizing was necessary for it to work; what was needed was just its simple activation. The life itself naturally organized the development of the gift, and this is why the depiction of it in this essay needed to be embedded in the events of that life.

A major point is at the center of the account. It can be seen that Claire felt the existence of pain in others, and I had sensed some of it. Pain is supposed to be purely subjective—that is, closed to the individual. I would say it is not so closed.

The ability to approach near enough to this, I believe, stemmed from actual friendship with my difficult opposite number, Claire—from an increasing odd and mutually amused familiarity between us, culminating in that sweet embrace after the fourth episode. Still, what had been going on in Claire in these episodes remained a mystery. If any others in the discipline have had those four-day episodes, they might not not be able to put them into words either. My own dark times—I have had them; I have clambered out of them with poetry, then gained at the end a sense of utter glory. It seems clear that the Inuit in the cold regions have latched onto some key that poets have also struggled to use.

It is Claire herself, her experience with her own personality, who is the hero of the piece. Her role and reputation in the village were always up for discussion. She was praised by many because of those gentle hands. "She has The Blessing," said a pillar of the local church. A few of the others said her healing did not work; they preferred her rival, whose hands were "real strong." I felt those strong hands myself. Claire was therefore sometimes on the defensive and wondered if her critics were out to get her. But always she "refused to doubt."

About future research into the four-day episode: we are anthropologists, after all. It is for us to probe, to reexamine the Inuit shamanic roots of Claire's work, to put her care for others in a context of a long line of gifted spirit workers. Anthopologists cannot but be researchers, but the truth is that they are also turning out to be something like midwives of their hosts' developing cultures. So we may hope that our researches may actually help our people. Reconsidering the four-day period, its very existence in Claire throws into doubt the possible next step, which might be psychiatric study. The doubt remains whether psychiatry would cover the shadowy psychic elements involved. I hold out more hope in anthropology, with its richness of data and its growing and flourishing humanism. Humanism itself can dissolve the barriers of the academic conventions and reach in and really embrace the humanity we are studying. For we are inescapably an embracing species. Then we will *feel*—perceive with our senses—those things we have been in the habit of calling *symbol*, representation, and metaphor in the ritual cultures of the peoples whose experience we may not have yet shared. And it is my argument that the proper study of such frontier phenomena as Claire defended will ultimately prove to supply the missing link in the study of ritual and symbol.

So the issues are indeed the actual presence of the anthropologist in the research scene, the possibly profound depths of her subject matter, the liveliness—unsterilized by inappropriate scientific superimpositions—to be found in almost every experience of a fieldworker, and the finding of words truly to convey the complexities to responding readers. Moreover, we are saved by the fact that even those words themselves come not from some all-knowing individual but derive from their nest in our own living culture. The natural social humanism of our bodies will continually bring anthropology back to its old subject matter.

REFERENCES CITED AND SUGGESTED READING

Abu-Lughod, Lila. 1986. *Veiled Sentiments: Honor and Poetry in a Bedouin Society*. Berkeley: University of California Press.

Andors, Phyllis. 1983. *The Unfinished Liberation of Chinese Women, 1949–1980*. Bloomington: Indiana University Press.

Angrosino, Michael V. 1981. *Quality Assurance for Community Care of Retarded Adults in Tennessee*. Nashville: Vanderbilt Institute for Public Policy Studies.

_____. 1989. *Documents of Interaction: Biography, Autobiography, and Life History in Social Science Perspective*. Gainesville: University of Florida Press.

_____. 1992a. Benjy's Tale: Faulkner and the Sociolinguistics of Mental Retardation. *RE Arts and Letters* 18:5–22.

_____. 1992b. Metaphors of Stigma: How Deinstitutionalized Mentally Retarded Adults See Themselves. *Journal of Contemporary Ethnography* 21:171–199.

_____. 1994. On the Bus with Vonnie Lee: Explorations in Life History and Metaphor. *Journal of Contemporary Ethnography* 23:14–28.

Angrosino, Michael V., and Lucinda J. Zagnoli. 1992. Gender Constructs and Social Identity: Implications for Community-based Care of Retarded Adults. In *Gender Constructs and Social Issues*, Tony L. Whitehead and Barbara Reid, editors. Urbana: University of Illinois Press.

Bacon, Francis. 1992. Essay on Friendship in *Bartlett's Familiar Quotations*, 16th ed. Boston: Little, Brown.

Beaver, Patricia. 1986 (reissued 1992). *Rural Community in the Appalachian South*. Prospect Heights, IL: Waveland Press.

Beaver, Patricia, Hou Lihui, and Wang Xue. 1995. Rural Chinese Women: Two Faces of Economic Reform. *Modern China* 21(2): 205–232.

Beaver, Patricia, and Burton Purrington, editors. 1984. *Cultural Adaptations to Mountain Environments*. Athens: University of Georgia Press.

Beaver, Patricia, and Melissa Schrift. 1994. Women Mentoring Women in China. *Anthropology and Humanism Quarterly* 18(2): 1–9.

Behar, Ruth. 1993. *Translated Woman: Crossing the Border with Esperanza's Story*. Boston: Beacon Press.

Behar, Ruth. 1994. No Returns. In *Her Face in the Mirror: Jewish Women on Mothers and Daughters*, Faye Moskowitz, editor. Boston: Beacon Press.
_____. 1995. *Bridges to Cuba*. Ann Arbor: University of Michigan Press.
Behar, Ruth, and Deborah A. Gordon, editors. 1995. *Women Writing Culture*. Berkeley: University of California Press.
Bowen, Elenore Smith. 1964. *Return to Laughter: An Anthropological Novel*. New York: Doubleday.
Briggs, Jean L. 1970. *Never in Anger: Portrait of an Eskimo Family*. Cambridge: Harvard University Press.
Casagrande, Joseph, editor. 1960. *The Company of Man*. New York: Harper and Brothers.
Croll, Elizabeth. 1978. *Feminism and Socialism in China*. London: Routledge and Kegan Paul.
Diamond, Stanley. 1974. *In Search of the Primitive: A Critique of Civilization*. New Brunswick: Transaction Books.
Edgerton, Robert, editor. 1984. *Lives in Process: Mildly Retarded Adults in a Large City*. Washington, D.C.: American Association on Mental Deficiency.
Farrer, Claire R. 1991. *Living Life's Circle: Mescalero Apache Cosmovision*. Albuquerque: University of New Mexico Press.
_____. 1994. *Thunder Rides a Black Horse: Mescalero Apaches and the Mythic Present*. Prospect Heights, IL: Waveland Press.
Farrer, Claire R., and Ray A. Williamson. 1992. *Earth and Sky: Visions of the Cosmos in Native American Folklore*. Albuquerque: University of New Mexico Press.
Fletcher, Alice C., and Francis La Flesche. 1911. *The Omaha Tribe*. Washington, D.C.: Twenty-seventh Annual Report of the Bureau of American Ethnology.
Foulks, E. F. 1972. *The Arctic Hysterias of the North Alaskan Eskimo*. Washington, D.C.: American Anthropological Association.
Geertz, Clifford. 1968. Thinking as a Moral Act: Ethical Dimensions of Fieldwork in the New States. *Antioch Review* 28:139–158.
Grindal, Bruce. 1972. *Growing Up in Two Worlds: Education and Transition Among the Sisala of Northern Ghana*. New York: Holt, Rhinehart and Winston.
_____. 1983. Into the Heart of Sisala Experience: Witnessing Death Divination. *Journal of Anthropological Research* 39(1): 60–80.
Hankiss, Agnes. 1981. Ontologies of the Self: On the Metaphorical Rearranging of One's Life History. In *Biography and Society: The Life History Approach in the Social Sciences*, Daniel Bertaux, editor. Beverly Hills: Sage.
Henry, Jules. 1964. *Jungle People*. New York: Vintage Books.
Huang, Shu-min. 1989. *The Spiral Road: Change in a Chinese Village Through the Eyes of a Communist Party Leader*. Boulder, CO: Westview Press.
Johnson, Kay Ann. 1983. *Women, the Family and Peasant Revolution in China*. Chicago: University of Chicago Press.
Mark, Joan. 1988. *A Stranger in Her Native Land: Alice Fletcher and the American Indians*. Lincoln: University of Nebraska Press.
Mead, Margaret. 1965. *The Changing Culture of an Indian Tribe*. New York: Capricorn Books.

Narayan, Kirin. 1986. Birds on a Branch: Girlfriends and Wedding Songs in Kangra. *Ethos* 14:47–75.

_____. 1989. *Storytellers, Saints and Scoundrels: Folk Narrative in Hindu Religious Teaching.* Philadelphia: University of Pennsylvania Press.

_____. 1994. *Love, Stars, and All That.* New York: Pocket Books.

Norton, C. S. 1989. *Life Metaphors: Stories of Ordinary Survival.* Carbondale: Southern Illinois University Press.

Peacock, James L., and Dorothy C. Holland. 1993. The Narrated Self: Life Stories in Process. *Ethos* 21:367–383.

Reck, Gregory G. 1978 (reissued 1986). *In the Shadow of Tlaloc: Life in a Mexican Village.* Prospect Heights, IL: Waveland Press.

_____. 1986. Celistino and His Discontents: A Metalogue with Civilization and Its Discontents. In *The Burden of Being Civilized: An Anthropological Perspective on the Discontents of Civilization,* Miles Richardson and Malcomb Webb, editors. Athens: University of Georgia Press.

_____. 1993. Narrative and Social Science: Reclaiming the Existential. *Issues in Integrative Studies* 11:63–74.

Reed, Robert Roy. 1990. Are Robert's Rules of Order Counterrevolutionary? Rhetoric and the Reconstruction of Portuguese Politics. *Anthropological Quarterly* 63:134–144.

_____. In press. From Utopian Hopes to Practical Politics. *Comparative Studies in Society and History.*

_____. In press. A Statistical Look at Political Candidates and Strategies in Rural Portugal. *Meredies.*

Reed, Robert Roy, and Jay Szklut. 1991. Community Anonymity in Anthropological Research: A Reassessment. In *Ethics and the Profession of Anthropology.* Philadelphia: University of Pennsylvania Press.

Ridington, Robin. 1984ms. Mottled as by Shadows: The Life and Death of a Sacred Symbol.

_____. 1988. Images of Cosmic Union: Omaha Ceremonies of Renewal. *History of Religions* 28(2): 135–150.

_____. 1988. *Trail to Heaven: Knowledge and Narrative in a Northern Native Community.* Iowa City: University of Iowa Press.

_____. 1990. *Little Bit Know Something: Stories in a Language of Anthropology.* Iowa City: University of Iowa Press.

_____. 1993. A Sacred Object as Text: Reclaiming the Sacred Pole of the Omaha Tribe. *American Indian Quarterly* 17(1): 83–99.

_____. 1994ms. All the Old Spirits Have Come Back to Greet Him: Realizing the Sacred Pole of the Omaha Tribe.

Salamone, Frank A. 1974. *Gods and Goods in Africa.* New Haven, CT: Human Relations Area Files.

_____. 1985. *Missionaries and Anthropologists. Studies in Third World Societies.* Williamsburg, VA: College of William and Mary Press.

_____. 1992. Art and Culture in Nigeria and the Diaspora. *Studies in Third World Societies.* Williamsburg, VA: College of William and Mary Press.

Sandstrom, Alan R. 1991. *Corn Is Our Blood: Culture and Ethnic Identity in a Contemporary Aztec Indian Village.* Norman: University of Oklahoma Press.

Sandstrom, Alan R., and Pamela Effrein Sandstrom. 1986. *Traditional Papermaking and Paper Cult Figures of Mexico.* Norman: University of Oklahoma Press.

Simonelli, Jeanne. 1986. *Two Boys, a Girl, and Enough! Reproductive and Economic Decisionmaking on the Mexican Periphery*. Boulder, CO: Westview Press.

_____. 1990. *Too Wet to Plow: The Family Farm in Transition*. New York: New Amsterdam Press.

Stacey, Judith. 1983. *Patriarchy and Socialist Revolution in China*. Berkeley: University of California Press.

Stewart, John O. 1989. *Drinkers, Drummers, and Decent Folk*. Albany: State University of New York Press.

Turner, Edith. 1986. Philip Kabwita, Ghost Doctor: The Ndembu in 1985. *Drama Review* 30(4): 12–35.

_____. 1987. *The Spirit and the Drum*. Tucson: University of Arizona Press.

_____. 1990. Experience and Poetics in Anthropological Writing. *Journal of the Steward Anthropological Society* 17:21–46.

_____. 1992. *Experiencing Ritual: A New Interpretation of African Healing*. Philadelphia: University of Pennsylvania Press.

Turner, Edith, and Victor Turner. 1978. *Image and Pilgrimage in Christian Culture: Anthropological Perspectives*. New York: Columbia University Press.

Turner, Victor. 1960. Muchona the Hornet, Interpreter of Religion. In *The Company of Man*, Joseph Casagrande, editor. New York: Harper and Brothers.

Welch, Roger. 1981. *Omaha Tribal Myths and Trickster Tales*. Chicago: Swallow Press.

Whittemore, R. D., Paul Koegel, and L. L. Langness. 1980. *The Life History Approach to Mental Retardation*. (Socio-Behavioral Working Paper No. 12.) Los Angeles: Mental Retardation Research Center, School of Medicine, University of California.

Wolf, Margery. 1985. *Revolution Postponed: Women in Contemporary China*. Stanford: Stanford University Press.

Wolff, Kurt H. 1964. Surrender and Community Study: The Study of Loma. In *Reflections on Community Studies*, A. J. Vidich et al., editors. New York: John Wiley and Sons.

Yang, Mayfair Mei-hu. 1988. The Modernity of Power in the Chinese Socialist Order. *Cultural Anthropology* 3:408–427.

ABOUT THE CONTRIBUTORS

MICHAEL ANGROSINO is professor of anthropology at the University of South Florida. He has conducted ethnographic research on ethnic identity in the Caribbean and also on mental health issues in the United States. Angrosino is the author of *Documents of Interaction: Biography, Autobiography, and Life History in Social Science Perspective* (1989). Papers related to the material in "Eutaw Jack"—"Metaphors of Stigma: How Deinstitutionalized Mentally Retarded Adults See Themselves (1992) and "On the Bus with Vonnie Lee: Explorations in Life History and Metaphor" (1994)—have appeared in the *Journal of Contemporary Ethnography*.

PATRICIA BEAVER is professor of anthropology at Appalachian State University in Boone, North Carolina. She has conducted research in Appalachia and the American South and more recently in China, focusing on families, gender issues, and the formation and maintenance of community. With an abiding interest in ethnographic writing, her principal publications on Appalachia include *Rural Community in the Appalachian South* (1986) and, co-edited with Burton Purrington, *Cultural Adaptations to Mountain Environments* (1984). Articles resulting from her work in China during the 1990–91 year are, co-authored with Hou Lihui and Wang Xue, "Rural Chinese Women: Two Faces of Economic Reform," forthcoming in *Modern China* (1995); and co-authored with Melissa Schrift, "Women Mentoring Women in China," in *Anthropology and Humanism Quarterly* (1994).

RUTH BEHAR was born in Havana in 1956 and came to live in New York with her family in 1962. She is professor of anthropology at the University of Michigan in Ann Arbor. Behar has traveled to Spain, Mexico, and Cuba and written on a range of cultural issues as a poet, essayist, editor, and ethnographer. Her most recent book is *Translated Woman: Crossing the Border with Esperanza's Story* (1993), an account of her friendship with a Mexican street peddler. Behar is the editor of *Bridges to Cuba* (1995), a forum she created for the voices of Cubans on the island and in the diaspora seeking reconciliation and a common culture and memory. She is also co-editor of *Women Writing Culture* (1995). Her short memoir piece, "No Returns," is included in the new anthology, *Her Face in the Mirror* (1994). She is currently writing a full-length memoir that explores the silences of her Jewish-Cuban family.

CLAIRE R. FARRER is professor of anthropology at California State University—Chico. She has worked with people from the Mescalero Apache Indian Reservation for over three decades. Her research and writing have ranged from children's play to clowning to ceremonialism to ethnoastronomy. In addition to scores of book chapters, journal articles, and magazine or newspaper articles, she has published six books, most recently *Thunder Rides a Black Horse* (1994), *Earth and Sky: Visions of the Cosmos in Native American Folklore* (1992, co-edited with Ray A. Williamson), and *Living Life's Circle: Mescalero Apache Cosmovision* (1991).

BRUCE GRINDAL is professor of anthropology at Florida State University. He was one of the founders of the Society for Humanistic Anthropology and served as the first editor of the *Anthropology and Humanism Quarterly*. Grindal has done research in West Africa and the American South, and his interests have focused largely on religion and ethnographic writing. His principal publications on the Sisala include *Growing Up in Two Worlds: Education and Social Transition among the Sisala of Northern Ghana* (1972) and "Into the Heart of Sisala Experience: Witnessing Death Divination" (1983).

KIRIN NARAYAN is associate professor of anthropology and South Asian Studies at the University of Wisconsin—Madison. Her research interests include religion, folklore, and gender. She has done fieldwork in Nasik, Western India, and Kangra, in the Himalayan foothills. Narayan is the author of *Storytellers, Saints and Scoundrels: Folk Narratives in Hindu Religious Teaching* (1989), which won the 1991 Victor Turner Prize and was co-winner of the 1991 Elsie Clews Parsons Prize for Folklore. She has also written a novel, *Love, Stars, and All That* (1994). A book about Urmila Devi Sood's folktales is under contract with Oxford University Press.

ROBERT ROY REED teaches part-time at The Ohio State University. His research interests are politics, religion, and movements of radical social change. His publications on rural Portugal include "Are Robert's Rules of Order Counterrevolutionary? Rhetoric and the Reconstruction of Portuguese Politics" (1990), "Community Anonymity in Anthropological Research" (1991, with Jay Szklut), and "A Statistical Look at Political Candidates and Strategies in Rural Portugal" (in press). He is presently preparing a book on village politics and the life and death of the Portuguese revolution.

GREGORY G. RECK is professor of anthropology at Appalachian State University. He has conducted field research in Mexico, southern Appalachia and India, focusing on issues of ethnicity, class, and socioeconomic change. He is a radical humanist who believes that anthropologists must struggle to create narrative forms of representation that reflect the passion of lived experience. Reck's publications reflect this interest in experimental forms of ethnographic writing; his perspectives on Mexico and narrative ethnography combine in his book *In the Shadow of Tlaloc: Life in a Mexican Village* (1978).

ROBIN RIDINGTON has done fieldwork with the Dunne-za of British Columbia and the Omaha tribe of Nebraska. He listens to stories, and he tells them. He is author of *Trail to Heaven: Knowledge and Narrative in a Northern Native Community* (1988) and *Little Bit Know Something: Stories in a Language of Anthropology* (1990). He is currently completing a book about the Sacred Pole of the Omaha tribe with Dennis Hastings, the Omaha tribal historian. It is called *Blessing for a Long Time*. Ridington lives on Retreat Island in British Columbia and is professor emeritus of anthropology at the University of British Columbia.

FRANK A. SALAMONE is professor of anthropology at Iona College in New Rochelle, New York. The tension between being in the field and being at home with his family is seen in many of his works, including the one in this collection. He has carried out fieldwork in Nigeria, Kenya, Great Britain, Venezuela, Ghana, Canada, and the United States. His studies have included jazz musicians and resettled Ugandan Asians as well as more traditional anthropological peoples. However, the overriding subject of his studies has been the manner in which human beings seek to forge identities that have meaning in an otherwise meaningless world.

ALAN R. SANDSTROM is professor of anthropology at Indiana University—Purdue University, Fort Wayne. He has conducted ethnographic research among Tibetans in the Himalayas of northern India and among Nahuas of northern Veracruz, Mexico. His interests include ethnic identity, economy, ecology, and religion. His major publications include *Traditional Papermaking and Paper Cult Figures of Mexico* (1986, with Pamela Effrein Sandstrom) and *Corn Is Our Blood: Culture and Ethnic Identity in a Contemporary Aztec Indian Village* (1991). He is also editor of the *Nahua Newsletter*, a multidisciplinary and international publication for scholars interested in the history, culture, and language of Nahuatl-speaking peoples.

JEANNE SIMONELLI is associate professor of anthropology at the State University of New York—Oneonta. Her field experiences are united by the broad theme of change and development in Mexico, Oklahoma, rural New York, and at Canyon de Chelly, Arizona. Resulting publications are directed at both the anthropological audience and the general public and include books, articles, and poetry. Her principal publications include *Too Wet to Plow: The Family Farm in Transition* (1992) and *Two Boys, a Girl, and Enough!: Reproductive and Economic Decisionmaking on the Mexican Periphery* (1986).

JOHN O. STEWART's interest in African diaspora studies has led to fieldwork in the Caribbean, the Southern United States, and Nigeria with a focus on religion, folklore, and public rituals. He is trained in literature and anthropology and has been working on the literary presentation of anthropology for some time. His major publication in this area is *Drinkers, Drummers, and Decent Folk* (1989). He is a former editor of the *Anthropology and Humanism Quarterly* and currently professor and director of African American and African Studies, University of California, Davis.

EDITH L. B. TURNER has been on the faculty of the department of anthropology at the University of Virginia since 1984. She has been in anthropology for forty-four years, her major interests being the Ndembu of Zambia, the Inuit of northern Alaska, symbolism, ritual as performed, and anthropological writing. Her significant publications include *Experiencing Ritual* (1992); "Experience and Poetics in Anthropological Writing," (1990); *The Spirit and the Drum* (1987); and *Image and Pilgrimage* (with Victor Turner, 1978). Her new monograph on Inuit healing, *The Hands Feel It*, is in the hands of a publisher.